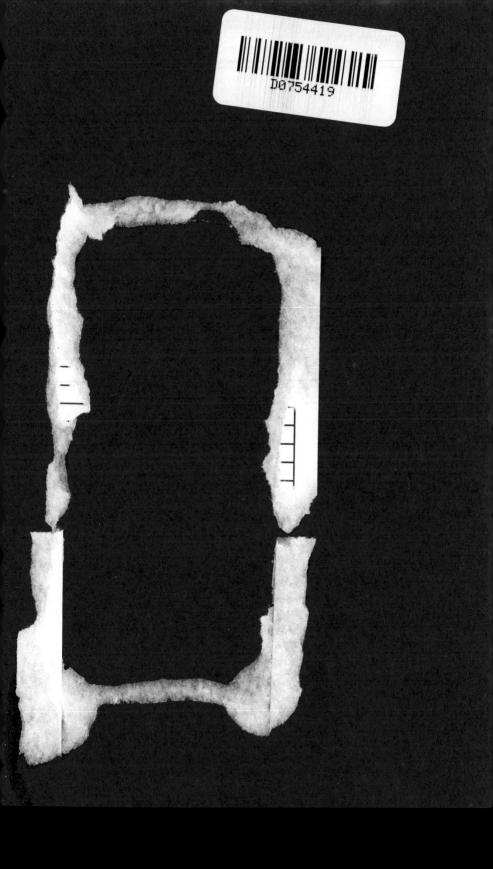

Metaphors of Evil

nightmare of history. Having been deserted by all the circus animals, the poetic imagination insists on returning, to use Yeats's words, to "the foul rag and bone shop" of the human heart, with little hope, however, for ladders of aspiration. The following chapters, too, are arranged along these lines. For each of the writers reveals the experience of deprivation, the means to cope with it, and the wish or demand for a ladder towards transcendence, an impossibility because of the insistent dominance of metaphors of evil which in their most harmless guise are shallow, empty husks, or mere surfaces.

I.
Metaphors of Evil and the Archetypal Energies of Creation and Destruction

As an implied analogy which imaginatively identifies one object with another, a metaphor establishes a connotative relationship between the word as intermediary of reality and the experience of reality. Metaphor diffuses and enriches the word as a literal sign and projects the ambiguity of human existence by combining that which can be said with that which remains unutterable. Repression and projection are both active in metaphors which always contain a mute point communicated through the "tenor and vehicle" (I. A. Richards) and enable the human being to repress and release pains and desires. On one end of the spectrum are those metaphors which have become so familiar that they give the illusion of accurate description and instant communication of truth, for instance, "war is hell." On the other end is the use of absolute metaphors which seem so unique that the word appears to be freed from its ethical and social context and seems to exist self-contained, separated, and authentic. The poet who uses metaphors this way wants to rescue them from the corruption of historical time. Yet the reality which metaphors seek to explain and the reality from which they seek to escape is always more powerful and overwhelming than the metaphors' impotent magic. Metaphors have never sufficed to communicate the mute point of the *summum bonum* or the *summum malum*. In the literature about the Nazi period, in the recorded memory of the victim-survivors, the creative imagination has been unable to approximate the reality of evil in historical time; and even the most empathetic reader cannot penetrate to the mute point encapsulated in the metaphor of evil.

Nevertheless, human beings employ the defense of language in their experience of extremity. As Paul Ricoeur argues in *Symbolism of Evil,* well as realize that it is not unique. But Nazism, and especially the experience of the holocaust, have been *perceived* as unique, as Lawrence Langer argues in *The Holocaust and the Literary Imagination*.[3] That it was and is perceived thus depends, I would argue, on two circumstances, apart from the fact that each individual in the unspeakable situation experienced his or her ordeal in a unique way. First of all, because the Nazis and Germany lost the war, the information about and the images of the holocaust no longer needed to be officially repressed and could be freely disseminated. Secondly, since the thoughtful individual realizes that such images are not the result of God's punishment or the temptations of the devil but originate with human beings, he or she feels the necessity to respond ethically to them. Such ethical responses are extremely complex, as the literature to be discussed in the following chapters reveals. The holocaust is evil; it cannot have any apologists. And the imagination of the literary artist whose language is German must somehow reveal an ethical-judicial attitude towards a situation which remains, in spite of all the physical reality of evil, unspeakable and indefinable through the symbolic system of a literary work.

The ethical-judicial attitude on the part of the author or poet does not, however, warrant self-righteousness, though characters within a literary work may have such an attitude and are criticized for it. The mode of irony therefore dominates all the works to be discussed. It manifests itself perhaps most brutally in the diary, where only the reader is retrospectively aware of the horribly ironic situation of the diarist. The survivor-victim and the witness, who by accident of time could not have been more than a bystander, feel themselves implicated, feel the guilt which the criminal often suppresses so successfully. The ironic mode results, however, not only because of the precarious balance between a judging and self-implicating attitude, but also because it is the appropriate negative mysticism of a godless time, or, to use Lukacs's words, a *docta ignorantia* that opposes preconceived meaning.[4]

Nazism and the holocaust validated Western literature's already prevalent ironic mode into which the projections of archetypal myths had been displaced. In this chapter I will retrace this process by beginning with a definition of metaphors of evil and their relation to the archetypal energies of creation and destruction. I will then show how the Nazi use of language and myth, and the historical reality that resulted from it, inevitably devalued religious, historical, social, and literary patterns so that they can no longer be accepted without adulteration, without irony. For the literary artist, irony actually becomes a defense against the me aware of the fundamental situation that underlies all the literary works I will discuss in this book: the reality of an unspeakable, though not inhuman, event, and the witness—bystander's knowledge of and defense systems against it. Kafka's story reveals that ''the heart of darkness'' can emerge aggressively with all its grotesque horror from behind the door of the most ordinary of bedrooms, but also that it can be shoved back into its darkness, that the door can be closed upon it, and that it may finally turn into nothing but a vacant flattened shell, readily discarded. As Gregor Samsa, the ''monstrous vermin,'' moves towards his eventually easy death, neither he nor his family ask why this misfortune has befallen them. The ordeal does not lead to insight but to repression. Normalcy is what the Samsas want. After Gregor's death, the family moves with ''dreams and good intentions'' into a future where Gregor will at best be referred to with the circumlocutions appropriate to a taboo. Yet, this conspiracy of silence is so typically human, for who would not repress the memory of a monstrous vermin within the human community? The nightmare ends and is forgotten until it emerges again at another time and place.

Was Gregor Samsa ever called an *Ungeziefer,* a vermin, a corruptive parasite who worms himself into the good graces of his family and employer? His metamorphosis indicates what could happen when signifier and signified become one, when naming makes being. Words, seemingly such flat and arbitrary constellations of signifying sounds, do harbor in their etymons, of whose meaning the casual speaker is unaware, the possibilities for complex modes of perception and action, for mythologies. As Ernst Cassirer points out, we have adapted to our environment by projecting a symbolic system between ourselves and reality, but there is a catch: ''No longer can man confront reality immediately; he cannot see it, as it were face to face. Physical reality seems to recede in proportion as man's symbolic activity advances. Instead of dealing with things themselves, man is in a sense constantly conversing with himself.''[2] This does not mean that he knows himself, for the symbolic system also effectively screens, for better or worse, the reality within.

Even when we know that symbolic systems are generated from within the human community, we continue, consciously or unconsciously, to live and die through our metaphors and mythologies. Symbolic systems generate historical reality, and new or modified systems allow us to cope with that reality through memory. A historical event such as Nazism is perceived therefore in terms of the archetypal pattern of a rise and fall, of a beginning, middle, and end which allows us to shelve the experience as

1

Metaphors and Myths of Evil in History and Literature: Projections and Reflections

Verbal universes compensate us for our human deprivations. Within their shelter we can contemplate the painful memories of the past and even turn them into nostalgia for a never possessed and yet lost Eden, or transform them into utopian visions projected into an obscure future. Created in the flick of a present moment and recreated in an ever recurring present by the attentive and creative reader, the literary work recalls and disguises the past as it simultaneously projects and screens our human hopes and fears. A regressive and progressive dialectic tension can, therefore, be perceived in each work. Kafka's enigmatic tales exemplify this clearly, and for this reason the intensely private vision of Kafka has often been seen as an oracle for our civilization. Kafka's tales reveal the milieu of a familiar world but rob that world of all comforting notions about space, time, and causality. Memory, through which we intend to give pattern and meaning to our lives, seems unimportant and is repressed or nonexistent. Compulsive repetition of attitudes and gestures is guaranteed. The apparently absolute metaphors of Kafka's world, absolute in the sense of having no external referent, take on a oracular numinosity that stimulates imagination and critical intellect and leads the uneasy reader to a plurality of interpretations that are at once valid and doubtful.

Kafka did not know about Nazism when he wrote ''The Metamorphosis.'' ''In the Penal Colony,'' and *The Trial;* but his private projections of the interrelationship between aggressor and victim, between hunter and hunted, have been viewed by Jean-Paul Sartre and George Steiner as prophetic foreshadowings of the destruction of the Jews.[1] Such misreadings by creative readers enrich the literary work in time with connotations it did not originally possess but which do not interfere with the radicals of its archetypes. In my case it was ''The Metamorphosis'' which first made

Part One

The Creative Imagination in the Trauma of
Historical Time

most frequent in the autobiographical accounts of those who were in the camps and eventually became survivor-witnesses. None of the diarists and autobiographers in the chapter "The Rage for Order: Autobiographical Accounts of the Self in the Nightmare of History" wrote in German, and it may seem strange to include them in a study of contemporary German literature. However, I deem such inclusion necessary, for the camp experience is that ultimate ground of evil from which all the metaphors, diversions, circumlocutions, and allegories of irony are generated. Though the survivor-witness selects what to record, recollect, and repress, he has been closest to the brink of the precipice. The fact of his experience provides the novelist, the playwright, and the lyric poet with a concrete metaphysics; for in his personal record are images of evil that, no matter how permutated, reach through the linguistic network of the ironic mode and emerge on occasion as demonic epiphanies of evil. Permutation begins in the record itself. Patterns emerge which the reader alone recognizes in retrospect in the diaries of Odd Nansen and Chaim Kaplan. Patterns and the consequent displacement of reality become even more pronounced in Elie Wiesel's *Night* and Tadeusz Borowski's *This Way for the Gas, Ladies and Gentlemen.*

As the point of view switches from the survivor-witness to the witness as bystander or fellow traveler, the extreme situation is even more displaced and disguised. Part two, "Uneasy Armchair Reading: The Ambiguous and Implicating Worlds of Lenz's *The German Lesson,* Grass's *Dog Years,* and Johnson's *Jahrestage,*" may easily lull the reader into believing that the unspeakable situation was peripheral and hence bearable, that is, if the reader allows himself to be tricked by the narrators of these thoroughly ironic novels. Siegfried Lenz constructs metaphors of evil on a narrow ground and shows a narrator who does not venture far beyond his provincial environment where the "pride of narrowness" spends its rage. In "Günter Grass's *Dog Years:* The Dark Side of Utopia," guilt expands from the idyllic and ironic world of childhood to the Nazi utopia, to the economic miracle of postwar Germany. The largest expansion of guilt occurs in Uwe Johnson's *Jahrestage* (Anniversaries). In this three volume novel Johnson reveals how guilt filters through the memory and desire of Gesine Cresspahl and shapes her present and future. Guilt is not limited to her, however, for it extends from a small provincial town to the Third Reich, to the British and Soviet occupation forces, to East and West Germany, and, finally, to the actions of the United States at home and in Vietnam. Gesine's record covers a year in New York spanning 20 August 1967 to 20 August other authors and poets influenced by the shadow of Nazism, notably, Heinrich Böll. The unspeakable situation wrought by the Nazis, its effect on private and public ethical values, and its effect on the creative activity of the imagination preoccupy all the writers and poets I will discuss. I have, therefore, included a brief summary of each author's attitude towards or involvement in history and politics and the effect of both on his or her poetics.

The seven chapters of *Metaphors of Evil* are separated into three parts. The first, "The Creative Imagination in the Trauma of Historical Time," discusses in chapter one the ambiguous powers of mythmaking in history and its effect on the literary imagination and analyzes in chapter two some autobiographical accounts by human beings caught in the nightmare of history. Both chapters emphasize the immediacy of history as a shaping force on perception and imagination. Subsequent chapters will be more concerned with the process of memory and repression and their formative influence on the present for the author and the work.

Giambattista Vico's statement that "every metaphor is a little myth" prompted me to title my study *Metaphors of Evil* instead of archetypes or symbols of evil. The metaphor of evil is more than a stylistic device. As a linguistic phenomenon, it is not only the nucleus of larger mythical structures but also illustrates the tendency to obscure and reveal the unspeakable. In my first chapter, "Metaphors and Myths of Evil in History and Literature: Projections and Reflections," I attempt to define the archetypal energy from which the basic metaphors of evil are generated and evolve into larger symbolic structures. The Nazis themselves contributed not a little to the evolution of such structures when they simplistically divided the world into the *we* and the *others,* an age-old tradition, of course. Their use of language and myth has made the literary artist skeptical of mythical patterns, including the one pattern that has remained meaningful to secular humanity: the process of individuation. The poet of the ironic mode is deeply aware that the individual caught in historical time will not crown and miter the self, will not reach an anagogic vision of integration. The ironist knows that Faust is simply criminal and that there is no transcendent place and time for judgment and sentence, for the inferno is in this world. I owe the concept of the interrelationship between myth and irony to the pluralistic criticism of Northrop Frye, which seems to me well suited as a means for the analysis of the nightmare and wish-fulfillment dreams projected through the content and form of the works I have chosen.

The inferno metaphor is present in almost every one of the works and is of time would allow us to escape the neuroses of history. Such a radical change in perception would perhaps only be possible for the scattered survivors of a global holocaust. Barring such an event, our memory and our fumbling, always inadequate, self-awareness must work together lest we forget and repeat.

Metaphors of Evil: Contemporary German Literature and the Shadow of Nazism is an analytical and critical attempt to determine the impact of the Nazi era on the literary imagination. This attempt is grounded in the critic's personal memory, in her living as well as intellectual experience. I am only a few years younger than most of the authors I will discuss, and to a great extent I share the ambiguity of their memories and the irony and skepticism with which they view ideologies. I also share their hesitation to emphasize German suffering during the war and during the immediate postwar period. The Nazis, who deprived the individual of all human and civil rights, also took from the Germans the right and basic human need to mourn one's dead and lament the destruction of cities. Their creation of the concentration camp kakotopia also took from the German literary artist the right to imagine that world and the suffering of its victims. Only those who, like Elie Wiesel, Nelly Sachs, or Paul Celan, were victims themselves can recite the kaddish for the dead. As a child I remember seeing the Star of David as a symbol of abuse attached to a human being. My questions regarding it were hushed; and something vaguely terrible, dangerous, and shameful began to attach itself to the word *Jew,* a word not understood except in relation to the swastika banners. Family and school did not discuss the word; silence and circumlocutions surrounded it. Much later I read about the historical reality of the concentration camps, and this intellectual, not experiential, knowledge served me for a time as a means to separate myself from the generation that lived as adults under Hitler. Since then, after many years and much reading, I realize that the guilt of the parent generation would have been mine, too. It is mine. It becomes mine whenever I listen to anecdotes about "that crazy time," whenever I hear those abusive words and phrases and only remain silent so as not to disturb the family peace. Moreover, my guilt is suspect, for I can afford to be guilty about a past in which I did not act because I was a child; and I neglect to become conscious of those extreme situations that I know exist but prefer not to become conscious of for the sake of my comfort.

Metaphors of Evil is not an attempt to survey post–World War II German literature; others have done so. Instead, it is an in-depth study of representative works whose metaphors and ironies can also be found in

Introduction

Another book spun off the Nazi impact on our civilization? Has not everything been said and recorded already? Yes, but the individual consciousness must think it through again. Each of the autobiographers, novelists, playwrights, and poets to be discussed in *Metaphors of Evil* has thought it through again; each filtered that time through his or her consciousness and projected it in the form of verbal expressions that inevitably make the leap from the chaotic reality of history to the illusion of order inherent in art. With different means, I, too, think that time through again as I move from historical facts to the interpretation of these facts and their literary metamorphoses. It is on the latter that my emotional and critical attention has concentrated but not at the expense of the former. The "rise and fall of the Third Reich" receives anecdotal, parabolic, and symbolic significance as it recedes into the past, an unavoidable and necessary process; but memory, without being paralyzed by the past, must keep it alive so that we can see our present motives and acts reflected in that time. The connections must, of course, be made through the awareness of each individual.

The Nazi era was no hiatus in our civilization, was no transcendent atrocious time: it was our time. From the vantage point of an ephemeral present moment, we presume to overlook the years 1933–45, overlook them in the sense of overseeing and neglecting. Blind to the significance of the present moment and living in the illusion of reprieve, we circle the casual rounds of daily existence. We can do this because we repress the memory or possibility of such an extreme situation, a repression that may well guarantee compulsive re-enactment of different traumatic times for the individual and the social community. Only the eradication of all historical consciousness and the abolishment of our particular perception

Why deny the obvious necessity of memory?

Marguerite Duras
Hiroshima Mon Amour

Auschwitz–Birkenau

Contents

Acknowledgments

Selections from *Night* by Elie Wiesel. Translated from the French by Stella Rodway. English translation © MacGibbon & Kee, 1960. Reprinted with the permission of Hill & Wang (now a division of Farrar, Straus and Giroux, Inc.).

Selections from *The German Lesson* by Siegfried Lenz. Translated by Ernst Kaiser and Eithne Wilkins. English translation © 1971 by Ernst Kaiser and Eithne Wilkins. Reprinted with permission of Hill & Wang (now a division of Farrar, Straus and Giroux, Inc.).

"In my Room" from *O the Chimneys* by Nelly Sachs. Translated from the German by Michael Hamburger. Copyright © 1967 by Farrar, Straus and Giroux, Inc.

"Landscape of Screams" from *O the Chimneys* by Nelly Sachs. Translated from the German by Hamida Bosmajian. English language translation Copyright © 1978 by Farrar, Straus and Giroux, Inc. Reprinted with the permission of Farrar, Straus and Giroux, Inc.

Excerpts from *Anniversaries* by Uwe Johnson are translated and reprinted by permission of Harcourt Brace Jovanovich, Inc.; Copyright © 1970, 1971 by Suhrkamp Verlag, English translation Copyright © 1974, 1975 by Uwe Johnson.

Library of Congress Cataloging in Publication Data

Bosmajian, Hamida.
  Metaphors of evil.

  Includes bibliographical references and index.
  1. German literature—20th century—History and criticism. 2. National socialism in literature. I. Title.
PT405.B625   830'.9'00914   79–22758
ISBN 0-87745-093-5
ISBN 0-87745-096-X pbk.

University of Iowa Press, Iowa City 52242
© 1979 by The University of Iowa
Printed in the United States of America

Hamida Bosmajian

Metaphors of Evil
Contemporary German Literature
and the Shadow of Nazism

University of Iowa Press Iowa City

1968—the day when the Warsaw Pact Nations occupied Prague.
The reader will feel far more uncomfortable in the third part of
Metaphors of Evil, "Confronting the Audience and Turning Away from
the Audience: Documentary Theater and Lyric Poetry." Documentary
drama confronts and implicates its audience aggressively while hermetic
poetry rejects the reader unless he or she is willing to go beyond the easy
language of commerce and exchange. Hochhuth and Weiss do, however,
share a common concern with Sachs and Celan. For playwrights and
poets imply eschatological yearnings through either the content or form
of their work; their ironic imaginations, however, tend to project such
yearnings as parodies of a sacred world view.

I have titled my sixth chapter "Rituals of Judgment: Hochhuth's *The
Deputy* and Weiss's *The Investigation.*" For, while the documentary
playwright is concerned with trial, judgment, and justice, it is only the
ritual of judgment that is possible in the ironic mode. Human beings
yearn for justice so that the unspeakable situation may receive meaning,
but justice, if it exists, lies beyond their ken. Hochhuth's Christian
tragedy enlarges the circle of guilt which Weiss concentrates within the
narrow space of a Frankfurt courtroom during the Auschwitz trials of
1964–65. In the words of witnesses, Auschwitz is remembered as a place
where the circles of evil constricted themselves on horizontal ground.
Nothing can alleviate the experience of that evil, and the documentary
play's ritual of judgment is merely a show.

Metaphysical questions are even more urgently asked by the lyric poet.
Repression, guilt, and memory are still the shaping causes of the poems
discussed in "Towards the Point of Constriction: Nelly Sachs's 'Landschaft aus Schreien' and Paul Celan's 'Engführung' "; *towards* again
implies the image of progressively constricted circularity from which the
lyric self emerges at a state of openness wherein it waits in suspension for
answers that will never come. Form and content of these poems are such
that they do not provide the meditative reader with answers; instead, they
offer possibilities for communion through and with the word. While
Sachs and Celan seem to turn away from immediate sociopolitical and
personal questions, while they seem to address the nothingness of the
cosmos for the sake of the silent dead, they crystallize at the same time the
metaphysics inherent in all of the works discussed in *Metaphors of Evil.*
Sachs and Celan precariously possess the alpha and omega of *logos,* the
word which, after having passed through the abuse of history, receives a
new force in their poems but is also thrown back to its impotent magic,
unable to provoke an answer from the universe.

As I hinted in the beginning, writing a book such as this is a quest; and, like all questers, I needed helpers without whom my task would have been far more arduous and prolonged. The works of many scholars have influenced me intellectually and will be duly noted in footnotes. An unseen power, the National Endowment for the Humanities, has extended itself to me in gracious largess through a Fellowship for Younger Humanists during the year 1973–74. Without that aid the project would have taken many more summers.

Special thanks are directed to my former teacher at the University of Connecticut, Wolfgang Paulsen, who is now at the University of Massachusetts. He has encouraged me through word and deed. I also wish to thank my friend Barrett Mandel at Rutgers University for his constructive and helpful criticism on my chapter about autobiography. On home ground, colleagues and friends have helped me in many ways. My thanks go to Joseph B. Monda, to James Reichmann, S. J., to Dolores Johnson, whose keen critique of the beginnings of my book I have kept in mind throughout, and to Kenneth MacLean who has helped me in my translations of the poems by Sachs and Celan. I also thank Seattle University's Committee for Research for their generous assistance in the final preparations of my manuscript.

Most of all, my gratitude goes to my husband, Haig Bosmajian, although my public stance prohibits me from indulging in sentiment. I will conclude with apologies to my son Harlan, whose mother image is that of a woman at her desk. To his frustrated inquiries as to why I must always write about the war, I would answer, if he understood German, with the lines of Bertolt Brecht:

> In mir streiten sich
> Die Begeisterung über den blühenden Apfelbaum
> Und das Entsetzen über die Reden des Anstreichers.
> Aber nur das zweite
> Drängt mich zum Schreibtisch.
>
> (At odds within me are
> The delight over the blooming apple tree
> And the horror over the speeches of the painter-trickster.
> But only the latter
> Urges me to my desk.)

Hamida Bosmajian
Seattle, 1979

"We are not . . . reduced to the ineffable when we try to dig beneath the myths of evil; we still come up with a language."[5] Ricoeur defines the language of fault as a complex of symbols clustering around the notions of impurity and defilement and oscillating between physical and ethical dirtiness, the "stain of sin." Ricoeur's examples are metaphors of evil which the literature about the unspeakable situation employs again and again, but the physical nature of fault is also hidden in words that appear quite abstract, for example, *rigor* and *chaos*. The etymons of rigor, rigidity, and the German *rigoros* suggest a stiff, unbending, authoritarian posture, a tensed concentration that is also expressed through the German *steif* and *starr* (stiff, i.e., *stipes*, post or tree trunk) as well as in the words *wrath, anger, anxiety*, or the German *Angst, Grimm*, and *Zorn*. The metaphors hidden in these words, which no longer seem metaphorical, suggest a physical or mental condition of distressful constriction whose pain and rage urge towards violent release.

Chaos only seems the opposite of constricted rigidity. One takes a rigidly defensive attitude as a retreat from chaos—the yawn, gape or chasm—but that retreat results in an anxious turmoil within. This process is the radical of the myth of creation where chaos is equated with evil and "salvation identical with creation itself" (Ricoeur, p. 172). Such ethical connotations are constructs of human consciousness which, after becoming aware of itself, fears everything of which it is not conscious. As Erich Neumann argues, "Chaos and the seemingly unshakable order of consciousness appear in humankind, for extra-human nature is as free from the Devil as it is from rigidity and chaos."[6] In the Judaic and Christian mystic tradition, creation, that is, form, comes into being after God retreats into an unbearable state of wrathful rigor. His energies demand to become manifest and individuated in a creation which offers relief but which is a catastrophe unless it is tempered by mercy or love. Orthodox views split that myth into the image of the life-giving God and the life-denying devil, who destroys because he cannot create. In Dante's vision he is the unhappiest and most repressed of beings, for the weight of the whole world lies upon him. As a demonic scapegoat he is the antithesis to Christ who took the sins of the world upon himself out of love and thus liberated himself. Metaphors and myths project the two sides of the rage for order and the rage for chaos. There is form as meaningful shape and form as rigidity; there is chaos as meaningless void and as the potential for all meaning.

Psychologically, the compressed aggressive-defensive posture of rigidity and the sense of chaotic emptiness are in a reciprocal relationship.

In order to get to the archetype from which all our metaphors of evil are generated, we must push towards the basic phenomenon to which both rigidity and chaos are related. But, as Jung points out, the "further down" the archetypes are, the more they become universalized and are "finally extinguished in the body's materiality, i.e., in chemical substances. Hence 'at bottom' the psyche is simply the world."[7] Because of consciousness and our ability to project, we experience a profound sense of lack over our impotence to retain our individual consciousness. Western civilization, at least, experiences the fact of death as an unnatural and punitive doom. Death reduces the body to the "merely physical," an incomprehensibility to the thinking and feeling consciousness. We cannot imagine ourselves dead, for such imagining is itself a contradiction to annihilation. The rigid corpse, void of life, is the final image of rigidity and chaos, an image associated with physical and ethical impurity and, therefore, part of that language of fault as defined by Ricoeur.

The archetype from which the metaphors of evil are generated is that tendency which causes a defensive-aggressive, hence rigid, attitude towards formlessness and chaos. It is the negative retreat from empathetic response and is manifested physically in the upright backbone, the stiff upper lip, the heavy heart, or the sense of total indifference to the outside world, the individual feeling himself no more than a bag of bones. How mental and physical conditions induce both chaos and rigidity can been seen in the example of the concentration camp inmate and his oppressor. The prisoner may eventually become completely apathetic to the world around him, while the SS man who reduced him to that state of physical deprivation had often felt an inner emptiness which he sought to escape by joining the Party. His work in the camp demanded that he repress all human feeling and become "as hard as steel" until he was as void of life as his victim, though for different reasons. What Henry V. Dicks calls in *Licensed Mass Murder* "the murderous enclave in the personality," which "remains for most of us a safely encapsulated area,"[8] was stimulated by Nazi death constellations to such an extent that, once its power was licensed, it broke forth with a violence that led to the creation of a catastrophic world.

The physical and psychological sense of rigidity and chaos finds its positive expression in the feeling that we have a self which is contained and centered but is also expansive as it takes the plurality of the world into itself and projects it again as personal vision. Through the objective other, whom we endow with meaning, we define and confirm ourselves, in this case not in opposition but in empathy. It is the feeling that expresses the sense of being alive. The feeling is extended cosmically in Beatrice's answer to Dante's question why God created the world: "Not to increase Its good . . . but that reflections of his reflection might declare 'I am' . . . new loves were born of the Eternal Love."[9] Yet it must be remembered that this loving and nonpossessive narcissism contrasts with the tortures of the damned; it feels no empathy for them. The demonic though human version of the divine Narcissus is the person who has been forced to see what should not be seen and defines himself by what he saw. Such is the image of young Eliezer Wiesel at the end of *Night* when he sees his alien image in a mirror and is locked in the unspeakable memories that reflect from a corpse-like face.

In spite of this, Wiesel dedicates his book to the memory of his beloved parents and sister. In one way or another, all the literary works which I will discuss in this study have at the core a failure of love. One hesitates to use the word *love,* abused as it has become. Theodor Adorno expresses a like hesitation before he points out that "every person today, without exception, feels not sufficiently loved because no one can love enough. The incapacity for an empathic identification was unquestionably the most important psychological reason that made it possible for Auschwitz to occur among relatively proper and harmless human beings."[10] The refusal to love, motivated by the failure to receive love, is the vicious circle that defines the ground of deprivation in the literature written in the shadow of Nazism. Moreover, there seems no remedy for it, for it is as impossible to fulfill the commandment of love in the New Testament as it is to obey every letter of the law in the Old Testament. The human being is bound to accumulate guilt in reality and in fictions about human reality. Usually incapable of loving our neighbor, humankind much more readily loves an ideology or a leader who promises to take care of our collective selves by permitting us to project and unleash our deprivations and anxieties onto a group that has been defined as "the others." Even the creative energy of the artist, which I am aligning here with life-giving forces, is not unadulterated. For the artist, too, creates out of deprivation and aggression and uses the same mythmaking energies that are used to create repressive political systems; however, he has less power and can, therefore, do less harm. As Paul Celan clearly realized, "Whatever word you speak, you are indebted to *Verderben,* to evil, destruction, annihilation."[11]

II.

Nazi Mythmaking and Its Effect on Traditional Literary Archetypes and Conventions

Although the responsible historian knows that the Nazi era did not begin on the evening of 12 September 1919 when Hitler went to his first meeting of the German Worker's Party, and did not end on 30 April 1945 when he committed suicide in Berlin, a mere glance at a chronological table of that time already stimulates patterns of interpretations. This is unavoidable since history is created by a symbolic interpretation of reality and becomes, after events occur, again symbolic. When historical reality leaves negative and guilt-laden memories, we develop either the tendency to shelve those memories into a legendary realm where they can be made exciting, or we view history with a deeply pessimistic attitude, as a vicious circle of dog years. Even the latter perception is mythical, for, as Cassirer argues, "History can live and breathe only in the human world." It does not aim at a conglomeration of facts but at the relation of these facts to a form of self-knowledge.[12] The word *Geschichte* communicates with its dual meanings of history and story the mythical impulse of history. The self-knowledge that can be gained from history seems at best the knowledge that in the study of history, too, memory screens control and represses recall.

The many documentaries made by and about the Nazis generally have the effect of turning that time into a pattern with beginning, middle, and end. Its iconic images fascinate us and yet separate that time from us. The pattern usually begins with images of social unrest in Germany. Hitler is still a face in the crowd; a white circle for identification surrounds his head and gives it a symbolic dimension as the unknown is marked and set off. Then follows a sequence showing Hitler before the crowd, which is at first disorganized but eventually evolves into uniformed and disciplined columns. The aimless marching of resounding boots, as we witness it in the propaganda film *Triumph of the Will,* is finally directed to the imperialist aims of the Nazis. In contrast to these masculine formations are the crowds of enthusiastic women rushing towards the Führer's car in Dionysian abandon while the Führer himself stands rigidly aware of his destiny. A few images of broken shop windows and anti-Semitic signs intimate the nightmare world of the Nazis. The end invariably shows the fiery collapse of Berlin, the broken shelters of the Nazis, and the liberation of the concentration camps—their pits revealed, their ghostly survivors tumbling forward. It is unlikely that this often repeated documentary ritual genuinely increases historical consciousness and self-knowledge. Instead it permits the viewer to secretly thrill over the unanimous crowds and the horror of destruction while leaving him secure in his moral righteousness. Those who lived at that time can on occasion be heard to say nostalgically, "Es war schon eine tolle Zeit" (What a mad but exciting time it was).

No postwar writers or poets whose concerns are ethical try to evoke such a thrill. Their concern is with the suffering of the victim and, even more, with the intellectual and emotional make-up of the survivor-victim and the bystander, the little fellow travelers of history. Historically important figures are generally absent from literary works. When they do appear, as in Hochhuth's *The Deputy,* heroic posturings emerge in spite of all the satiric attacks and ironic understatements. The demythologizing of the Nazis has been the unwritten program of the poet whose language is German, and this, too, raises problems. For while the concept of the banality of evil explains much about the bureaucrats, who after all put Nazi rhetoric into action, it overlooks the fact that the pseudo-religious symbols and hyperboles of the Nazis, the wide-screen effect of their displays on grand occasions, were power symbols that transferred their potency to men and women who felt insignificant unless they rallied around the symbols of the Party.

Detlev Grieswelle argues in his excellent study of Nazi propaganda that we can only understand the effect of Hitler's rhetoric if we view it as sermons of political faith uttered by a preacher who defined himself as a secular savior.[13] He did not argue with the failing policies of the Weimar Republic by countering them with carefully worked out and constructive political and economic programs; he invented, instead, the magic word *System* for the Republic and directed against it the full force of his rhetoric of negation: "Germany needs an iron broom to sweep everything away," he told his audiences (Grieswelle, p. 79). His favorite images have mythical and eschatological connotations. There is his death-linked imagery of fault—slave chains, shame, rotting corpses, swamp, leeches, plagues, poison, vermin, bacilli, parasites, worms—and, contrasting with it, the language of renewal and resurrection—growth, sun, blooming, awake, rebirth, liberation, purification, paradise, resurrection. Such patterns were already set by 1922–23 when he related the following apocalyptic vision to his listeners: "Blast furnaces may explode, coal mines may be flooded, houses may burn to ashes—if only a people *[Volk]* rises behind them strong, unshakable, determined till the end! For when the German people will resurrect again then everything else will be resurrected. But if everything stood and a people succumbs to an inner corruption, then chimneys, industries, and oceans of houses are nothing but the gravestones of this people" (Grieswelle, p. 78). One cannot deny the archetypal validity and appeal of such language; it has, however, nothing to do with the rational discourse that most governments pretend to apply to political decision making. By the time thousands chant "ein Reich, ein Volk, ein Führer," the dichotomy of "Deutschland erwache" (Germany awake) and "Juda verrecke" (Juda die) has been established, while the savior and his disciples call to those they wish to save and reject those they wish to destroy.

Nazism displaced the concept of a transcendent god into the image of the German Aryan; thus, as Grieswelle points out, the borderline between religion and politics vanished as the Christian god became one with the interests of the nation (pp. 185-86). This displacement abolished the built-in safeguard of Christian anagogic thought, namely, that the heaven of the blessed and the hell of the damned are projections of love and hate over which mankind basically has no power, placing them beyond time and space. When these projections are displaced into historical time, then a Dante needs no longer to create an inferno; Auschwitz will have become its realization. Hitler's use of apocalyptic and demonic images devalued, therefore, the eschatological vocabulary of Christianity, and it devalued political discourse by diverting attention from the economic and social realities that are the concern of politics. Nevertheless, the disastrous success of this language was undeniable until the mythologizers themselves became trapped in the myths they concocted.

The structure of Nazi mythology can be divided into Hitler's utopia and Jewish kakotopia, the latter being both the world in which Jews were allowed to live and the world designated for Jews, the concentration camp. Legends about Hitler spread throughout the course of the movement and seem to the detached observer nothing but obvious propaganda of sentimental *Kitsch* aimed at momentary effectiveness. Such *Kitsch* became, however, the *miranda* of power during the Nuremberg Party rallies or shrank to the gruesome grotesquery of the orchestra at Auschwitz playing for those who were about to die.

The messiah myth defines Hitler as early as 1924 in a sentimental story about "a lonely wanderer walking across the Bavarian mountains" in 1919. He "taught people to understand their misery and hope for future salvation." When the people of an isolated hamlet pledged their support, "Adolf Hitler got up and looked at the people. And at this hour God was in his heart" (Grieswelle, pp. 46–47). As the following editorial reveals, he is the rejected cornerstone and the unknown savior who emerges from the midst of a people: "He was a torchbearer, preacher, and evangelist. They wanted to follow him and go his way. Even if it meant the cross. His way was hard and strewn with thorns. But everyone wanted to walk it. His example was an obligation. His work was sacrifice, fulfillment, and devotion. He came to us unknown. A God gave him the grace to awaken us. And a tongue to speak movingly. Behind him arose a people. Out of him they formed a future. . . ."[14] But Hitler was no passively suffering Christ; instead he was the Aryan dragon slayer as savior. Many poems and street songs project that image, implicit in the composition of an elementary school pupil: "As Jesus liberated men from sin and hell, so Hitler saved the German people from ruin. Jesus and Hitler were persecuted, but while Jesus was crucified, Hitler was raised to be chancellor. . . . Jesus built for heaven, Hitler for the German earth."[15] While these religious metaphors were effective propaganda, Hitler respected in actuality only the centralized power of the Catholic Church, a rival who he vowed to destroy after the war. He felt only contempt for the ethics of Christianity which he saw as "the systematic cultivation of human failure."[16]

As a member and the leader of the *Volksgemeinschaft* (racial and national community), the Führer was its perfect manifestation, while his idealized follower was a white, blond, masculine body ablaze in sunlight and reflecting through physical purity that most important "fanatical purity" of his inner nature, devoting itself in absolute faith and obedience to the Führer. The attempt to realize this transfiguration of an ordinary human being resulted in a person who was asked to repress all humane feelings for the sake of an iron will and granite strength, metaphors of rigidity that are clearly projected in the parade goose step during which the marchers fixed their eyes on the reviewing Führer. A noninvolved onlooker readily sees these steps as those of a fanatic marionette. The linguist Viktor Klemperer, for example, records his impressions of a drum major who kicked so high that he almost seemed suspended in this tense, unnatural pose: "Here I saw fanaticism in its specifically National Socialist manifestation; this mute figure communicated to me for the first time the language of the Third Reich."[17] The Nazis themselves viewed such rigidity as order. For instance, in a report published in *Das Reich,* the chaotic conditions in the Warsaw ghetto, brought about by the supposedly degenerate nature of its inhabitants, are contrasted with an image of Nazi discipline: "Sometimes one can meet a troop of German soldiers marching to the accompaniment of tuneful music. Then it seems as if the ordering principle, which represents the power of this space, steps into the foreground of daily life.''[18] In her poem ''What secret cravings of the blood'' Nelly Sachs comprehends metaphorically this particular manifestation of rigidity and chaos brought about by the ''terrible puppeteer'': ''Arms up and down,/Legs up and down/And the setting sun of Sinai's people/As the red carpet underfoot.''[19]

By identifying the Jews with satanic forces of disorder, Hitler found an even more effective means of attack than the one against the Weimar *System.* As devil, a Jew could be attacked collectively and individually. He was both capitalist and bolshevik. Economically, his status was one of *Schuld* (guilt and indebtedness); politically, it was one of seduction and betrayal. In the early parts of *Mein Kampf,* Hitler begins his association of Jews with the physically and ethically impure language of fault: ''The cleanliness of this people, moral and otherwise, I must say, is a point in itself. By their very exterior you could tell that these were no lovers of water, and, to your distress, you often knew it with your eyes closed. Later I often grew sick to my stomach from the smell of these caftan-wearers. Added to this, there was their unclean dress and their generally unheroic appearance.''[20] Nazi metaphors of evil followed the pattern of those used by many societies throughout history whenever human beings were defined as *the others.* Eventually, Hitler's image of the obscure ghetto Jew extended to all Jews and finally to all who differed from the Nazi concept of man. Defined by a language of death with its associations of dirt, anality, and corrupt sexuality, *the other* had to be exorcized and placed into a locale suitable to its nature. The gruesome *Endlösung* (final solution) was to become the *Erlösung* (salvation) of the German people. As Goebbels wrote in an editorial for *Das Reich* on 16 November 1941, ''The Jews must be separated from the German racial community . . . that is an elementary law of racial, natural, and social hygiene.''[21]

The parody of Western ideas of progress and of all utopian thinking was realized in the kakotopia of the concentration camp, a word once part of the administrative rhetoric of the Nazis, but now denoting a stark though incomprehensible reality. As an excremental place it was set off from the rest of the world (or so it seemed) and became a state in itself. Yet deception masked even here the reality of the gas chamber (shower), the pit, the crematoriums, and the ashes (the workers, the factory, the product). Today, Auschwitz and Dachau are museums that preserve the past by enclosing it in images and symbols, thus sheltering the living consciousness from attempting to approximate the meaning of such museum pieces. Although the deaths of thousands was the daily routine of the camps while they existed, it was mythmaking that lead to their construction, and it is mythmaking that makes them comprehensible to us. Yet when the reality of the camp was about to be instituted, it was to be done in the evasive and euphemistic language of bureaucrats. The reader will find no mythical and apocalyptic images in the minutes of the Wannsee Conference held in Berlin on 20 January 1942, but only the casually deceptive language of the banality of evil: "Under suitable management, related to the final solution, the Jews will be put to work in an appropriate manner in the eastern territories. In huge work columns, separated by sex, the work-able Jews will be led into these areas while building roads; through this a large part will, without doubt, fall out due to natural depreciation. The final residue, since it constitutes the most resilient part, will have to be treated appropriately because it must be viewed, as a natural selection, as the germ cell of a Jewish reconstitution after liberation (see historical experience)."[22]

Such language seems to have repressed aggression as it turns death into an agenda for a meeting of efficient managers. The nightmare that is created by them is best expressed, not through the metaphor of the inferno, but through the metaphor of the factory where all guilt is abolished because everybody is merely part of a machine. The banality of evil is, however, again enormous; for while the petty followers of the Third Reich may have found no great destiny, they found numerous haphazard and planned opportunities in which their licensed power allowed them to willfully vent their aggressions. Mythical projections and banal reality obviously contain the potential for ironic perception. They are thus perceived in literature written in the shadow of Nazism, a literature where irony also functions as a defense and screen against an undesirable world which irony is incapable of transforming.

III.
The Ironic Mode as an Expression of and Defense against the Nightmare of History

The words *rigidity* and *chaos* are understood as antitheses to form, reverberating with life and unindividuated, life-giving potential. Yet when the negative denotations of rigidity and chaos are manifested in images, our need to give meaning is so insistent that we see the rigid, life-emptied corpse, the stare of the madman, of the harrowed and emaciated human being as an expression of spirituality in which all spirit is gone. Similarly, the aggressive-defensive posture of the repressed individual, shut off from all empathetic responses to the world, can be seen in its sullen and stubborn silence as an expression of integrity, thoughtfulness, and even profundity. Images and metaphors of evil suggest parodies of desirable states of being and are, therefore, ironic. In Dante's cosmic romance of the self, evil is obviously a parody of the good that ultimately controls evil. But when the projections of romance are displaced into historical time and space, parody becomes increasingly ambiguous, and the individual's power to clearly separate good and evil is reduced, as is the power to act and to create. The result is the mode of irony as Northrop Frye defined it. [23] It is a mode that has been part of Western literature for a long time and that has begun more recently to undermine the myth of meaning itself.

The creative imagination is caught in ironies as it seeks to give expression to an unspeakable situation that is at the same time absolute as a historical fact. To write or to remain silent is the first choice the poet has to make; for writing will inevitably be done at the expense of the victims, while silence represses victims and persecutors to the state of a taboo. Secondly, language, the poet's medium, has been corrupted in its course through time. Connotative meanings charged with memories of abuses and cruelties have attached themselves to words whose archetypal connotations were once the very stuff of poetry. Historical events which displaced the inferno into the ghetto or concentration camp, the purgatorio into the world of the compromising and directionless bystander, and the paradiso into the rigid formations of a party rally of persecutors, have limited the freedom of artistic choice; for no longer can merely anything in reality be subject to mimesis in a work of art. On the one hand, the creative imagination is compelled by its ethical-judicial involvement in historical time to bear witness against that time; on the other hand, it is conscious of its impotence to do so. The witness role is not the role of the judge; it is the role of limited vision and power. But it is the only role possible, for there is no judicial sentence that can redeem the unspeakable situation. Desire for redemption is, however, the secret motivation of the poet writing in the ironic mode; it is the ultimate irony.

German writers and poets who want to preserve the memory of Auschwitz in their work will be criticized if they do so and if they do not. For they are not qualified to write about events in which they did not take part, and yet it is demanded of them that they take a stand. Playwright and novelist Martin Walser argues that those who were not in the camp know little about the nature of an SS man and even less about the ordeal of the inmates: "We cannot imagine a situation where people are totally without rights. We cannot put ourselves in place of the 'inmates' because the measure of their suffering goes beyond any known concept and we can, therefore, make for ourselves no human image of those who inflicted that suffering."[24] Nevertheless, as Hans Egon Holthusen declares, the obligation to write remains a necessity for an entire generation of writers for whom the past remains "unmastered": "This past, as we all know, has not faded or become indifferent in two decades, but rather stronger, more terrifying, more unbearable, and, one would like to add, more incomprehensible."[25] One cannot master the past and remain conscious of it, for mastering implies repression. Dwelling on a pathological past does not necessarily lead to consciousness but may be merely a ritual of confession. Hans Magnus Enzensberger has been very critical of this: "The reality of Auschwitz shall be exorcized as if it were the past, specifically the national past and not a common present and future."[26]

No matter how engaged and ethically committed literature is, the process of metaphorically displacing reality will inevitably raise the question of a conflict between aesthetics and ethics. Theodor Adorno feels that "it is characteristic for such literature that it hints, intentionally or unintentionally, that the essentially human flourishes in extreme situations because they supposedly reveal the essence of man."[27] One alternative is silence, as George Steiner suggests;[28] however, there are two kinds of silence. The first comes from too much knowledge, while the second is a refusal to become aware. This second silence is the escape into which memory and guilt are repressed until they discharge themselves again in defensive wrath. To varying degrees, both kinds of silence are present in any work of literature because of the repression and projection process that characterizes metaphoric constructs. When readers are stunned by an image that seems to reveal so much, they need only ask themselves what has been omitted in order to discover how much has been consigned to silence.

For the literary artist who is Jewish, the choice of writing in the German language is often problematical and conscious. As exiled poets they are deprived of a sense of at-homeness and yet need a language that will house their thoughts and memories of home and exile. Without using the word *deutsch*, Peter Weiss argues in his autobiography that the language he chose after the war was as absolutely free as he was. But his choice of words contradicts that freedom, for his language was a language from the past: "The language which asserted itself now was the language I had learned at the beginning of my life, the natural language which was my tool, which belonged only to me, and which had nothing to do with the land where I grew up. This language was present wherever I went and wherever I would be. . . . I could carry the language with me, the lightest of luggage. In this moment the war was overcome.''[29] For Celan, language also is a possession but is laden with all the abuses and enrichments that agglutinate to it in historical time: ''It, language, remained: yes, in spite of all. But it had to go through its own answerlessness, go through a terrible muteness, go through the thousand darknesses of death-bringing speech. It went through and had no words for what happened; but it went through these happenings. Went through and was allowed to emerge into the light of day again, 'enriched' by it all.''[30] Words may become burdened with guilt, but they still retain an openness for new meanings as well as the possibility to express ''the quite other'' as the poet Celan ''goes with his existence to language, wounded by reality and seeking reality.'' The poet chooses the abused language and makes it his own by defining his world and vision through it; as soon as the direction of the poet's work is outward towards the affairs of humankind, however, the tension between language as a private treasure and as abused public property reasserts itself.

The abuse of language is, of course, a continual process and is not limited to a specific political movement. However, for the German-speaking individual who is conscious of language and history, certain words immediately create a state of tension. This is the case when the words *Deutscher* and *Jude* are juxtaposed, especially in confrontations between two generations of Germans. Likewise, no writer conscious of the Nazi meanings of *Blut und Boden* (blood and soil), of *Volksgemeinschaft* or *braun,* can use such words naively. *Braun* retains its traditional associations with the color of earth, the nut brown of fall, the brown of human skin; but there also looms the connotation of the excremental brown of the brown battalions in the Horst Wessel song. Hence, Günter Grass's lyric, elegiac catalogue about the color brown in *Dog Years* ends with that excremental brown, and Siegfried Lenz shows in *The German Lesson* how the painter Nansen became a decent man by developing an allergy to the color brown. Basic words have become ironical, and the single use of such a word suffices to undercut any nostalgic memory. Words and names spark a nervous reaction, as, for example, in Johnson's *Jahrestage,* where Gesine Cresspahl's immediate reaction to the name Roosevelt is the correction that he was not really the head of the international Jewish conspiracy.

The ironic poet is aware that archetypal images of totality and wholeness are projections of human dreams, language, and artistic creation and that ''at bottom'' the archetypes are ''extinguished in the body's materiality.'' Hence, ''the Orcus is above,'' as one of the characters in *Dog Years* admonishes. Hell is not a downward transcendence; it is experienced in the horizontal space of human time wherein an individual's damnation or salvation is delimited. The ironic imagination finds that words like *hell* or *inferno* no longer heighten the familiar or illuminate the incomprehensible. Rather, they are reduced to clichés whose conventionality serves as a bridging effort between poet and reader. The reader is asked to muster all the associations that have accrued to these words in order to vaguely intimate the trauma of the unspeakable situation, the physical reality, the overcrowdedness, stench, filth, and chaos of camp or ghetto. The insufficiency of the inferno metaphor becomes immediately apparent when we consider the inhabitants of that secular world where demons and damned were individuals deprived of individuality.

In Dante's hell the damned are locked rigidly in their egocentric individuality. Their identities are defined and named; they are not hollow men. In control of his ideas about the nature of good and evil, Dante dreamed a nightmare of perverted desire for us over six hundred years ago which we realized in the twentieth century. He appeals to the creative imagination not merely because he provides conventional analogies. The ironic literary artist is aware that Dante projected a fantastically sadistic vision through which he moved innocently and securely in the knowledge that his infernal system was officially licensed. In fact, however, it is Dante's imagination which decides who will be saved and who will be damned, and thus, he is a far greater overreacher than Faust. As unmoved mover, Dante the poet watches himself walk through hell, teaches himself to repress all empathy, and praises himself when he kicks one of the damned paralyzed in ice. The Dante enthusiast has to admit that Dante's education in hell is similar to that of the SS guard in the camp: he has to become hardened against those who have been condemned as the others. The difference is that Dante knew that if such tortures should ever be displaced into historical time, their perpetrators would find themselves punished with everlasting pain, a state of being they themselves desire. Only a god is allowed to create an inferno.

In the camps, human beings transformed compassion into aggressive flare-ups or voided themselves of empathy and, without emotion, deprived their victims of life. Licensed with power, the persecutor usually did not view the powerless victim as sinner; in retrospect, the persecutor, when brought to judgment, appears strangely void of personality, fixed though he might be in ritualistic denials or rationalizations of sin and guilt. The perpetrators of the holocaust undermined a cherished high mimetic myth, namely, the notion of the personhood of the great sinner so well exemplified in the medieval Faust legend. Irony was always part of that legend, but it has now become so dominant that it overwhelms any grandeur the person of Faust possessed for Marlowe or Goethe.

The poetic imagination has been aware that Faust externalized his shadow in Mephistopheles who then could seduce Faust's all-too-ready will. The persistence of that convenient split is evident in an essay, written in 1947, wherein the Germans are seen collectively as Faust and Hitler is seen as the Mephistopheles who led them astray: "The satanism of Hitlerism is the nightside of German idealism which, through a lost war and a present undermined with social crises, had reached a dead end."[31] The ironic German Thomas Mann does not make use of such flattering constellations of despair but realizes that shadow qualities are banalities which trouble the person of the artist as they troubled the Faust-Mephisto-Hitler personality. Recognizing this kinship, he writes in "A Brother": "For must I not, however much it hurts, regard the man [Hitler] as an artist phenomenon? Mortifyingly enough, it is all there: . . . the bad conscience, the sense of guilt, the anger at everything . . . the obstinate need for self-justification, self-proof, the urge to dominate and subdue, the dream of seeing the whole world, abased with fear and love, admiration and remorse, at the feet of the once despised."[32] The difference between Thomas Mann and his brother Hitler is that the ironic poet is conscious of his questionable kinship with the trickster.

In the ironic mode, consciousness is much desired and discussed, but it remains a dead end or is unattainable for the trickster and his or her constantly shifting and ambiguous roles. The trickster-self fills the void with words and creates through them a questionable vision that serves as a screen against the painful sense of deprivation and guilt, first experienced on the personal level as the denial or betrayal of love, and later transferred to the political and historical sphere. Reflections lead to painful awareness, and such awareness can be meliorated and repressed by the desire for action through myths of positive change. Yet the reader is aware that such tentative yearnings, as they can be found in Weiss's *The Investigation* or Johnson's *Jahrestage,* repress guilt through a utopian vision which sees the concentration camps as mere excesses of capitalism. In a world where no god worries over and prepares the individual's salvation or damnation, there remains a choice of nightmares: a degree of consciousness at the price of feeling impotent in historical time, whose guilts the conscious individual wants to escape, or the repression and denial of guilt as the individual projects hopes into the future, thus insuring that the past will invariably repeat itself in spite of all good intentions. The Orcus of history has no three-headed demon at the center and no way out towards a purgation of sin and guilt. Hells are created now and then, here and there; and the memory of them may be encapsuled as an unspeakable catastrophe, or they may be shelved in museum images that are mere shells unless the imagination reanimates them.

The creative imagination of the ironist is "in the know" about such ironies which keep it from making the commitment that any belief demands. The ironic poet and his or her personae are witnesses of evil who threaten to expose what they have seen and heard. Their power is that of a trickster who could become a civilizing agent; but, because they also want to belong to the human community, they use the screens, disguises, and repressions that humanity always employs. The ironist as trickster is finally as self-deceptive as those whom he wishes to expose.

Being in the know, the ironist is necessarily exiled and isolated from the unreflective human condition, but so dear is the power of knowledge that he or she is willing to pay that price. What the ironist knows is the secret life of the others, the life they want to repress, forget, or rationalize. By knowing about the sins of the world, the ironist takes those sins upon himself and becomes a kind of *pharmakos*, a scapegoat guilty because he is part of a guilty society, but less guilty than those who refuse to become aware. For example, Siggi Jepsen, the narrator of *The German Lesson*, realizes that he is in a reformatory in place of his father who never learned to see, never found a new word, and from whom he will always be exiled. Siggi's consciousness is the consciousness of the reflective witness and thus is necessarily a partial vision that reveals another refraction in the prism of irony, namely, that consciousness does not need to mean consciousness of self but merely consciousness of the faults of others as these relate to the self. The final joke that world and time play on the ironic exile is that he is one of us; proud and insistent on his notion of separate identity, he is a parody of individuality as he is continually subjected to external pressures to which he succumbs more frequently than he would like to admit. For the time being, he will remain with us at the bottom of Socrates' cave.

Lacking that cosmic extension of self which "conceives all things in a single volume bound by Love, of which the universe is scattered leaves" (*Paradiso,* XXXIII), the ironist becomes a little god who gathers his fragmented perception into a fiction of order; for only in that order is any sort of transcendence possible. Here, as Lukacs argued, irony becomes a corrective to the world's fragility since "inadequate relations can transform themselves into a fanciful yet well-ordered round of misunderstandings and cross purposes, within which everything is seen as many-sided, within which things appear isolated yet connected, full of value and yet totally void of it, as abstract fragments and as concrete autonomous life, as flowering and as decaying, as the infliction of suffering and as suffering itself.''[33] Although Lukacs's definition was written before the momentous reality of Nazism, his words continue to apply to literature written in the shadow of Nazism. Even as it insists on emptiness, rigidity, and chaos, even as it insists on the impotence of language, the literary work cannot avoid meaning, a meaning that is given to it by the nature of the language that shapes it. The language of the ironist carries its own meaning, and the ironist speaks only in so far as he artfully and fatefully complies with his language in his attempt to reveal his ethical-judicial attitude by means of metaphors of evil.

IV.
Literary Form as a Means to Approximate and Escape from Historical Reality

Verbal universes compensate us for our human deprivations. As recorded in a book, knowledge about holocausts will always be more or less peripheral knowledge, for the center of the conflagration consumes all who find themselves therein. As signs and symbols, words—sometimes the very words that brought the extreme situation to pass—reverberate with the memory of horror and simultaneously screen that memory. Herein lies the truth contained in all literature concerning extreme situations in general and, in particular, in the unspeakable situation brought about by Nazism. The survivor-witness and the witness as bystander somehow need to repress and compensate for their knowledge of evil. The literary artists discussed in the following chapters engage in this process, a process that includes the yearning for transcendence as the means towards an ultimate escape from memory. But the memory of the reality of evil and humankind's reaction to it delimits, corrupts, and finally denies the possibility of transcendence.

In order to keep the reality of the extreme situation before my own and the reader's mind, I will first discuss the record of four nonfictional witnesses who were at the precipice of the conflagration. These records were not written in German. The concentrationary universe was international, and not many wrote about it in German, Ernst Wiechert's *Der Totenwald* being a questionable exception. For those whose native language was German, its use often became problematical after survival and liberation. The literary form which communicates the impact of the concentrationary universe with greatest immediacy is the diary. Odd Nansen's *Day after Day* and Chaim Kaplan's *Warsaw Diary* sprang from the diarists' need to respond to the moment as it occurred in order to forestall forgetting. The diarist does not hesitate to record gruesome and grotesquely real moments which may appear sensational from the more distant perspective of the autobiographer. Yet because the diary follows day after day, the outrageous becomes part of the daily routine, recurring with the same predictability as roll call or the search for food. In retrospect, the reader of a diary is aware of how the diarist unconsciously shaped the narrative pattern and theme of his record. The diarist found himself in a situation which he tried to make comprehensible through a language whose topography is conventional and which attempts to locate what is finally inexpressible.

Immediacy of observation combined with accessible language would make the diary appear to be a highly reliable record; but, in order to write, the diarist at least needs minimal distance, perhaps only the wall of his barrack which separates him from being consumed by the holocaust. He also has the minimal choice of what to include and what to exclude; through this choice, as well as through occasional visionary glimpses of a better life, he can transcend to some degree of weight of the hours. Finally, it is only the diary itself, however, which provides a measure of transcendence wherein he records the world of camp or ghetto, a world he knows will end sometime, either because of his death or his liberation.

The autobiographer recollects and shapes his experience from a more distant point of view in time. As a survivor, his memory selects, condenses, and interprets experience. However shocking the details of an autobiography may be, they can be viewed as part of the autobiographer's individuation process in an evil time. Thus, Elie Wiesel's *Night* is the record of a downward transcendence experienced by a fifteen year old who was cast into Auschwitz and stripped of everything he loved. He discovers strength only in rebellion against the silent, absent God of his fathers and in his care for his weak, earthly father. Wiesel records the memory of his losses in a book whose pattern ritualistically repeats the ordeal but condenses lived experience into the *Wahrheit of Dichtung,* the inevitable consequence of repression, recollection, and artistic choice. Such extended repetition was not possible for Tadeusz Borowski, a Polish political prisoner at Auschwitz. At best he can collect memory points and reflections in the form of short stories gathered in English under the title *This Way for the Gas, Ladies and Gentlemen.* Yet each of his stories is a ritualistic, physical or mental tracing and retracing of the constricted ground of evil.

When the unspeakable situation has not been personally experienced, the ethical-judicial attitude of the literary artist bars the creative imagination from imitating actions and experiences it has not lived through. This especially affects the novel whose traditional alignment with history would make it an obvious genre for including mimeses of the concentrationary universe; but in the ironic web of the contemporary German novel, direction is at best discovered through indirection. Siegfried Lenz's *The German Lesson,* Günter Grass's *Dog Years,* and Uwe Johnson's *Jahrestage* refer to ghetto or camp through memories of photographs, intimations, allegories, and ambiguous circumlocutions. These novelists emphasize the anxieties, dreams, and failures of men and women who were children during the Nazi years, who stood and watched how their elders compromised and betrayed, and who were during those years somehow deprived of love themselves. The narrators of these three novels all write as autobiographers or diarists. They feel compelled to record and, in the process of recording, carefully touch the deprivation they experienced on the familial level, a deprivation that prepared them for adult displacements and projections of childhood trauma into historical time.

Thus, at the core of each narrative consciousness lies an encapsuled and painful sense of lack that could once more discharge itself into a catastrophic creation if the opportunity were given. In *The German Lesson,* metaphors of evil remain on a narrow, provincial ground; that ground, however, is emblematic for Germany as a whole. Because of the limited topography and because of Siggi Jepsen's youth, he can become more genuinely conscious of his selfhood than the narrators of Grass and Johnson. But Siggi also realizes that consciousness in and of itself is of no use; it does not reform the world that he knows so well. When the geographical horizon expands, personal awareness decreases as expansion becomes a device that screens the memory of painful deprivation and the sense of guilt for being thought unlovable. Grass's three profit-motivated narrators lose themselves in the pluralistic society of West Germany, while Johnson's Gesine Cresspahl seeks to escape her provincial origins by moving to New York where she believes that she can live consciously by reading the *New York Times,* whose information explosions make her aware of the global proportions of guilt in the past and present (the year 1967–68). The greater the narrator's rational expansion of consciousness is, the more his or her discomfort with civilization increases. The facts of past and present are perceived as "knowledge" and begin to define the narrator, thus making him or her a "prosthetic god" whose defense is the guilt of others. It is a troublesome and brittle defense whose many details depress. Occasionally, the narrator desires to break all defenses and penetrate to the core of the original ground of deprivation or to escape it altogether by projecting utopian political dreams which will be corrupted in historical time. Expressed in words, painful memories and wishful dreams of friendship and community turn out to be mere verbal utterances.

The possibility of seeing clearly and the dream for a better life through a new social and political mode are the only means for transcendence in these thoroughly secular novels. Here, the Nazi era does not overwhelm; rather, the novelist de-demonizes it by portraying ordinary men and women whose personalities are such that, if they were given licensed absolute power, they could commit the crimes committed in ghetto or camp. Nevertheless, the Nazi era is a constant, dreadful presence in the childhood of the narrators. This dread is most obviously and chronologically delineated in *Jahrestage;* Gesine becomes conscious of it, however, only after she reconstructs her childhood and becomes aware of how personal and political attitudes and actions reciprocally influence each other. In Grass's novel, the dread implodes into the bourgeois kitchen and into the mound of bones and ashes from the concentration camp Stutthof. In *The German Lesson* it is constricted into the closed Gestapo car that periodically appears in the novel. While such images of bottled-up dread do not communicate the suffering of those caught in the center of the nightmare of history, they are the only means with which the novelist can communicate that dread. The reader of these deeply ironic novels will not be horrified; rather, he will remain comfortably settled in an armchair, impervious to the realization that our world is a variable to the world projected by the ironist.

The documentary playwright on the other hand addresses, attacks, and often shocks a collective audience into recognizing the evil of the past and its variables in the present. Because the characters of a drama are literally embodied on the stage, the playwright can conceal himself much more than the novelist. Especially through the reliance on documents, the creative imagination of the playwright can project much more deeply the extreme situation and humankind's reaction to it, without violating the ethical-judicial directive that he may not invent such situations. Yet even Hochhuth's *The Deputy* and Weiss's *The Investigation* reveal the horrors of the camp peripherally, primarily through witnesses for whom the play becomes a ritual of judgment. There is no justice for the perpetrators and victims of the concentrationary universe; there is only the ritual of confessions of sufferings on the part of the victims or the rigid denial of fault and failure of empathy on the part of the perpetrators or bystanders. Both plays are parodies and inversions of Dante's cosmos and of the medieval mystery and morality play; and both express, in their use of these conventions, the yearning for an absolute and just judge who alone could give meaning to suffering.

In their hermetic poetry, Nelly Sachs and Paul Celan turn away from an obviously defined audience and address "the something quite other." Words used in hermetic poetry only seem to be the familiar language of signifier and signified but are actually centripetally locked into their multilayered universe of meanings. The inclusive language of these two poets becomes a hieroglyphic and sacred language with which the user addresses the deity, a deity that remains absent. In Sachs's "Landschaft aus Schreien" and Celan's "Engführung," hermetic language is charged with an ethical-judicial awareness of history. The lyric voice of both poets bears witness to the dead who no longer exist and who cannot speak for themselves; but its efforts to communicate, to establish contact, fail. Carefully chosen words alone contain the memory of evil, of the loss of love, and the desire for healing so that death would once more be part of the natural rhythm of life rather than a state of being. Given the isolation and limitations of the human being in the mode of irony, such demands drive the lyric self to a point of constriction where nothing is set free, where the self comes to a dead end. At that point, the self can merely retract its steps and design another turn in the labyrinth of words, whose surfaces seem too deceptively familiar as if they were nothing but husks protecting a void.

2

The Rage for Order: Autobiographical Accounts of the Self in the Nightmare of History

The destiny of the concentrationary universe in inconceivably remote. Measureless expanses of laws and offices, of meandering corridors and stacks of papers, where a whole genus of office workers, preoccupied and pale, lives and dies, human typewriters, isolating the camp and letting nothing leak through to the outside world except a vague and awesome terror of inhuman realms. At the center of this empire, forever invisible, a brain unifies and controls all the police resources of the Reich—and Europe—and dominates with absolute will every possible aspect of the camps—the brain of Himmler and his intimates.[1]

David Rousset, philosopher, French resistance worker, and inmate of three concentration camps, mythologizes here the bureaucracy behind the camps into the Kafkaesque cosmos of the concentrationary universe. In this universe the unspeakable event came about through the will of the Führer and through words used in laws, propaganda slogans, and obscene expletives. Words created the reality of the SS state and the other kingdom, the camp. It was precisely that power of words that Himmler feared when he told a group of SS men that the events in the camps must remain "a never recorded and never to be recorded glorious page of our history."[2] Totalitarian will wants to abolish its movement through historical time; and if Himmler had had his way, millions of Jews and other undesirables would have disappeared without any verbal record into the crematoriums and burial pits, into the abyss of unrecorded time. It was not to be. Words and the symbolic structures that the human mind shapes through them became the nemesis of the Nazis, for few historical atrocities have ever been as thoroughly documented, analyzed, and written about as the concentrationary universe.

The diary or autobiography of the victim-survivor as witness is written in a language whose familiarity of phrase makes the unspeakable situation accessible to the reader. It is a language that is outer-directed in its historical and ethical orientation and as such seems to be the antithesis to the intense inner-directedness of the hermetic language in the poetry of Nelly Sachs and Paul Celan. Yet, because each of the works to be discussed in this chapter is an expression of the same historical event as perceived by different personalities, the social aspects of language are more or less subtly subverted by the displacements, memory screens, and projections with which the victim-survivor manages to cope with the unspeakable situation. Thus, each diary or autobiography also has a centripetal movement which makes it a unique and self-contained linguistic universe. As records, Chaim Kaplan's *Warsaw Diary* and Odd Nansen's *Day after Day* seem to use familiar language that fixes experiences immediately after they occur. The language of Elie Wiesel's *Night* while still outer-directed by the familiarity of its metaphors, becomes much more centripetal, primarily because of the central image of the eyes into which the memory of the unspeakable situation contracts. Such contraction is also present in Tadeusz Borowski's short stories, whose language fluctuates between intensely realistic and objectified descriptions of human behavior at Auschwitz and demonically apocalyptic image constellations through which the narrator defends himself against the memory of Auschwitz. Nevertheless, given the pattern of the historical experience of the camp, the narrative of diarist and autobiographer follows lines that can be summarized as an ironic and perverse inversion of the conventional quest pattern, an inversion that markedly affects the traditional definition of autobiography.

I.
The Rage for Order: Metaphoric Perception of Catastrophe.

In a sense, all the works to be discussed here are defenses against horror; for even as the memory of horror is being retained, horror is given shape, is being controlled by the autobiographer. Horror is a response that comes suddenly over those whose beings are still somehow intact, and it threatens those beings with physical and psychological disintegration unless defenses are soon established. Therefore, horror particularly overwhelmed the newcomer who suddenly entered the antiworld of the camp. Old timers became used to the horror to a certain extent and developed what Erich Kahler calls "the splitting of consciousness," a transpersonal objective perception that allowed them to withdraw as much as possible from the experience of their own pain and the pain of others.[3] This splitting of consciousness is, of course, applicable to victims and persecutors alike, as well as to most of us as we turn away from the recurring horrors of historical time and retract our steps from the abyss.

The ritual of daily routine is one of the first means preventing the individual from succumbing to the experience of horror. The camp, an anarchic world of chaos and death where anything was possible, had at the same time a predictable and rigid routine; part of that routine was the daily ritual of roll call, whose main function was to terrorize the prisoner into rigid attention in summer heat or winter cold. In his record of and meditation about events, the diarist responds to the immediacy of the moment, while the autobiographer recalls such moments through memory and reflection from a more distant point of view in time. Thus, the literature which sprang from the experience of the camps inevitably contributed to the shaping of a myth of the camp experience, the myth of a secular hell. Today, what was once so very real has already taken on the aura of something distant, of a "once upon a time" horror story, a metaphor and myth of evil.

The autobiographer and diarist are witnesses who, in order to retain memory and somehow give that memory meaning, record out of a sense of personal need. Yet they realize that they cannot do justice either to reality or its victims. Like the historian, the autobiographer is finally no mere accumulator of facts but, rather, a creator of symbolic patterns that synthesize and articulate experience. Language was instrumental in the catastrophic creation of the camp world, and the language of the survivor becomes the means of coping with that catastrophe by containing its chaos within a book. The metaphors of antiworlds as applied to the camp and the prisoner's horribly ironic quest in that world are two conventional means with which the survivor-victim can comprehend and communicate catastrophic experiences.

"In extremely varied cultural contexts," writes Eliade, "we constantly find the same cosmological schema and the same ritual scenario: settling a territory is equivalent to founding a world."[4] The Warsaw Ghetto, Treblinka, and Auschwitz were such staked-out territories in conquered Poland. Here settlements were established that were the antithesis of the sheltering nest, the refuge, the loved, sacred place that is the clearing in the wilderness, the form out of chaos. Instead, the camp became the obscene place with all the perverted sacredness that attaches itself to the obscene. It was a tabooed place, an autonomous state existing in time but simultaneously outside of time. Because it was so alien, the outsider could repress its existence even though the camp always depended on outside contact. Eugen Kogon points to the perverted Darwinism of the camps and their absolute lack of justice, the first requisite of an ordered state: "The concentration camp was a world in and of itself—an order into which man was thrown with all his virtues and vices (more vices than virtues) to fight for bare existence and mere survival."[5] This separate and secret place fulfilled its function not only as a center for the destruction of life but also as a means to spread anxiety and terror through the land, feelings much stronger than those of the traditional fear of hell. For no matter how much the indifferent person suppressed the knowledge of the camp, he or she knew that it was very real. It was the nadir of the new Reich envisioned by the Nazis, and at the bottom of its hierarchy were the Jews, who had been defined as the epitome of evil.

At one point, all accounts of the concentrationary universe attempt to convey the physical reality of camp or ghetto either through analogy with the Christian, especially Dantean, concept of hell or through analogy with the utopian polis of reason and light to which camp and ghetto are the kakotopian counterpart. Nightmare and dream of European thought are thus demythologized by being displaced into historical reality, thereby returning to the point of origin from whence they generated: the fear of disintegration, death. Before the victims met death, they were *durch den Schmutz gezogen* (pulled through the dirt) so that, by appearing physically dirty and deprived, their emaciated bodies looked as if they had done something wrong, looked like criminals in need of punishment. As a cloacal hell, the camp received all those whom the Nazis considered the excrement of Europe. The camp, as anus of the world, turned the Jews, as Richard Rubinstein and others noted, into feces, the devil's food, his gold and weapon.[6] At the same time, the anal, aggressive world of the camp was a world of boredom and indifference, of the banality of evil. Oppressor and oppressed were in the same evil ditches, Dante's *malebolge,* getting used to it and chewing the cud of death endlessly with the same dull motions. Only a few of the damned managed to save remnants of human dignity, while many either vented their aggressive feelings away from the oppressor towards their fellow sufferers or resigned themselves to the death-in-life state of the *Mussulmann,* a Moslem, in the sense of being indifferent or fatalistic. The breakdown of the inferno analogy occurs, however, when we ask who the sinners in this inferno were. From the Nazi point of view, they were the inmates, but for us they are the Nazis who, like Dante's sinners, have proven themselves incapable of raising sin and guilt into a consciousness of fault.

As a parody of the secular utopian city, the camp mocked the ideas of progress so prevalent in advanced industrial societies. It mocked the tradition of the Greek polis and the yearning for the New Jerusalem, envisioned by the victim over and against suffering; and it mocked Nuremberg, the city of Nazi party rallies impeccably organized and punctuated by the marching boot as an expression of the "Triumph of the Will." As the antipode of the city as progressive community, Auschwitz, with its vast complex of industries, exploited every part of the human being and finally reduced the human body itself to products. The monuments of the kakotopian city—the furnace, the pit, the chimneys of the crematoriums—were, to the newcomer, images of horror to which many eventually became indifferent. Escape, as the taunting remarks of the Nazis reveal, was possible only through the chimneys, a grotesque parody of what Eliade has defined as the fundamental mystical experience, namely, the transcendence of the human condition through the twofold image of breaking the roof and flight.[7] As Nelly Sachs and Paul Celan say so often, Israel's body found its grave as smoke in air. That smoke, however, did not leave Auschwitz but hung as a polluted cloud over the camp and became, along with the miasma of the surrounding swamp, an indelible figuration of evil in the experience and memory of humankind.

In all the works to be discussed here, the lived experience of the inmate is expressed in terms of an archetypal quest pattern. Deportation was a perverted and ironic quest journey into an externalized dark night for body and soul that ended for most in a meaningless death, at best offering a word, a phrase, or a muted insight to those who survived. As the territorial definition of the camp became the antithesis to the ideal city, the "quest" became the antithesis to the process of individuation. The radical of every quest is the struggle of life against death, but the deportee could engage in this quest only if he or she was given time to struggle. Yet the quest metaphor in concentration camp literature is an expression of the rage for order, a very real and necessary illusion with which the individual can reconstruct the accumulations of the past as he projects patterns for life into the void of the future. Nevertheless, we choose our memories, especially when we have been victimized by traumatic experiences. Experience is thus made dense in *Dichtung* (fiction) that reverberates with intimations of the *Wahrheit* (the truth of reality). Literature created by former concentration camp inmates is, therefore, grounded in the experience of historical reality and controlled through the choice and condensation of certain events in that experience. Because reality swallowed the individual so totally, it, rather than the individual, provided the pattern along which the diaries and autobiographies are written. First, there is life before the ordeal, an innocent and ignorant life expressed poignantly in the notion of business as usual. After the victims have been collected comes the journey in the cattle wagon where they begin to intimate what is in store for them. Arrival at the camp provokes an illusion of reprieve: "Thank God this terrible journey is over." The self is almost immediately traumatized and, if it survives this stage, attempts to establish a pattern for survival. The final stage is liberation and the demands it makes on the former inmate to cope with the fact of survival. All this is, of course, deeply ironic, for the people forced to go on this quest were ordinary men and women who had no desire for heroics or any sort of challenge to their bodies and souls. Hence, so many deluded themselves that nothing could really happen to them, an all too human delusion that persisted to the moment of deportation and even to the moment of selection in the camp.

If the prisoner survived initial selection as well as the trauma of being brutally initiated into the camp world, he or she (though women had fewer chances of survival) would begin a process of adjustment in the camp until the status of "old timer" had been achieved. All records point out how prisoner and persecutor alike were dehumanized, how all human responses, especially emotions, were deadened. The *Mussulmann* no longer lifted his feet while walking but glided along like an automaton; the camp had swallowed him and any concept of selfhood. The SS man, as powerful as the *Mussulmann* was powerless, shared with the latter the quality of an automaton. As one commentator pointed out, the SS man who accepted the idea of the superman "must abandon all moral order; he condemns himself to act as an automaton. And it has frequently been demonstrated that he did not even find it unpleasant to be in motion like an automaton."[8] While the *Mussulmann* had been voided of all will power, the will to power in the SS officer contracted into tensed rigidity and at best projected bored indifference or discharged itself in willful and brutal acts of gratuitous violence.

Absolute power and absolute powerlessness offer temptations that are unthinkable to the individual in ordinary circumstances. The persecutor is allowed to vent aggression by almost any means against the powerless, whose abjectness is to him in and of itself a provocation; and the powerless will on occasion do anything to regain a reprieve from death. Compared to the numbers that died, only a fraction carried away the prize of life. Even this was not unambiguous, for survival itself affects the individual with a sense of stain. Hence, all autobiographical accounts of the camp experience express the writer's need to gain relief, perhaps only temporarily, through the confession of the experience. Sometimes the confession attempts to metamorphose the camp experience into a hell through which one had to pass in order to eventually work for a progressive, secular paradise. Examples of such autobiographical statements are David Rousset's *The Other Kingdom* and Bruno Bettelheim's *The Informed Heart*. The autobiographies I have chosen to discuss offer no externally defined set of values through which the writer could make life liveable after the extreme situation. Rather, they reveal the individual in an often agonizing search for meaning, for the extreme situation had challenged if not destroyed all belief. The diaries reveal this search on a day to day basis as the human being is caught in and has to form an attitude to each moment.

Traditional autobiography reveals much introspection and self-analysis. In James Olney's words, the reader of an autobiography looks for "a characteristic way of perceiving, of organizing and of understanding, an individual way of feeling and expressing that one can somehow relate to oneself."[9] The implication is that we are to ourselves the center of the world and reflect the manifoldness of that world in the metaphors of the self. Autobiographies of former concentration camp inmates also show a characteristic way of perceiving and organizing experience. The extreme situation, however, is one into which the individual is cast and which bears down upon him with sudden, tremendous physical and psychological pressures. Ordinary pressures such as familial tensions and conflicts or identity crises disappear as the individual is thrown into an environment that threatens to consume him. The destructive reality of the concentrationary universe cannot be incorporated and absorbed by the human being as can less problematical situations. The concentration camp inmate had to make a concerted effort to preserve in the core of his or her being some contrasting way of thinking that at least maintained a remnant of selfhood. This inner core had to remain detached from the world of the camp; as a result, the autobiographer does not reveal himself with the depth into which an autobiographer delves under more normal circumstances. He cannot reveal himself because he cannot identify with and incorporate the world in which he lived into his own being. At least he cannot do so rationally.

James Olney writes in his study on autobiography, "If a man suffers a sudden shock or fright, then, whether or not he acts 'out of character', I

think most people would agree from experience, that for the moment he is
not his normal self. Extreme pain and extreme anger can also, in a sense,
cause an apparent disjunction of selfhood."[10] For the concentration
camp inmate this disjunction became a state of being. In order to survive
he had to adjust himself with incredible speed to a situation into which he
was literally thrown and which was totally alien to him. A disjunction
between his present and former self took place; later, after his liberation,
he had to further modify his self and screen his memories.While imprisoned he had to be constantly aware of everything around him and yet
pretend to see nothing. If he wanted to remain somehow intact and not
become a *Mussulmann,* he had to observe himself sideways, that is,
askance and with a certain sense of disapproval. For this reason, all
accounts by former inmates must by necessity be an identification with a
world of stain and guilt; it cannot be otherwise no mater how much that
identification is screened. The choice of rhetorical form often makes it
appear as if the individual is totally detached. This is particularly true
when that form is rational, descriptive, and professes to be objective, as,
for example, in Kogon's *The SS State.* Rational structuring prevents the
identification with a guilty world; but the more personal and emotional an
account becomes, as in the case of Wiesel's *Night,* the more the world of
stain and guilt is absorbed by the individual and threatens to destroy him.

Defined as a defilement, the inmate was subjected to verbal and
physical rituals of uncleanliness by the Nazis. Some accepted the definition they were given, others asked the question "Have we really sinned
more than other people?" Still others developed the apparently cooperative yet observant self that retained, in spite of the split, some sense of
personhood. These became guilty, not through the accusations of the
Nazis, but by what they saw within themselves, in others, and in the
environment. The drive for survival caused a sense, if not of sin, then of
guilt. This sense of guilt was internalized and developed after liberation,
unless totally repressed, into consciousness and conscience. With these
two qualities man becomes again the measure of himself. As Ricoeur
asserts, "The promotion of guilt marks the entry of man into the circle of
condemnation; the meaning of that condemnation appears only after the
event to the 'justified' conscience; it is granted to that conscience to
understand its past condemnation as a sort of pedagogy; but to a conscience still kept under the guard of the law, its meaning is unknown."[11]
Thus, an inmate could look on while someone was being strangled with
the handle of a shovel. After liberation, the survivor-victim will give such
moments ethical connotations they did not have when they occurred, but

which they need to have so that the justified conscience can transcend callousness.

The autobiographers and diarists I will discuss dwell little on their personal physical and mental agonies, not only for the above reasons but also because dwelling on such suffering would make the autobiographer guilty against those who succumbed. Also, very few autobiographers admit to any depths the feelings of hate and frustrated aggression they felt for the Nazis. Such emotions were real; but because they could not be directed against the oppressor, they turned towards fellow inmates or reflected back to the person who felt them. Though the former inmate may have expiated or repressed his experience, he is not free of it since he is driven to record his memories and reflections in a book. This confessional quality is shared by the inmate with more traditional autobiographies. "Most autobiographies," writes Northrop Frye, "are inspired by a creative, and therefore fictional impulse to select only those events and experiences in a writer's life that go to build up an integrated pattern. This pattern may be something larger than himself with which he has come to identify himself, or simply the coherence of his character and attitude. We may call this very important form of prose fiction the confession form."[12]

We have come full circle. The world of the camp with all its associations of fault was created through language. It became real; but as reality it blinded the individual who found himself in its historical time, a time where continual fear of annihilation deadened feelings and blocked most positive emotions. Many survivors could not talk or write about their experiences until several years later. As the antiworld and the prisoner's quest in it are brought into the consciousness and light of speech, the sufferer reveals his own consciousness and conscience and gains, at least momentarily, symbolic power over memory.

II.

In That Time and That Place: The Diaries of Odd Nansen and Chaim Kaplan

The writing of a diary requires at least a shell of privacy for a few moments during the day. In the camps, such a shell was denied to almost everybody, and this total lack of privacy contributed much to the suffering of the inmates. Among the few diaries that have come to us from women and men in the extreme situation are Odd Nansen's *Day after Day* and Chaim Kaplan's *Warsaw Diary*, both distinguished by their intense perceptions and sensitive language. Both writers were habitual diarists; and after both became caught in the extreme situation, this habit not only provided relief in a personal sense but became a crucial device to retain the immediacy of the moment. Kaplan never had the chance to reread his diary after the evil time had passed. But Nansen had that chance, and when he read his diary for the first time, he was surprised at the tricks memory had already begun to play with him: ''Much was worse than I seemed to remember. And yet I know that words are too pale to describe most of it. And another thing: What my companions and I saw and experienced is little and pale in comparison with what many, many others saw and lived through in the worst camps.''[13] Kaplan records how the community of the ghetto is subjected to ever increasing constriction until the inhabitants find their only escape in death, the final destination of the diarist himself. Nansen's record is primarily that of a man who remained at the periphery of the extreme situation because of his privileged position as a Norwegian and who struggled to remain a decent man by channeling his consciousness and guilt into empathy with those whose suffering exceeded his.

Both writers could isolate themselves spatially from the horror of ghetto or camp. Nansen, who was arrested in January 1942 and who stayed in Sachsenhausen and Neuengamme from 1943-1945, had some privacy as a Norwegian and kept his diary hidden inside hollowed-out bread boards. Kaplan had his room in an apartment from which he could view the chaos in the streets of the ghetto. When Kaplan's diary ends, this protective shell is taken from him, and time, which liberates Nansen, destroys him. Both writers are intensely aware of time and are driven to record and shape historical vicissitudes, thus attempting to make them somehow meaningful. Kaplan is especially conscious of his mission: ''I sense within me the magnitude of this hour, and my responsibility toward it, and I have an inner awareness that I am fulfilling a national obligation, a historic obligation that I am not free to relinquish. My words are not rewritten; momentary reflexes shape them. Perhaps their value lies in this. Be it as it may, I am sure that Providence sent me to fulfill this mission. My record will serve as source material for the future historian.''[14]

Unlike Kaplan's communal mission, Nansen's motive is at first a private one. Unable to write the truth about the camps to his wife, he records what he sees so that she will be able to understand him later. In his postscript, however, he realizes that the diary transcended the private motive and became a record against forgetfulness that all should read. He has little hope for the future, for hardly anywhere does he see evidence of man acting with civilizing love, the only means towards a better way of life as far as Nansen is concerned. The enemy of this love is not hate but the indifference among humankind: "The worst you can commit today, against yourself and society, is to forget what happened and sink back into indifference. What happened was worse than you have any idea of—and it was the indifference of mankind that let it take place!" Both diarists write in spite of the final impotence of the word. When we have read their chronicles of wasted time, we realize that, though the moments in time were chaotic, they converge once again into an overall pattern in the diaries, namely, the time before the extreme situation, the camp world and humankind's adjustment to it, and the end of bondage either through death or liberation.

Nansen is the perfect example of an individual who looks askance at himself. Because of his privileged status, he and his fellow Norwegians smugly define themselves as a group over and against those less fortunate than they. Moreover, in order to maintain privilege, they actively participate in anti-Semitism since it is profitable and easily cooperated with: "And so we lounge our own way, grocers in spirit and, in fact, Jews as that word is understood when we use it as a term of abuse—and we nearly always do, not least in this place. At any rate, one would suppose we'd be above that. But no! we howl with the Germans and with others: 'Verdammte Juden!'" (p. 518) Nansen's rigorous criticism of himself and others shows that he is fully aware of what the right attitude ought to be. To compensate for his privilege and failings, Nansen develops a compulsive need to go to the Jewish quarters in order to learn about greater miseries and to hear, at least second hand, about the horrors of Auschwitz (p. 437). Imprisoned in one of the lesser circles of hell, he wants to remain the man of conscience who feels compelled to learn about the lower depths so as not to become guilty of what he considers the worst moral evil, indifference and sloth.

On 11 February 1945 he decides to make his attitude visible in spite of the risks; he wants to act, to help, and only discovers his own helplessness. His next day's entry expresses a deep sense of futility and a sense of shame for having been praised for his impotent gesture: "The language is exhausted. I have exhausted myself. There are no words left to describe the horrors I have seen with my own eyes. How am I to give even a reflection of the hell I plunged in yesterday?" (p. 545) "Dante's inferno could not have been worse" when nearly one thousand Jews arrived, attacked the garbage cans, and were beaten down by young hoods of a *Sonderabteilung* of the *Wehrmacht* (soldiers imprisoned most likely because of theft). In an ecstasy of violence the young men become "living devils" and "roaring lions" as they beat, laughing fiendishly, the bleeding skeletons (p. 546). Nansen, the man of consciousness and conscience, leaves his comfortable periphery and goes into the circle of the damned in order to aid one of them: "I went over to him, took him under the arms and raised him. He was light as a child" (p. 546). Nansen realizes that his action is no more than a pitiful gesture because all are doomed. Nevertheless, his act is recognized with astonishment, for the Jew and his friend cannot believe that a Norwegian would aid them:

> They simply stared at me, both of them, with big surprised eyes, then he raised his arm with an effort, as though mastering all his failing strength; his hand reached the level of my head; there he let it sink, and slowly his bony hand slid down over my face. It was his last caress, and he gurgled something which his friend translated with: 'He says you are a decent man.' Then he collapsed along the wall and on to the ground, and I think he died there and then, but I don't know, for I was hurrying off with my face burning. 'A *decent man!*' I who hadn't even dared to try to stop his tormentor. I who hadn't even dared to risk my own skin by going into the camp and collecting food for those starving skeletons! 'A *decent man!*' If only I could ever raise myself up again from this shadow-life in this sink of degradation, and be a decent man! [pp. 547–48]

The human response to his futile attempt evokes in Nansen a deep sense of shame over undeserved praise and the realization that it is impossible to ever love one's neighbor enough. It becomes clear to Nansen that, under certain circumstances, the simplest human gesture merely contrasts more violently to the lovelessness of the world.

Nansen always describes the evil of the camps in human terms and avoids abstraction by focusing on the specific moment, the specific individual through whom evil manifests itself. He notes that, while we often exaggerate events in ordinary life, in the world of the camp events told from mouth to mouth do "by no means always grow worse in reality": "The plain fact is that reality is stronger, more dramatic, and far more gruesome than one can grasp on hearing it recapitulated; normal human imagination falls short, therefore a second-hand account is always paler and more plausible" (p. 553). Nansen is a person who remains capable of experiencing horror. Whenever he thinks that the sights around him have become habitual, he is shocked again into consciousness.

Among Nansen's last and most disturbing impressions is a Jewish child who had worked as an errand boy at Auschwitz and to whom the horror of destruction had become so habitual that he no longer experienced it as such. He is less than ten years old, and his angelic face, which is at the same time a mockery of the divine child, robs Nansen of his last illusions over the possibility of innocence. Completely in the know about death and destruction and yet remaining grotesquely innocent, the child is a riddle to the decent man: "Death and destruction, murder, torture and all the deviltry of man are familiar to him. Such was his world picture— the only one he had a chance of forming. He knew nothing of life—and death—but what he had seen in Hell! Yet I couldn't make out any stamp, in that little face, of all the horrors he has lived among" (p. 556). The child knows how to please, but his hands are in constant nervous motion and unconsciously reveal the effect hell has had on him. His prereflective consciousness has absorbed the world, but to Nansen to whom the death and corruption of that world indicate the absolute moral failing of man, the child's acceptance of horror is shocking. He attempts to instruct the boy morally but realizes that it would take years "to save his little soul." After the desire to create a better world for this boy momentarily overwhelms him, he realizes that this, too, would be futile. All that is left is the impression he had of the child: "Even though I am pretty thoroughly hardened by this life here and in the German concentration camps altogether, and used to hearing both this and that, these little smiling replies of his came down on me like bombs" (p. 557).

On 27–28 April 1945 Nansen is free in Denmark, and the last entry of his diary is that of a stunned man who has lost his power of words and is "out of contact with reality." Asked to write to his wife, he comments, "One might have thought it would be easy. . . . But no, it seemed to me impossible, insuperable! Every word became a great intrusive toad, and Kari and the children, all that is dear to me, all that I have been longing for for years with all my soul, more remote than ever. I felt like crying with despair and rage." As life becomes ordinary again, the person who has been in the extreme situation remains locked in the closed circuit of his memories, unable to share them with anyone. For this reason, Nansen attempts to universalize the experience in his postscript, expanding the concentration camp to a global community of guilt and suffering. "Can you picture it?" he often asks the reader, to whom he offers the "front of human kindness" as the only battleground against misery and guilt.

Unlike Nansen's chronicle, Chaim Kaplan's *Warsaw Diary* is unfinished and open-ended but leaves the reader with an overpowering sense of conclusiveness as the author's impending deportation and inevitable death (in 1943) encroach upon the record.[15] Kaplan's diary reveals an introverted and reflective elderly man, a man who, however, keeps his own experiences in the background in order to fully perceive and reflect upon the myriad manifestations of the ghetto from its inception to its eventual dissolution. Caught in that time and place, Kaplan could not know all the facts that brought about this particular reality for the Jews in Warsaw. When reading his book, one gets the lasting impression of a man sitting in his room in the Warsaw Ghetto of conquered Poland during the Second World War, a war fought by three contending powers: the old democratic world, fascism, and communism. Surrounding this set of boxed-in aggressions is a silent and indifferent universe to which Kaplan often directs his gaze and question in vain. In his final reference to the once benign force of the cosmos, he concludes, "In these two days the emptiness of the ghetto has been filled with cries and wails. If they found no way to the God of Israel it is a sign that He doesn't exist" (p. 383).

Beginning with his entry of 1 September 1939, Kaplan is conscious that a new era in history has begun and that it is the beginning of the end for Nazism and perhaps for the Jews unless the free nations rise and defend their liberty. He thus projects the definite beginning, middle, and end of the ordeal, after which humankind will move once again into the light of freedom, democracy, or the formation of the State of Israel. At present, however, a darkness that gains symbolic dimensions reigns in a blacked-out Warsaw: "Great Warsaw, from its center to its suburbs, is cloaked in a terrible darkness, comparable to the plague that was visited upon Egypt—darkness so thick that it can be felt" (p. 25). People hide in their houses so that "our noisy gay city seems to have stopped breathing." As yet Kaplan is unaware that this is only the beginning, for this lack of air and breath will become a state of being as the ghetto is built and more and more people are forced to exist on its narrowing ground. At that point Kaplan writes, "I do not exaggerate when I say that we have reached a state of lack of breath. There simply is no air. Every minute is like a thousand years. Every day is like a never ending eternity" (p. 362). Time ceases to exist for the Jews as they are forced into a converging point of suffering where they can only make labyrinthian turns but no progression. As Kaplan perceives the stark reality of the ghetto, as its gruesome images bear down upon him, his comprehensive faculties force rigidity and chaos into traditional metaphors whose familiarity functions to make the present comprehensible to him and somewhat accessible to his future readers.

The metaphor of the forbidden city, the cloaca of humanity, the antithesis to Eden, becomes the historical actuality of the Warsaw Ghetto which condenses into a demonic epiphany. Time reveals the circles of hell, for before it becomes a roofless prison, it seems as if the ghetto might lead to "a Jewish state with all the attributes that pertain to any state" as people try to establish the routine of business as usual. In the spring of 1942, however, Kaplan is keenly aware that Eden is outside where "there are trees and beautiful ploughed fields, forests and streams, hills and valleys, 'full of splendor, they radiate brightness.' " This is a world from which the ghetto dweller is infinitely distant, a vision of pastoral innocence from which he may be separated by a mere fence: "It is now three years since we have seen the grass growing and the flowers in blossom. Even before we were shoved into the ghetto we were forbidden to enter the city parks. Inside the parks there was space and breath. Outside, the Jewish children—beautiful little ones, the children of the masses—would find a place for their games and toys on the stone sidewalks outside the fence. Within the limits of the ghetto there is not a single garden. . . . We have been robbed of every tree and flower" (p. 353).

As time moves from one point of constriction to another, Kaplan believes repeatedly that he and his fellow sufferers have reached the nadir of their ordeal and that the upward turn of their existence must come soon; for "on the very day the Temple was destroyed, the Messiah was born" (p. 285). The metaphor of hell is both end and beginning. After Warsaw has been bombarded he writes, "Dante's description of the Inferno is mild compared to the inferno raging in the streets of Warsaw" (p. 29). After the ghetto has been closed and the point of constriction narrowed, Kaplan wonders if the sight of external evil is not some objective correlative to an inner condition: "I gazed at the Dantean scenes of Warsaw, and could not stop thinking: are we really guiltier than any nation? Have we sinned more than any other people? Will we really die? Are we doomed to total destruction? Nobody in the world is concerned for us, nobody shares our plight" (p. 210). The metaphor of hell explains nothing, for the ghetto's inhabitants have obviously sinned no more or less than other people. Kaplan does not know that the constriction furthers the aims of the Nazis to eventually destroy all inhabitants. The reader perceives the terrible irony whenever Kaplan wonders about the future or when he complains that the Nazis have turned off the gas. In the beginning of his chronicle, he writes, "I have seen Warsaw in its utter devastation. Woe is me!" But after innumerable miseries have come to pass, he concludes, "Blessed is the eye which has not beheld all this." The mere absence of the sight of evil defines the good life.

The roads of the ghetto, too, take on a metaphorical quality as people move backward and forward in frantic activity that eventually leads nowhere. In the early days, "the streets have begun to resemble a fair. . . . everywhere selling and bargaining, trade and barter are going on under the sky" (p. 50), as all give themselves to the illusion that business can go on as usual. As time passes, it becomes clear that these streets are not the arteries that bring the stuff of life to a body politic but are intestinal labyrinths wherein human beings are drained of life until they can be carted off as waste. In the winter of 1942, the last winter in the ghetto, Kaplan perceives the cloacal city: "Frozen water and sewage pipes have forced us to make latrines out of stairways and yards. We are surrounded by stinking filth, and when the spring thaw melts the frozen dung heaps who knows what ghastly diseases will be let loose on us then?" (p. 299). Even at night the streets are silently crowded, as "the whole ghetto seems like some eerie underworld inhabited by ghosts intent on strange pursuits" (p. 284). But these ghosts no longer care for each other, locked in their own misery: "There is crowding and congestion on the sidewalks. One person shoves another on the side and shoulder without malice and without any apology. . . . They all share the same fate. In everyone's face the terrible happenings of which he himself is subject are reflected. A certain silent sorrow is cast on all faces" (p. 110). Finally, all normal conduct ceases, the dead begin to line the streets, and the living scurry into hideaways whenever a Nazi walks the streets looking for a victim (p. 350). Wholesale destruction has begun; however, the exact form it will take remains a rumor. When Kaplan prepares himself to go to the collection point, the reader becomes fully aware that the ghetto is "suspended over nothingness" (p. 377), that only death reigns: "There is the silence of death in the streets of the ghetto all through the day. The fear of death is in the eyes of the few people who pass by on the sidewalk opposite our window. Everyone presses himself against the wall and draws into himself so that they will not detect his existence or his presence" (p. 399).

The *Warsaw Diary* reveals to us a walled-in humanity with all its frailties and occasional goodness. The evils of ordinary life become intensified in this microcosm as the rich hoard luxuries and the poor roam greedily through the streets until death overtakes them both. Kaplan does not spare his people invectives, and only rarely does he set a memorial for a good man. It is hard to be a good man in the ghetto. Outside, the Poles generally support the anti-Semitic measures of the Nazis who have unleashed all the brutality of absolute power. Kaplan defines the Nazis as beasts and psychopaths (pp. 9, 50, 69): "A poison of diseased hatred permeates the blood of the Nazis, and therefore all their stupid decrees, the fruits of this hatred, are doomed to failure. Such an awareness saves us from despair" (p. 120). In spite of external evidence, Kaplan cannot afford to admit that the deeds of the Nazis are manifestations of human potential for evil. Here the language used by the victim is similar to but differently motivated than the language used by the oppressor. The familiar associative cluster of images by which evil is seem as permeating the biological being of the evil-doer is used by Kaplan to "save us from despair." To admit that the Nazis are human would mean that they be included in the humanity of the ghetto dweller who by definition would then have to admit the possibility of atrocious depravity within himself; such an admission would lead to despair. Language alone provides the powerless with the futile magic of exorcism and with the secret knowledge that the oppressor will fail.

Language is impotent but is also the only means to preserve at least an inkling of the agony of actual experience. As Kaplan states in his purpose sentences, "It is difficult to write, but I consider it an obligation and am determined to fulfill it. I will write a scroll of agony in order to remember the past in the future" (p. 30). Self-contained as a scroll whose content is antithetical to the law content of the Torah, Kaplan's diary is a defense against the overwhelming influence of a reality that chokes his breath and cannot possibly be contained in a book. Kaplan does not indulge in self-revelations; we know nothing about his hunger, his pains, or his fear of death. Often he reacts angrily at the evil time but remains open and vulnerable to it in order to recreate it. Shortly before he will be sent to Treblinka, his last concern is for his diary: "If my life ends, what will become of my diary?" It is the concern of a parent who, in continual agony, gave birth to a child, the link with the future; and, in order to reach the empathetic thou which will receive the child, the writer shapes his work through familiar language. Implicit in that language, however, is also the problem of repetition and compulsion as the metaphors of Eden and hell, of every man and man as beast catching us in circles of associations.

III.

The Metaphysics of the Autobiographer's Creative Consciousness: Elie Wiesel and Tadeusz Borowski

"Humankind cannot bear very much reality." When applied to the autobiographies about the concentrationary universe, T.S. Eliot's insight in "Burnt Norton" defines not a Platonic reality, but a reality in which body and soul were annihilated to the body's carbon. Lawrence Langer quotes Elie Wiesel as saying that the event of the holocaust "seems unreal as if it occurred on a different planet," and he adds, "Perhaps what we tell about what happened and what really happened has nothing to do with the other." The autobiographer, who has not used the extreme situation as an infernal experience from whose center of gravity he was led to a "progressive" vision of future humanity, is more often than not the artist and can offer only a consciousness of negation, a downward transcendence of profoundest irony.

In Elie Wiesel's *Night* and in Borowski's collection of short stories, the illusion of reprieve of the diarist writing in his defined space is absent. The autobiographer of the concentration camp is a survivor who has received an extended reprieve from death, but that reprieve has not liberated him. As a matter of fact, it can contribute to make life so unlivable that the survivor seeks death through suicide, as Borowski did on 1 July 1951. With compulsive repetitiveness, the autobiographer must return to the memory of deprivation even as that memory is bound to take on fictional aspects, one of the main reasons why Wiesel and Borowski use a first person narrative in which the narrator's name varies slightly from the author's—Elie becomes Eliezer, Tadeusz becomes Tadek. The self looks askance at itself in that time, and the reader is aware of the distance between narrator and author. In *Night* that distance is created between the fifteen-year-old boy who runs to the synagogue of his village "to weep over the destruction of the Temple" at a time when the Nazis are closing in on Hungary[17] and the adult writer-narrator who reflects on that illusory innocence. Tadek and Tadeusz Borowski are less distant from each other; both are young adults, and both agree on the universal implications of Auschwitz. Both autobiographers were swallowed by the experience no matter what defenses they attempted to construct. The reader knows that Auschwitz forced itself into the struggling, vulnerable, and open consciousness of two young human beings and brought about a physical and psychological suffocation and paralysis, leading each consciousness to a point of constriction in its memory from which it tries to extricate, but cannot liberate itself, through art. Wiesel retraces the ground of deprivation because of the love and guilt he feels over the loss of his family, and he does so by shaping his recollections in terms of a parodic quest pattern. Borowski, a political prisoner at Auschwitz, survived because he cooperated. His stories, while they can be arranged to give the illusion of beginning, middle, and end, are really memory shards in which he retraces his guilt, reacts aggressively against it, and mocks himself profoundly as an artist in a world of stone.

Since Lawrence Langer has written an extensive analysis of the parody of the quest in Wiesel's *Night,* [18] I will focus mainly on how metaphors of evil define Eliezer's experience in Auschwitz as well as the rupture of dialogue between himself and the god of his fathers. Both writers describe the extreme situation in accessible language. Wiesel's language is influenced by his religious education, and it is able to provoke in the reader a deep feeling of sorrow. Borowski's language, however, stuns the relief that comes with tears. He attempts mimesis through cool understatement and the juxtaposition of opposites, or he reflects with brutal irony or flagrant aggression against this world of stone. I will analyze Borowski's constricted memory points in the short story "This Way for the Gas, Ladies and Gentlemen" and in the sketches "A Visit" and "The World of Stone."

In *Night,* time ends for young Eliezer in the spring of 1944 when he and his family are torn from their idyllic world in Sighet and transported to Auschwitz. His mother and sisters die immediately, and Eliezer begins work in the Buna factories. During the evacuation of Auschwitz, Eliezer, his father, and a multitude of prisoners are driven on the run through a raging blizzard, eventually herded into open cattle wagons which transport them to Buchenwald. It is there that his father, the mainstay of Eliezer's existence, dies. On the eve of 28 January 1945 (the first date since he left Sighet), time begins again for Eliezer as he looks at his dying father for the last time and climbs into the bunk above him. The next morning his father is gone: "They must have taken him away before dawn and carried him to the crematory. He may still have been breathing. There were no prayers at his grave" (p. 124). If time before the concentrationary universe was one of Edenic innocence and ignorance, time after the experience defines knowledge of a world so totally fallen that, for Eliezer, at least there is no hope for redemption after liberation. He is locked in his memory of the antiworld: "From the depths of the mirror a corpse gazed at me. The look in his eyes, as they stared into mine, has never left me" (p. 127). Wiesel's autobiography is about the origin of that look.

The language of *Night* is deceptively simple, language that gives the reader the illusion of understanding the unspeakable situation. The familiar linguistic signals, however, reverberate and urge the discovery of a revelation of experience and truth behind the image as sign. It is the language of a religious imagination, demonstrated in the first chapter by the passion with which Eliezer studied not only the law of the Talmud but also the mysticism of the Kabbalah (pp. 12–14). In the final analysis, *Night* is not an attempt to realistically detail the experience of Auschwitz but rather to show how that experience transformed the religious personality's relation to God. The relation to God is brought about through the language of prayer, as Moché, the mystic Beadle of Sighet, tells Eliezer: "Man raises himself towards God by the questions he asks of Him . . . that is the true dialogue. Man questions God and God answers. But we don't understand His answers. We can't understand them. Because they come from the depths of the soul, and they stay there until death. You will find the true answers, Eliezer, only within yourself" (p. 14).

This is the most important thematic statement in *Night*. It defines the complex inner-outer relationship of the ego to the larger self; it defines the narrator and his language, in which the familiar phrase "depth of the soul" becomes a leitmotif. Charged with affirmation or negation, the phrase is used in all crucial moments of Eliezer's experience. Moché is unaware of the problems his definition can and will cause the boy; he is unaware that the "true dialogue" will be a monologue, a failure of communication. In Wiesel's autobiography, the creature finds himself in a catastrophic creation and concludes that the creator must have withdrawn defensively from that chaos. The creature, too, after viewing and absorbing the chaos, withdraws with defensive aggressiveness into a rigid posture. As Harold Bloom points out in *Kabbalah and Criticism,* "Such a concentration sets up defensive reactions in the self, making the subsequent creation a catastrophe, and rendering . . . representation a hopeless quest."[19] The narrator's defensive reaction is that he, unlike the Creator, does not want his linguistic creation to be catastrophic but wants to shape it with a rage for order by means of a language that is obviously defective in its "imagery of limitation" (Bloom, p. 77). Yet the familiar order of the narrator's linguistic cosmos reverberates, and the reader, receptive to these reverberations, will break the familiar vessels of the images in *Night* and approximate the catastrophe that underlies them. Such approximation necessarily involves a misreading; for the reader's defenses against the catastrophe in *Night* are likewise provoked, and the true dialogue becomes impossible.

Eliezer's experience at Auschwitz-Buna is shaped by the gradual stripping from him of everything he loves. There is the blind struggle for existence at all cost, but along with it the meaning for life is lost. As the boy deteriorates physically, as he is stripped of his flesh, he loses his potential for love as a force in a meaningful life. To be sure, this takes a long time, for love is strong. But in the end, however, only emptiness remains. During the first selection upon his arrival at Birkenau, he is as yet unaware that the stripping process has begun—"men to the left, women to the right." His mother and sister disappear forever. His father, who was somewhat on the periphery of Eliezer's world in Sighet, now becomes for him the fulcrum, the one stable point with which Eliezer can align himself even after his commitment to his father becomes hardly more than a conditioned reflex.

The reader of *Night* has to remain conscious of the fact that the events Eliezer witnesses in the inferno are experienced by him as a child. Although he is not innocent in the sense of being unreflective (for he had studied and interpreted the scriptures too much), he is still innocent in that the world into which he is cast is at first totally alien and incomprehensible to him. The child is father of the man and as such holds the promise for the future. In the concentration camps, that future was demolished and the innocence of the child perverted. The child in the camp did not only hear stories about evil such as the destruction of the Temple, over which he could weep with the empathy that distance permits, but the child lived in what has become for the twentieth century a myth of evil. The camp was never a metaphor for the child. His first consciousness of evil is aroused by the sight of infant damnation that pales all images of the slaughter of the innocent: a lorry filled with babies is emptied into a burning pit. "In the depths of my heart, I bade farewell to my father, to the whole universe; and in spite of myself, the words formed themselves and issued from my lips: '. . . May His name be blessed and magnified . . . ' " (p. 44). Eliezer can still pray, prayer that has already become a reflex action.

Eliezer's rebellion against God is initiated by witnessing two hangings. The first, the execution of a heroic Polish youth, affects him hardly at all; the second, the hanging of an angelic-looking child, affects him deeply. On the eve of Rosh Hashanah, however, when hundreds of men prostrate themselves with love before their invisible and powerful God, "like trees before the tempest," Eliezer accuses God of breaking His covenant with men (p. 79). He does not deny the existence of God; he contracts away from God, as God has withdrawn from him: "My eyes

were open and I was alone—terribly alone in a world without God and
without man. Without love or mercy. I had ceased to be anything but
ashes, yet I felt myself stronger than the Almighty to whom my life had
been tied for so long." Until now, his ego had identified with the
archetypal symbols of his religion which he had projected, not only as an
energy within "the depths of his soul," but also as existing externally. As
a religious but powerless human being, he felt empathy at the sight of
suffering, an onrush of powerful emotion that ought to be felt by the all-
powerful god he had projected. Since the god remains silent, no matter
how much the believer demonstrates love, Eliezer rejects the god through
his ego's expression of will. With hope gone, his will makes him strong
and allows him to say no to a cosmic system that is contradicted by the
reality of Auschwitz. He turns to his weak, earthly father instead and
achieves with him a wordless moment of perfect communion of love, a
primal communication of touch assuring that the other is really there.

Even the bond with the earthly father is threatened, however, by the
temptation that he might be better off without him. This temptation
develops during the evacuation of Auschwitz as the inmates are forced to
run through the snow and are eventually transported, snow and ice
encrusted, on open cattle wagons. Torn between the need to protect and
reject his parent, Eliezer projects images of how other sons treat their
fathers. The most horrible of these images occurs in the cattle wagon
when a nameless son, crazed with starvation, creeps towards his father
who is chewing a crust of bread. He beats his father down only to be
himself killed by his starving fellow prisoners. Eliezer, however, saves
his father from being thrown out as dead from the cattle wagon, but increasingly these rescues become the prolonging of a death of which the
son does not want to be guilty. He can never given enough love to keep
his father alive; love is no longer enough, just as hate will not suffice to
avenge the camp experience. He will be left with guilt because he
survives, but at the time of his father's death he only feels drained: "And,
in the depths of my being, in the recesses of my weakened conscience
could I have searched it, I might perhaps have found something like—
free at last!" (p. 124)

Having struggled between life and death for so long, he looks into a
mirror at the end of his ordeal: "From the depths of the mirror, a corpse
gazed back at me. The look in his eyes, as they stared into mine, has never
left me." The image communicates the demonic epiphany of a Narcissus
locked into the closed circuit of experiences that have robbed him of all
interest in and love for life. He cannot love the world, and, since the

world is reflected in his eyes, he cannot love himself. But Wiesel writes
"a corpse" and "his eyes," and this implies that the reflection is
experienced as *the other,* a life-saving disjunction which turns the camp
experience at that moment into memory and all which the process of
memory entails. The look in the mirror holds a memory of a loveless
world, but it is in memory of a loved family who died in the camp that the
book is created. In the re-creation of the struggle to maintain love and in
the eventual defeat of love, the catastrophe is once more enacted: the
mother once more carries the sister to the gas chamber, God is once more
rejected, the father dies once more. But this time it happens in a verbal
structure, in a record that preserves and stalls forgetfulness. *Night* is an
homage to such love and its struggle; it is also, however, a denial of
forgiveness and expiation, for the look of the corpse never leaves the
autobiographer who incorporated the world of Auschwitz into his very
being.

In Tadeusz Borowski's "This Way for the Gas, Ladies and Gentlemen," we see again how a young man, the narrator Tadek, incorporated
Auschwitz. Tadek is not a religious person; there arises no rebellious
energy against his god from the depths of his being. Instead, after having
had to deny his question "Are we good people?" throughout an inter-
minable day during which he fought his nausea through three transports
of victims, he succumbs finally to the momentary relief of a violent
vomiting.[20] This release parallels Eliezer's rebellion from the depths of
his being; however, Eliezer's guilt concentrates primarily on his father,
Tadek, who works at the ramp, actively participates in sending
thousands to their deaths. Yet the nonmetaphysically inclined Tadek also
arrives at metaphysical intimations; for the magnitude of decreation
around him evokes such resonances in "This Way for the Gas," inter-
nalizes them in "A Visit," and disgorges them in aggressive apocalyptic
visions in "The World of Stone."

The uncreating world of the concentrationary universe is a world of lies
and deceit, as is already evident in the title of "This Way for the Gas,
Ladies and Gentlemen," and is confirmed as the reader becomes conscious of the fact that within the twenty pages of this short story 15,000
people have been gassed. Speed intensifies throughout the narrative as
Tadek races through the account of his participation in preparing the
victims of three transports for their deaths. In the beginning he and his
compeers seem to eagerly await the first transport, for also at the ramp is
"Canada," the land of plenty, where the inmates get supplies for survival. The narrator's tone is objective, casual, and cynical. A detachment

of inmates does not hesitate to drink the water intended for the people on the transport. The oppressors, while highly visible, remain anonymous officers, SS men, guards. Anonymity protects persecutors and cooperative victims alike. An eager busy-ness pervades the ramp: crews are given work instructions, "motor cycles drive up, delivering SS officers, bemedalled, glittering with brass . . . some have brought their briefcases, others held thin flexible whips. This gives them an air of military readiness and agility" as they talk about home and families (p. 35). "We lie against the rails in the narrow streaks of shade, breathe unevenly, occasionally exchange a few words in our various tongues, and gaze listlessly at the majestic men in green uniforms, at the green leaves, and at the church steeple of a distant village." Complicity is established through the air of expectancy between the two groups and is repressed with an attitude of negligent apathy. Typical of Borowski's style is the climactic but ironic use of parallelisms. The church steeple obviously points to something that transcends this world. But whatever that might be, it has no contact with the two groups of men who conspire within this confined, narrow ground of evil.

If the camp is "sealed off tight" (p. 29), the wagons of the transport intensify constriction; when "the bolts crack, the doors fall open," and the people and their belongings spill from the wagon. As they breathe the fresh air with relief, however, they inhale with it the illusion of reprieve that the SS and the work crew try to maintain (p. 37). One SS man is particularly courteous as he urges good will and cooperation, but his whip flies as a woman, caught in the illusion of reprieve, attempts to recover her purse. She is destined for the gas chamber, for behind her walks her little girl affectionately calling her "Mamele" and thus defining her as a mother. It was too bothersome to separate mothers from children, no matter how "workable" the mothers might be.

After the wagons have been emptied, the inmates must clean up the "Schweinerei" (pig's mess); the physical and moral stain must appear to have been removed. Among the human refuse in the wagon, Tadek finds "squashed, trampled infants, naked little monsters, with enormous heads and bloated bellies. We carry them out like chickens, holding several in each hand. 'Don't take them to the trucks, pass them on to the women,' says the S.S. man, lighting his cigarette. His cigarette lighter is not working properly; he examines it carefully" (p. 39). Pity is consistently undercut as the narrator moves from infants to monsters, to chickens, and to the seemingly unaffected diversionary attitude of the SS man who sees but does not choose to see. Shocked, the women refuse to take the little bodies; but a tall, grey-haired woman accepts them and addresses Tadek as "my poor boy," a personalized phrase that overwhelms him, not with tears, but with intense, physical fatigue and with the refusal to look at people individually. When he addresses a fellow inmate, his words spill forth aggressively: "I feel no pity. I am not sorry they are going to the gas chamber. Damn them all! I could throw myself at them and beat them with my fists. . . ." His compeer assures him that such an attitude is almost healthy (p. 40).

With the arrival of the second transport brutality increases and deception diminishes. A woman, aware that she would go to the gas chamber if defined as a mother, denies her child but is killed by a Russian inmate. As Tadek once again struggles with nausea, there emerges from the train a girl that belongs to another time and world. She "descends lightly from the train, hops to the gravel, looks around inquiringly as if somewhat surprised. Her soft, blond hair has fallen on her shoulders in a torrent." Her wise and mature look defines her as in the know as she insists on going to the gas chamber. She is a totally absurd but true appearance of personhood and dignity in this world of deceit; her knowledge, however, leads her to seek death. Once again, only the human being can contain such knowledge, for there is no god who contains or refuses to contain so much suffering.

This is particularly evident after Tadek has cleaned up the wagons of the second transport and rests against the rails: "The sun has leaned low over the horizon and illuminates the ramp with a reddish glow: the shadows of the trees have become elongated, ghostlike. In the silence that settles over nature at this time of day, the human cries seem to rise all the way to the sky" (p. 45). No ear will receive the cries that rise from this constricted and seemingly eternal narrow ground. Tadek, who sees all this, describes it in a language resonant with religious connotations, a language similar to the images of Nelly Sachs in "Landscape of Screams"; for the precision of Borowski's attempt to imitate reality and Sachs's precise use of the literalness of the word approximate each other.

Sachs also refers to the "woe tendrils of the smallest children" in her poem, and just such a tendril of sound is emitted from a motherless little girl who falls out of the window of the third transport:

> Stunned, she lies still for a moment, then stands up and begins walking around in a circle, faster and faster, waving her rigid arms in the air, breathing loudly and spasmodically, whining in a faint voice. Her mind has given way in the inferno inside the train. The whining is hard on the nerves: an S.S. man approaches calmly, his heavy boot strikes

between her shoulders. She falls. Holding her down with his foot, he draws his revolver, fires once, then again. She remains face down, kicking the gravel with her feet, until she stiffens. They proceed to unseal the train. [pp. 47–48]

Tadek, as nervously tense as the SS, appears to approve of this action, but shortly afterwards, when a corpse's fingers close around his hand, he screams, breaks down, and vomits. In a final image he describes the translucent morning sky against which "great columns of smoke rise from the crematoria and merge above into a huge black river . . . ," the black milk of morning that the voices of Celan's "Todesfuge" drink and drink. Contrasting with this image of dissolution is the rigidity of "a heavily armed S.S. detachment . . . . The men march briskly, in step, shoulder to shoulder, one mass one will" (p. 49).

Nausea is a momentary and illusory relief for a man who has made such a world part of his being that his sense of ego has been lost. In the sketches "A Visit" and "The World of Stone," Tadek describes the state of such a man after liberation. He admits in "A Visit" that "I have never been able to look at myself" (p. 176), a realization which Wiesel communicated through the eyes of the corpse, the unfamiliar other that rose from the depths of the mirror. Self-knowledge is a myth for the former concentration camp inmate, for his self is constituted of what he saw. "A Visit" is a visit of the people who claimed his kinship, as is evident in the twice-repeated whisper of a dying man: "Brother, brother." Tadek had to fail as his brother's keeper, for he had thousands of brothers and sisters who claimed his kinship. As the repetition of "I saw, I saw, I saw" reveals, Tadek has only been able to fulfill the final request of the victims, namely, that he remember what happened. He is now housed in his memory but is unhoused in his present world as he sits "in someone else's room," where in a moment he will feel "homesick for the people I saw then." He can visit them all, and they will be his visitation. Because he is defined through them alone, because there is no room for self-knowledge, his consciousness is nothing but a house for the memory of the victims. The world that once swallowed him is now contained within him.

In "The World of Stone" the alienated narrator reacts aggressively against the "intimate immensity" (Bachelard) of himself as the anagogic container of the world of Auschwitz. Growing within him "like a foetus inside a womb" is the terrible knowledge and foreboding that "the Infinite Universe is inflating at incredible speed." He wants to retain it like "a miser," afraid that solid matter will dissolve into emptiness like a

"fleeting sound." Demonic knowledge crowds and pressures the confines of his being, a knowledge that cannot be transformed into the logos
of speech because it would not generate an individualized creation;
rather, it would generate a chaos of emptiness, reminiscent of smoke and
air or the cries that rose all the way to the sky from the ground of
Auschwitz.

With this knowledge in him, he walks "on hot summer afternoons . . .
long, lonely strolls through the poorest districts of my city," where he
enjoys inhaling "the stale crumb-dry dust of the ruins." At minimum
subsistence level, life is returning to the illusion of normality, an illusion
he does not want to share. Instead he falls into a demonic reverie in which
he expresses his terrible knowledge through a futile exorcism:

> Through half-open eyes I see with satisfaction that once again a gust of
> the cosmic gale has blown the crowd into the air, all the way up to the
> treetops, sucked the human bodies into a huge whirlpool, twisted their
> lips open with terror, mingled the children's rosy cheeks with the hairy
> chests of the men, entwined the clenched fists with strips of women's
> dresses, thrown snow-white thighs on the top, like foam, with hats and
> fragments of heads tangled in hair-like seaweed peeping from below.
> And I see that this weird snarl, this gigantic stew concocted out of the
> human crowd, flows along the street, down the gutter, and seeps into
> space with a loud gurgle, like water into a sewer. [p. 179]

The visionary with his half-open eyes reacts aggressively to the blindness
of the outside world and to the pressure of memory which becomes so
dense that it seems as if his physical being has coagulated and stiffened
(p. 178). Where he once took in the world with "wide-open, astonished
eyes," he is now the demonic daydreamer caught between repression and
emergence of memory; he transforms the horizontal life of the sidewalk
into an apocalypse which satisfies him because it affirms that the world of
his memory is the real world. His vision of a cosmic gale is, however, no
divine pneuma. Rather, it is a funneled sucking into an upward-down-
ward transcendence wherein human beings once more are as contorted as
the victims of the gas chamber. The center of this whirlpool is again a
point of constriction "that seeps into space with a loud gurgle, like water
into a sewer." Humanity is waste water, but only as a simile. It seeps into
space, the universe he had feared would slip through his hands like water,
and disappears with a loud gurgle that will be no more than a fleeting
sound.

Tadek is left with the choice of chaos as void or a world of stone, the latter symbolized by the "massive cool building made of granite" where he works. But granite does not protect him; he knows it "cannot keep the world from swelling and bursting like an over-ripe pomegranate, leaving behind but a handful of contracted, grey, dry ashes," an image which is a grotesque inversion of Mallarmé's "Afternoon of a Faun." In Borowski's world of stone there may be a volcanic eruption of aggression, there may be ashes, but no queen of love visits the daydreamer.

Tadek concludes that, because the world has not yet blown away, he intends to write and "grasp the true significance of the events and people I have seen." His matter is great and worthy of "an immortal epic," but the act of writing would mean a concession to the illusion of normality in which he does not want to participate. Tadek and the other victim-survivors of the concentrationary universe have not left us, who are still caught in the illusion of reprieve, the conclusive comfort of a great epic. They have left us partial visions, short stories, sketches, and fragments and retained "with a miser's piercing anxiety" (p. 177) the world which swallowed them and which they swallowed with open eyes.

Part Two

Uneasy Armchair Reading: The Ambiguous
and Implicating Worlds of Lenz's *The German
Lesson*, Grass's *Dog Years*, and Johnson's
Jahrestage

3

Siegfried Lenz's *The German Lesson:* Metaphors of Evil on a Narrow Ground

Like Grass and Johnson, Siegfried Lenz came from a geographical area to which he can no longer return. Born 17 March 1926 in Lyck, East Prussia, the son of a "patient official," he "began to play the game" at the age of ten, as he tells us in his autobiographical sketch "Ich zum Beispiel," when he became a Pimpf, a member of the youngest group in the Hitler Youth.[1] As Pimpf and high school student, he was primarily a witness, and it is the awareness of this role which is so important in his life and art: "I was thirteen when the war began: a student, a Pimpf, a patient curb-liner who asked no questions, who cheered when told, as if cheering were a matter of course like eating. . . . I had been converted to external obedience. I began to see that one had to learn, to understand, before one acted. So I became condemned to be a curb-lining minor" (p. 14). This external obedience covers another, more real part of young Lenz's self. There are his fantasies of rather grotesque adventures in which he dives to the bottom of Lyck Lake to fight battles for the black fish king in order to win his fish-lipped daughter (p. 10). There is his German literature teacher who introduces Lenz and a select group of students to forbidden authors like Heinrich Heine and Thomas Mann. The teacher's view that all literature is an expression of the suffering of the author reappears in Lenz's own attitude towards his craft. Young Lenz shares with others the split personality of people living in oppressive societies, a split fully revealed in the problematic childhood and youth of Siggi Jepsen in *The German Lesson.*

Lenz soon becomes acquainted with the idea of duty; but after joining the navy at the end of the war, he learns to see what duty wrought: the breakdown of duty which began for him with the assassination attempt on Hitler, after which he *sees* things as they really are (p. 24). Lenz, the curb-liner, becomes as an adult a *Mitwisser,* an accessory in the know about the events of his time.[2] His literary work is the projection of the socially and historically conscious *Mitwisser* who is motivated to write against the universal desire to repress and forget "our shame, our pressing tasks"; he has no illusions, however, about the effectiveness of a work of art in bringing about change (p. 32). Art is a risky, complex, and subversive dialogue between writer and reader. For truth, argues Lenz, is undogmatic; it is something that is suddenly revealed to the consciousness like the flash of a knife and can, therefore, be only insufficiently expressed in words (p. 49). Lenz's second motivation for writing, at least for the social and historical consciousness of his writing, is to give voice to those whom history consigns to silence. As he pointed out upon accepting the Bremen Prize for literature in 1962, "In our world the artist, too, is an accessory . . . . It seems to me that his work is only then justified when he admits to being an accessory, when he does not overlook the silence to which others are condemned" (p. 204).

Those condemned to silence are not in Lenz's case the victims of extreme situations but are those whom the power of authoritarian language silences. Yet so insecure and brittle is authoritarianism that a single word is a threat, a crisis (p. 203). Lenz, therefore, sees it as his task to "expose the world through language in such a way that nobody is guiltless" (p. 203). By this he accomplishes two things: he defends the integrity of language, and he pledges his solidarity with those who are powerless, with the many who only suffer history and who are even denied hope (pp. 203–4). The reader of Lenz's essays soon becomes aware how general his discussions of past and present problems are, and it is no surprise when Lenz admits that an author's rightful place is between two chairs (p. 36). A social democrat, he is no advocate of revolution, and he tries not to alienate his audience. He compromises by repressing the specifics of past brutalities. Nevertheless, he hopes that the risky encounter between author and reader will somehow come about as both hover between repression and awareness.

Will the reader of *The German Lesson* be open to the risk of encounter? In the novel, Siggi cannot even find a reader among those who are personally interested in him. Lenz's novel does not shock the casual armchair readers, secure in their pride of narrowness and their belief that "after all, one does have to do one's duty."[3] Lenz and his narrator pay a price as ironists; for many will read the novel as a *Heimatroman,* a novel about local color and nostalgia for the North German landscape and its quaint people, not realizing that this *Heimat,* which exiles Siggi, is a demonic narrow ground. At best, the reader will realize the truth about human beings caught in certain situations (p. 197). The *Mitwisser* child, Siggi, is in such a situation as he observes the power struggle between the policeman Jepsen and the painter Nansen, a struggle begun by Jepsen, who has succumbed to the dehumanization of authoritarianism and who tries to rob others of their life-affirming energies. Yet because the struggle is between two equal opponents, the painter winning out in the end, it does not parallel the struggle between a Jew and an SS guard. The victim in the novel is Siggi, the child who is consigned to silence until he begins to write a confession about his sufferings.

Siggi's choice to finally write about the struggle he witnessed as well as his own role in that struggle is an ethically important choice for Lenz, for whom the silent noncommitted are losers without defeat (p. 54). In his emphasis on choice and attitude he pleads for the informed heart; but as an artist he knows that such daylight hopes necessarily repress what he calls "the indivisible dark nucleus" in humankind, causing those actions that give rise to the question "How could our friendly neighbor have done such things?" This dark nucleus is revealed in the extreme situation when man has either total power or total lack of power over his fellow men (p. 55). In this case, Lenz argues, the possibility of free choice is shaken when we are reduced to the alternatives of either living and becoming guilty or dying and remaining guiltless. Many chose the first, because that choice was supported by the law (p. 55). It is this law which enables the policeman Jepsen to break the law of friendship with the motto "Whoever does his duty, does not need to worry, even if times should change."[4] Again, Lenz does not use the word *Nazi* in his essay on the dark nucleus but applies his observations to history in general. In this way he meliorates the specific atrocity of the camps built by the Nazis, permitting his reader to live with that memory in terms of a universal guilt, but at the same time implying the hope for the risk of recognition.

The same rhetoric is evident in his essay "Der Lagermensch" (the camp man), where he defines the camp experience as a universal phenomenon. The camp is seen as a world of exiles who are wrenched from their secure existence and thrown into the point zero world of the camp, needing to take stock of themselves in order to retain their identity. The camp may be the nightmare world of the concentration camp, or it may be a progressive reformatory; it nevertheless is a camp and by definition does violence to the individual. The generalization becomes too comfortable; for the concentration camp has murder as its ultimate aim, while the reformatory aims at an adjustment which at least allows for hope. Siggi's experience in the reformatory, no matter how that institution is satirized, cannot be put on the same denominator with a Nazi camp, a place where no one would allow Siggi to write his autobiography as therapy. In the end, however, Lenz's generalizations in this essay serve not as much to make the reader conscious of the past as to warn against all coercive forces, the "protective measures with which Leviathan silences doubters and opponents": "Because the shadow of the camp is ubiquitous and because the future is something to be continually ascertained, it is recommended that we do not react to the camp with resignation, but, as is proper, with opposition" (p. 61). Lenz offers no ideology with which the camp world could be opposed, for any closed system of thought would by definition perpetuate the camp world. The reader gathers from Lenz's writings that the only opposition is mental and spiritual.

The camp is an obviously demonic and destructive narrow ground. The narrow ground of a small town in a provincial setting may appear as the sheltering space; but in keeping with the ironic mode of the novel, it is more likely the ground where the neuroses of history manifest themselves on a microcosmic scale. In this sense *The German Lesson* is no *Heimatroman*. Lenz argues that this narrowness is an advantage and has been crucial for writers of world literature, for here "the great is revealed through the small . . . " (p. 91). The province is nostalgically and satirically used in his novel, circumscribed space reflecting the mental attitude of the people. As has been pointed out in one study, "The horizon is purposefully limited and correlates with the title *Deutschstunde* and its irony: the narrow, limited ability to see is distilled within a small space which becomes symbolic for the land and the time, symbolic for Germany."[5] As an inversion of the sentimental tradition of the *Heimatroman, The German Lesson* also satirizes the arrogance of Nazi esthetic theory, whose insistence on "blood and soil" as well as on the "healthy affirmation of life" excludes the painter Nansen's canvasses as *artfremd* (alien in a racial sense). Such exclusion is evident precisely because the canvasses reveal that "the land not only has its surface, it has its dangerous depths, and everything that lies there threatens you" (pp. 411, 344). Siggi fears this depth and yet attempts to bring it into the logos of speech, for only in the work of art can the sickness of the province and the world achieve an illusory sense of wholeness.

I.

The Fable of *The German Lesson*

Although he is fully aware of the insufficiencies and limitations of his craft, Lenz insists on the validity of storytelling as an art form: "We tell stories whenever we notice that something is blocked from us which we would like to possess; in this sense a story is an attempt at appropriation through recantation" (p. 92, *Widerruf*, i.e., to say again and to reject). Memory makes us conscious of the shaping influence of the past but cannot free us from that past. Lenz argues, "When one goes in search of the truth, one can hope to achieve only the insight that everything was in vain. In and of itself the search is not sufficient. What is important, I think, is that we maintain the need to be overpowered by the truth in certain situations. In the moment of such overpowering we experience all our potentialities, and is it therefore surprising that the limits of communicability are reached at such moments?" (p. 50) Siggi Jepsen experiences this dilemma. He feels confident about certain truths and themes, "but all these quite attractive subjects turned out to be not at all up my street as soon as I began to do what we had to do, 'organizing the material.' Essays had to be 'organized.' Introduction, exposition, body, evaluation: that was the escalator on which the whole thing had to roll" (pp. 461, 387). As organized experience, art conceals the dangerous depths of its truth. *The German Lesson* is a very well-structured novel, but its ambiguity and cunning are already evident in the title, which means German lesson or German hour, a lesson for Germans or the hour to become conscious of being German.

At the outset, Siggi tells the reader about his problems over the theme topic "the joys of duty," assigned during the officially scheduled German lesson at the reformatory. Because he had too much to say, he turned in blank pages. Now, locked in a small room overlooking the Elbe River in winter time, he reflects on the German teacher's inability to understand that "the anchor of memory could not grasp anywhere, would not tighten the chain, but that it would drag along, deep down at the bottom, rattling and clattering, at most throwing up mud, so that there was no peace, only turbulence, and it was impossible to cast a net over the things of the past" (pp. 15, 13). Immediately before his arrest at the end of the novel, Siggi dreams that his father and the painter, now in total agreement, attempt to catch him in a net (pp. 527, 441), the net of the past that they have made for him and that he has such difficulty recapturing. Anchor, net, ship, and the image of diving become basic metaphors for Siggi's journey into himself. He mocks the metaphors of science, the "cognitive block" (pp. 17, 15) of psychiatric jargon, because he wants to define himself rather than be defined. Yet he does not even realize how much the images he perceives from his window correspond to his cognitive block: "Twice the *Emmy Guspel* has come steaming past, for she has to keep the ice moving and prevent the piling up of floes; a clod of ice midstream might cause a thrombosis, paralysing the traffic on the river" (pp. 20, 17). It is the punitive ritual inflicted by a pedant, the "You will sit here until you are finished" that ironically provides the discipline and impetus for Siggi's autobiography. He accepts the institutional punishment totally until it is internalized and becomes a joyful duty; yet it is different from his father's obsession with duty in that it does not destroy or block creativity but allows it to flow freely.

The German Lesson falls into two time periods. The war years 1943–45 and the postwar years 1945–53 are years when Siggi's consciousness is prereflective. The two war years are given the most attention since they are the cause of Siggi's illness, while the postwar years are relevant because they reveal the outward manifestations of Siggi's illness. The year 1953–54 is the year when Siggi's consciousness becomes reflective. Driven to understand himself, Siggi realizes that he can only cope with the paralyzing influence of the past if he is willing to go backward in order to move forward (pp. 20, 18). The specific chronology of the novel is important in this process. Siggi is born on 25 September 1933, and ten years later, on a Friday in April, the policeman Jepsen informs his friend Max Ludwig Nansen that he may no longer paint. This establishes the central conflict of the novel: the confrontations between Jepsen and Nansen, their mutual attempts to trick and elude each other in the narrow space of the novel—the painter's house at Bleekenwarf, the home and office of the policeman of Rugbüll, and the old mill, the private hideaway of Siggi who witnesses the games of the adults. After an additional ten years, Siggi, now at the reformatory for juveniles, begins his *Strafarbeit,* a punitive assignment which he will finish on 25 September 1954 when the law says that he has come of age. Officialdom considers him at that point "rehabilitated" and releases him from the institution.

Throughout the novel the public duties of the policeman Jepsen come into conflict with his private obligations, or rather, his public duties provide ready-made solutions for his inability to cope with his private problems. Yet he is trapped, for he can neither fulfill the letter of the law nor the law of love. The conflict with Nansen reveals this most clearly.

When both were young, Nansen saved Jepsen from drowning, a rather symbolic death, for Jepsen will never again dive below surfaces. The painter therefore has a claim on Jepsen's love which Jepsen resents and refuses to meet. Nansen has his revenge, unconscious as it may be, for he is able to draw all of Jepsen's children into his sphere of influence. When Klaas, the eldest, wounds himself in order to avoid being sent to the front and deserts the army, Nansen shelters him. Hilke outrages her parents when she poses seminude for Nansen's painting "Dancer of the Waves," another manifestation of diseased art. Siggi himself falls victim to the conflict between the two men when his father wants to use him as a spy against Nansen. Torn by his feelings of love, loyalty, obligation, and fear for both men, Siggi develops the split personality of the individual caught in an extreme situation. By trying to see and not to see at the same time, he betrays both men. Siggi learns from Nansen how unconscious content is made conscious and controlled in art. Such knowledge, however, no matter how intuitive, is forbidden according to the rigid rule of the father, and Siggi has to repress that which attracts him; he has to repress the truth. He also represses his own fears of his father until they flicker forth in the shape of hallucinatory flames threatening any painting of which his father may disapprove. Then Siggi will "secure" the painting by taking possession of it. This possessing, defined as stealing by the adult world, is punished both by his father, the painter, and finally by the public authorities. At that point Siggi becomes an exile.

No matter how profoundly Siggi may reflect upon the past, the present, too, intrudes upon his voluntary and solitary confinement and forces him to define attitudes. He includes these intrusions in his narrative, and they reveal that the past repeats itself with variations. The enlightened director of the institution and the psychologist Wolfgang Mackenroth vie for Siggi's soul. The former tries to stop the penalty when he realizes that Siggi's composition is taking on "threatening proportions"; the latter uses Siggi as a case study for his dissertation. Siggi maintains himself against this competition for his allegiance and against the competition between the inmate-librarian Ole Plötz (again the connotation of suddenness, *plötzlich*) and Joswig the keeper, an individual in spite of institutional rules. Siggi remains noncommittal when Plötz asks him to join an escape; and when a second attempt is planned, Joswig asks Siggi's advice as to how it can be stopped. Betrayal seems unavoidable, but Siggi solves the dilemma in trickster fashion by inventing a joke that harms no one and keeps him from becoming entangled in guilt.

Since his early years, Siggi has developed the ability to see the

possibilities of truth on either of two sides. His education in seeing is
sometimes brought about through paintings but also through set verbal
constructs such as Mackenroth's thesis or the funeral eulogy for Ditte, the
painter's wife. Seeing can be learned by looking through a microscope at
school or by sitting on top of the old mill and watching the ludicrous
behavior of the adults below. Whatever the position of the perceiver,
slanted vision is unavoidable, as the chapter "Seeing" indicates. Nansen, allowed to paint again, is engaged in a self-portrait in which everything is equivocal. For, as he argues, "seeing is a sort of mutual
swapping. What that produces is mutual transformation. Take the rivulets in the flats, take the skyline, the moat, the larkspur: the moment you
get hold of them, they get hold of you. There's mutual recognition.
Another thing that seeing means is coming closer, diminishing the
distance between. What else? Balthasar [the painter's imaginary alter ego]
thinks all that's not enough. He insists that seeing is also exposure.
Something gets laid bare in such a way that nobody in the whole world
can pretend he doesn't understand. I don't know, I have something
against this stripping game. You can strip all the skins of an onion until
nothing is left. I tell you: one begins to see when one stops playing the
beholder and simply invents what one needs: this tree, this wave, this
beach'' (pp. 402, 336). This quote is crucial for Nansen and Siggi, for the
latter, too, wants to see and is simultaneously afraid to discover that
seeing, in the sense of analysis, will reveal an emptiness that destroys.
For this reason, he sees and invents what makes life livable. The object
lesson for this theory is revealed at the end of the chapter when Nansen
and Siggi watch the homecoming of the farmer Isenbüttel. His legs have
been amputated, and he has been tied to a narrow board on wheels. His
wife, Hilde, visibly pregnant by her POW farmhand, meets him and
wordlessly starts pulling the cart. Both see enough (pp. 419, 352). Siggi
and Nansen watch the two disappear into the horizon: "We stood there on
the dyke for a long time, turning our backs to the sea, watching those two
people becoming smaller and smaller, watching them turn into a single
body which then became also smaller and smaller, until there was nothing
left but a far-off scarcely recognizable movement on the ground'' (pp.
420, 352). The scene is emblematic for Siggi's quest. The images of his
memory reveal a truth, but that truth has no consoling constancy. It is
perceived by the reflective consciousness during a moment in time, and
then that which appears as a central point disappears into the periphery of
human experience.

II.

Siggi's Point of View: The Demonic Child as Witness

Technically, the point of view of *The German Lesson* is that of a witness-narrator who observes the struggle between the antagonists of the novel and who is profoundly affected by what he sees. Furthermore, the central consciousness of the novel is that of a twenty-year-old who is distant from and yet near enough to the events in his childhood that memory and repression are of equal importance. The childhood memories of a youth also emphasize the personal over the historical. As Albrecht Weber argues, given his age, Siggi is not aware of the historical events that brought the Nazis to power, nor is he aware of the Nazi period itself. Because of its lack of analysis, his youthful perspective communicates a directness which becomes accusatory while simultaneously maintaining a distant and ironical point of view: "He must reveal the past as present because it continues to live, duplicate itself, affect, because it is virulent."[6] Although his experiences and conflicts take place on a narrow ground, Siggi's intelligence, imagination, and introvertedness universalize these experiences. Lenz takes care to show the reader that Siggi is intelligent, always the first in his class, without being ambitious. He excelled in all subjects except religion (pp. 321, 269), as his psychologist Mackenroth's dissertation reveals. Mackenroth also points out that Siggi had a tendency to ask questions that would embarrass adults and that he had a distinctly artistic bent which the painter encouraged by permitting Siggi to watch him at work for hours on end. The narrator's qualifications are carefully established, including his heightened sensibilities, at first manifesting themselves in the ability to see the demonic dimension of the world in which he lives, and later leading to his peculiar second sight, by means of which he can detect those works of art that are "threatened" by repressive forces.

Lenz is not to be identified with his narrator, for he views the narrator with a distance comparable to that with which Siggi himself recalls his childhood. Yet author and narrator share many values and seem to speak at times with one voice. The reader becomes especially aware of the distance between the two in those parts of the novel which deal with Siggi's situation in the present, where Siggi is often unable to recognize how he repeats behavior patterns established in his past. Siggi is also unable or unwilling to interpret or analyze objects, scenes, people, and situations. He views and describes them precisely and thus gives them a phenomenological numinosity that provokes interpretation from the reader. To a great extent, the novel is a collection of keenly perceived images whose meaning the narrator intuits but does not raise into his rational consciousness. At the end, Siggi is left with many questions and no satisfactory answers:

> And I ask who is it that knocks on our doors in thunderstorms or sends puffs of smoke jerking out of stoves; and I ask why they so belittle those who are afflicted in body and mind, and why they regard anyone who has second sight with awe, even indeed with dread. Who is it that brings us our darkness and our murky days, who is boiling his bubbling broth in the peat bogs, drawing the mist around his shoulders, who groans in the rafters, whistles in the pots, hurls the crows in midflight down upon the fields? That is what I ask. And I ask myself why they leave the stranger there outside, scorning his help. And why they cannot turn back half-way and have a change of heart—that is what I ask myself. Who blackens the willows in the night? Who batters against the door of the shed? And I ask why it is that down our way they see farther and deeper at evening than by day, and why they are so fanatical in the performance of tasks they have taken on. Their taciturn gluttony, their smugness, their local lore *[Heimatkunde]*, the element in which they live and move and have their being: to these as well I put my questions. And I put my questions to their way of walking and of standing, to their glances and their words. And whatever I learn from any of it does not satisfy me. [pp. 556, 467–68]

Although Siggi includes Mackenroth's report for objectivity's sake, although he includes his sister Hilke's objections that they did also have fun with their father and that the painter, too, used to be taciturn for days, what he reveals in his summary questions indicts once more that sinister fairy-tale world that beset him as a child. Facile psychological rationalizations cannot evaporate the feelings provoked in such a world. They can at best repress or rationalize Siggi's troubled memories, but Siggi does not want to forget. He never excelled in religion; he did not need to. The nonrational was not placed for him in some subterranean or transcendent world; it was right in his world, and he had to come to terms with it. This is the reason why demonic images abound not only in Nansen's paintings but also in Siggi's world. They have come back from their supernatural displacements to their point of origin, the human heart and mind. Seeing is mutual swapping: the world is perceived and in turn influences the perceiver. The child perceives the forbidden, is involved in it, fears his secret and the secrets of others, and becomes the tricky child in order to manage in such a world. Siggi is a demonic child, not as obviously as Oskar Matzerath in Grass's *Tin Drum,* but is an understated demon, an *eiron* who is the nemesis of the adult world.[7]

Siggi has two demonic characteristics: ubiquitousness and shut-upness. As he moves from Rugbüll to Bleekenwarf and back, Lenz often used the colloquial word *flitzte* (moved rapidly and suddenly), with its connotations of flying like an arrow, and *blitzte* (flashed like lightening), the sudden eruption of consciousness, as when Siggi wonders during a meeting of the antagonists whether or not they were aware of a *blitz-schnelle Erinnerung,* a flash of memory about an event that would always tie them together (pp. 34, 27). Siggi is the child that has seen everything and eventually must tell what he has seen. He is the *eiron* who is in the know, whose knowledge gives him power but isolates him from the community that has no interest in that knowledge. Nansen is aware of the demonic in Siggi, as he is conscious of the demonic in everyone. He paints the boy as the son of the hay-devil and has a nickname for him, Witt-Witt. The name suggests wit and its associations with knowledge and irony; but it is also the call of the sandpiper that runs hither and thither between sea and shore, thus indicating Siggi's speed as well as his inno-cence and easily frightened nature. As a child, Siggi is of little account in the adult world. He can come physically close to adult confrontations, a closeness that would be considered eavesdropping if he were older. He is compulsively drawn to the confrontations between the two men he loves; he witnesses the betrayal of a friendship, and in the course of his young life, he is forced to betray both men. Thus, he becomes a *Mitwisser,* an accomplice in a guilty society. He is, however, also the victim of this society, which remains oblivious to guilt and its possible creative uses.

By speaking about his experiences, Siggi attempts to overcome the demonic forces of repression. As a child he was silent, officially aligning himself with the forces of the law that provided for his physical well-being. To an extent he even identifies and cooperates with the repressive father, but he also yearns for the creative powers that, while repressed, can never be repressed completely. They often emerge on Nansen's canvasses or in Siggi's dreams as "sick" images precisely because they reveal what happens when living and positive urges are repressed. When a child is refused love or is forced to pervert love, it feels guilt and wonders what it did wrong; for if it had not done wrong it would be loved. In Siggi's case, to love the father means to obey his command against Nansen, whom Siggi also loves. The failure of love is inevitable; the Jepsen household reinforces lovelessness repeatedly. The mother, Gud-run Jepsen, is incapable of showing love and shuts herself in her bedroom most of the time. In contrast, the Nansen household welcomes children. Nansen and Ditte adopt two children, and Ditte remains in Siggi's memory as the image of a woman leaning out the window with handfuls of cake for the children outside. The sullen silence of Siggi's parents, however, enhances the child's sense of guilt and makes him tremble before the unmovable father. As events are witnessed but not comprehended, as the child becomes increasingly guilty and yet compulsively watches the same scene over and over again, and as that guilt cannot be raised into the light of speech, the child becomes the encapsulated little demon acting, however, as far as those around him are concerned, like a bright and eager child who is perhaps somewhat too old for his years.

Motion in terms of pursuit is one-half of the demonic quality in the novel, but the motion leads each time to the moment of dead-end confrontation, usually expressed in the pose of stubborn and sullen pride. Another type of confrontation is expressed in those moments of epiphany when Siggi is suddenly faced with an image in reality or art that communicates to him a grotesque metaphysics; he does not understand the metaphysics rationally or analytically but grasps it imaginatively and intuitively as the image impresses itself on his memory. The form of the image both controls and reveals the demonic. An example of how Siggi exercises such discovery and control over his threatening world is the occasion of the birthday party of Teo Busbeck, the painter's friend. Siggi suddenly comes upon the invited guests and sees them transformed into creatures that express their essential nature:

> The silence made me suspicious . . . . But when I had gone in, hesitantly, and looked around, I got quite a shock, as anybody might have who'd expected, like me, to find the room empty. At the narrow, endlessly long birthday table there was a solemn congregation of sea-animals, all gray with age, sitting there in silence drinking coffee and gobbling madeira cake, nutcake and shortcake, sunk deep in stubborn contemplation. There were stiff-legged lobsters, prawns, and crabs crouching on the haughty, carved Bleekenwarf chairs; now and then one could hear the dry creaking of heavily armored limbs or the clatter of a cup set down on the table by a lobster's bony pincers; some of them gave me a look out of indifferent eyes, those eyes on long stalks, imperturbable with—if you know what I mean—the monumental indifference of certain deities. And at the same time this silent congregation of sea-animals definitely resembled people I knew . . . . [pp. 75, 60–61]

This silent, underwater world is peopled by beings who have not yet evolved as humans; however, the child is well aware that they are the people of his world. As water creatures they are brittle and dry, rigidly armored in external skeletons whose density encrusts a dangerous depth, dangerous because of its emptiness and indifference. At the same time, the gathered creatures are nothing but members of a birthday party. The ordinary always provides the possibility of confrontation with the disturbing, as when Siggi discovers that, beneath each orderly numbered day on the calendar in the reformatory, Ole Plötz's talented hand has drawn sexually suggestive pictures (pp. 195, 162). Unlike his father, Siggi does not consider it his duty to report Plötz's aggressive creativity.

Siggi becomes the guard and eventually the hoarder of Nansen's persecuted art. Nansen's art is sick because it projects truthfully the vacuously demonic world that underlies the daily existence of the people and their landscape. Their demonic quality is the result of the inverted and perverted energies of life that have not been allowed to flow and express themselves freely. Nansen's paintings are grotesques whose demonic forms the perceiver tends to interpret and give spiritual meaning. A perceiver like Siggi creates meanings for them, and it is not surprising that three of the paintings are actually crucial for Siggi's development. They are "Suddenly at the Beach," a portrait of his brother Klaas encountering a demon on a beach; "Dancer of the Waves," a Dionysian portrait of Hilke; and "Garden with Masks," a mysterious canvas that projects the primal situation in the novel. "Suddenly at the Beach" was begun in September 1939, the beginning of the Second World War, and thus takes on the larger significance of chaos suddenly bursting upon reality. As an interpreter of reality, Nansen shows again and again the emergence of chaos over the artificial and rigid world created by man, and he captures both chaos and rigidity in the frozen moment revealed within the confines of the canvas. Klaas encounters on the beach a universal though ludicrous demon who evokes from him a silent scream of fear, for the figure also suggests the father whom he and Siggi fear so much. When Jepsen catches Nansen several years later at work on the painting, the painter tears the canvas; but Siggi manages to get hold of the pieces, which contain for him a multitude of possible meanings (pp. 224, 185). As he glues them on the window shade used for obligatory blackouts, the cracked painting becomes symbolic: the blackout shade hides the fragmented unit of what has been forbidden. This incident initiates Siggi's increasingly frantic attempts to save the painter's threatened work from the policeman, who continues his persecution even after the war when Siggi catches him burning some of the painter's sketches (pp. 438, 368). Jepsen reacts viciously to Siggi's reproaches and once again makes a pact with him: "I did not threaten him and did not tell him how much I hated him, yet he must have felt it, for he stepped towards me and said: you'll only need to keep out of everything; we'll understand each other as always, if you only keep out" (pp. 439, 369). Consigned to be a *Mitwisser,* his knowledge choked, Siggi's illness begins to take threatening proportions as he sees open flames approaching any painting whose content officialdom would repress.

Although Nansen himself rejects Siggi as a disturbed child, Siggi's hallucinations are justified, especially when Jepsen becomes enraged over "Dancer of the Waves." Siggi steals the painting and hides it in the attic. Here, suffering under oppressive headaches, he contemplates the dancer of the waves among the discarded items of the Jepsen household: "Hilke dancing for me among the little tumbling waves. And all at once she was a personal concern of mine, there under the red sky, her hair loose. All at once it was important for me to understand her, there in that short striped skirt, with those pointed breasts, this Hilke did not cease dancing, despite her exhaustion. Alone there by the dazzling beach. Nobody, nobody would ever see this picture again, that was settled, and the other pictures, too, were only for me now. I had found out something about myself and what I needed in order to live with myself" (pp. 492, 413). Siggi, the unhappy little dragon, hoards the loved and forbidden image in his cave, possessively excluding it from the rest of the world because he alone can understand its value. The sexual abandon of Hilke is caught in the painting in a moment of paralyzed frenzy, a pitch of tension that finds no release and indirectly reflects Siggi's state; Siggi is, however, not aware of this.

Siggi is also not conscious of the sexual connotations that pervade several scenes with his sister, who sees him as nothing but a younger brother. When one considers that the narrative takes the main character through puberty, it is suprising that any overt sexual feelings or experiences are absent from the novel. But in the cosmos of Siggi's story the life-affirming qualities of sex are repressed and, if admitted, would be reduced to the joys of duty. They emerge only subversively under calendar leaves or in innocently demonic scenes, as when Siggi goes to catch plaice with his sister. She cuts her foot, and he sucks the wound, "pressing slightly with my tongue, and gradually all taste disappeared. Then I opened my eyes and saw Hilke lying there in front of me, nodding at me appreciatively" (pp. 289, 241). Such human contact is valuable to the child; and when Siggi eventually hoards the painting of Hilke, he tries to possess by force what reality denies him, namely, that quiet bower that provides a retreat from a loveless world. Displaced into the ironic mode, the romantic retreat becomes a dusty attic where the princess and the incestuous dragon are a policeman's son and daughter, each expressing in their own way repressed emotions in a shut-up and confined space. The dragon-self is only overcome when Siggi extends himself in empathy, as he does to Mackenroth, who interrupts this memory to tell Siggi about his love affair with his landlady. Siggi decides to help the psychologist with his work, and in this sense the dragon comes out of the cave, giving instead of hoarding.

Just before his arrest, Siggi ponders Nansen's painting "Garden with Masks," displayed in an exhibition which officially honors Nansen. Spellbound, he sees an intensely colorful garden into which three masks, two male and one female, are suspended on green cords. The masks appear vaguely familiar to Siggi: "There was a terrible certainty emanating from them, some enigmatic authority. The eye-slits were earth-brown, the sky behind them was bright and cloudless. Were these masks a menace to the garden?" (pp. 512, 428) Siggi begins to hallucinate before the painting as he conjures up a "breath of wind" which sets the picture in motion. His imagination multiplies the masks, and in a sudden onrush of aggressive feeling he wishes he had a stick to strike off all the masks on the bushes and branches. "I wanted to behead everything the way one beheads flowers and afterwards, for all I care, cart them off to the compost-heap" (pp. 512, 429). Repression has finally unleashed itself in destructive emotion, but Siggi is hindered from acting on his vision. At that point he is arrested by plainclothes men who wear "the stamp of reliability and professional suspiciousness" (pp. 513, 429), and Siggi realizes how many things try "to camouflage themselves when confronted by those dangling masks. The presence of the masks in the garden seemed to be all that was needed to make everything pretend to be something else." As he is dragged away, he sees "hidden among the flowers, two eyes gazing spellbound at the dangling masks." Again, he does not interpret the painting for his reader but simply reveals the vision of the garden, which is, like all other important paintings, a mystical epiphany for him. It is a garden of corrupted innocence, for it is repressed by the masks and can flower only in exotic corruption. The rigid and empty masks transform the garden into a fallen world where nothing can be as it was meant to be. To whom do the masks belong? From Nansen's point of view they may be the masks of himself, Ditte, and Teo Busbeck as observed by the eyes of Jepsen; but from Siggi's point of view they may well be the masks of Jepsen, Gudrun, and Nansen, summarizing the impenetrable adult world possessed with a mysterious knowledge that the young man cannot comprehend but to which he is yet inexorably drawn. All of this may be illusion, however, for the ultimate demonic quality of the masks is that they hide no horror at all, only emptiness. If they could be knocked off, they would simply be discarded, and Siggi's aggression would have spent itself on empty shells.

The hyperboles which Siggi-Lenz is so careful to avoid are expressed in Nansen's paintings, while the narrative reveals the demonic in understated and displaced metaphors of shut-upness. This shut-upness constitutes the metaphysics of Siggi's world, a metaphysics that knows no transcendence or even the desire for transcendence. His metaphysics remains locked into itself, except for occasional flare-ups when the pressure becomes unbearable and chaos encroaches upon the tedious emptiness of existence. The novel reveals the demonic very much in the way Kierkegaard discusses it in his *Concept of Dread,* in the metaphoric terms of shut-upness and sudden leap; for Kierkegaard the shut-up is vacuity and tediousness. In this lies the indictment of certain people in *The German Lesson,* for what is shut-up, what is confined to the "pride of narrowness," is emptiness. It is the suspicion that the land and its people do not have what Teo Busbeck calls "dangerous depth," which would provide profundity and plenitude, but rather consist only of surfaces. As Nansen says, "I know there is this uneasiness, but what makes everything so uneasy is moods—perhaps this whole countryside consists of nothing but moods, and anyone who knows and understands it all is perhaps less disconcerted by it" (pp. 411, 344). Although Nansen projects profundity through the surfaces in his paintings, he does not like to go beneath the surface; for this reason he can still feel at home with land and people in spite of Jepsen's hounding. Siggi, however, as an intense and repressed child, is afraid until he finds what Kierkegaard calls the good, namely, expansion that is free-flowing and communicative: "The more definitely conscience is in this way developed in a man, the more he is expanded, even though in other respects he shuts himself off from the world."[8] This is Siggi's situation as he is locked in the room in the reformatory and finds words to describe the past. Pride, the arrogance of narrowness, is basically the fear to be outgoing, to communicate and speak the saving word to others, thus bringing about one's own salvation. This is why the policeman Jepsen will be unredeemed, for he cannot find the creative word: "Not once did he go through the trouble of trying to put it any differently—every time he talked about his experiences, people got full value; he always managed to repeat it word for word'' (pp. 429, 360). After his outbursts, he sinks back into silent sullenness, shut-up into himself and refusing to understand. This is also the silence of Gudrun Jepsen locked in her room, the silence of the closed Gestapo car, and the silence of the images in Nansen's paintings.

But there is also the silence and emptiness that desires to be filled, the silence of the empty canvas, the silence of the empty page that Siggi at first cannot enscribe because he has too much to say. As he is shut in and given his penance, he expands in memories, and his duty becomes a creative joy sufficient unto itself. It is the counterforce to the repression that prohibits painting or music. Creative force is also a demand, but it is a positive duty. Yet because the world of this novel is an ironic world, the creative joy prevails only while it is in the process of expressing itself; it does not redeem anything permanently. Nansen's pleasure lies in the act of painting; the finished work is almost incomprehensible to him. Siggi asks himself what he should do with his filled copybooks: "I could give them to Hilke or to Wolfgang Mackenroth or to the indifferently flowing Elbe. I could toss them into a potato-fire or sell them for re-cycling. Possibilities. There are possibilities, but will I make use of them?"[9] The process of writing has taught him one thing, namely, that "time heals nothing, really nothing." He realizes that he is still tied to Rugbüll, that when it comes to Rugbüll he has run aground *(scheitern an Rugbüll)*. As he watches an English cable-laying ship in its efforts to establish international technological communication, he concludes that his "cable . . . would never extend beyond Rugbüll." He has no plans. On the day of his release he will string his copybooks on a line (like fish) and go to the director's office. There lies no territory ahead for this young narrator, who is unlikely even to find an echo or a listener for his effort to find words. Hilke promises to read the *Strafarbeit* soon; director Himpel has read it but already needs to refresh his memory when Siggi comes for a conference. He will read "pensively, occasionally nodding approval, he will leaf through it, without really stopping to read" (pp. 560, 471).

III.
The Antagonists Jepsen and Nansen

A. Jepsen, the "Polizeiposten" of Rugbüll

"I gazed through the wide bay window beyond the piano and saw the Elbe, saw two crows flying, fighting for something flabby, dangling, perhaps a piece of gut, tearing it away from each other, trying to swallow it, until it dropped on an ice floe and was snatched away by a watchful gull'' (pp. 16–17, 14). Siggi observes this scene as he looks out of the window in the director's office after having been called in for failing to write about the joys of duty. The image on the river fascinates him, and after finishing the novel, the reader cannot help but interpret the image as mirroring the conflict between Jepsen and Nansen. Siggi is caught between both of them until both drop him and leave him to another interested person, the director of the reformatory, who wants to remake Siggi into a well-adjusted citizen in a democratic society.

Siggi frequently calls his father ''der Polizeiposten Rugbüll'' and thereby reduces him to a sturdy, stubborn, and stunted object, a post. Jepsen, of course, identifies himself as such, but for the child that definition provides a critical detachment. There are repeated references to posts in the novel: Klaas, hospitalized with a self-inflicted wound, is only nursed in order to be made ready for the post—his execution; at the end of the novel Siggi sits by a weathered post on which is nailed a ''no trespassing'' sign put up by the Juvenile Welfare Society (pp. 555, 466). Posts are unambiguous markers, and along with the name Rugbüll, with its connotations of criticizing and bullishness (rügen and Bulle), they emphasize the thick-headed and stunted mentality of Jepsen. Basically, Jepsen is insecure, but his post gives him an external self-definition through which he can indulge in the joys or, rather, the obsession of duty. His motivation to persecute Nansen is far more complex than simple loyalty to the Hitler regime and the desire to adhere to the letter of the law. As a representative of law and order he enacts in his narrow sphere the collective evil that pervaded Hitler's Germany. Although Jepsen commits no murder, no overtly sadistic acts, the law allows him to vent his silent rage and wrath, by means of which he betrays the demands made by humane relationships. It is only because Jepsen is not given absolute power over those who are absolutely powerless that he remains for the reader a tolerable if not pathetic human being.

The origin of Jepsen's wrath can be seen in his unwillingness to comply with the law of empathetic love. As a child, Jepsen was saved from drowning by Nansen, who was eight years older. The friendship between the two men became, therefore, cemented through their mutual encounter with death. The experience is symbolically important for Jepsen; for while diving is a conscious exploration of depth, as can be seen in Lenz's novel Mann im Strom, or metaphorically in Siggi's exploration of the past, drowning is a helpless and passive floundering indicating that Jepsen will never be able to dive into unexplored regions of the self. Instead, he covers dangerous depths with "no trespassing" signs of duty, while Nansen insists on surfacing images of fear and dread which Jepsen considers, accurately from his point of view, a sick activity. Nansen always emerges with what Jepsen wishes to hide. Moreover, the knowledge that he owes his life to Nansen increases Jepsen's aggression, for that debt seems to be a perpetual claim for love. Jepsen, who cannot fulfill that claim, wants to be quits and free of it.

The "Polizeiposten" Jepsen has been analyzed as an example of the little man as cog in the machine of authoritarianism. He is the Eichmann self in all its banality of evil, for whom Kant's categorical imperative has come to mean duty and obedience to the state to which the individual surrenders his selfhood and always acts in such a way that the Führer would approve.[10] Hannah Arendt demonstrates the perversity of this, for Kant's law was closely "bound up with man's faculty of judgment which rules out blind obedience." Arendt shows that another twist occurs when the law-abiding citizen acts, not only in obedience to the laws, but as if he were the originator of them.[11] In this way, duty becomes a perverted joy, for under the guise of duty the individual "can just let go" and release his aggressions under the aegis of an ego-law cathexis. In the case of Jepsen, the word *duty* becomes a sign-post of self-definition in the dangerous depths of the guilt-aggression syndrome and its resulting spiritual emptiness. Without doubt or hesitation he follows his appointed rounds between Rugbüll and Bleekenwarf, for the rhetoric of this novel defines him in such a way that he seems to have no other duty as a policeman than the duty of seeing to it that Nansen does not paint. Only when one of his children disobeys the law of the state does he momentarily divert from the center of his aggressive energies. After the war, when his ego can no longer adhere to the law of the state, his sense of duty becomes internalized almost as a religion that has lost its affiliation with the church: "A man has to keep faith *[treu bleiben]* with himself. That he has got to carry out his duty even when circumstances alter. I mean a duty that he knows he has" (pp. 439, 369).

In spite of the *Kadavergehorsam* and his post mentality, Jepsen is by no means a drab personality. To Siggi he appears as demonic, as do the images in Nansen's paintings. There is his repressed aggression which can flare up at any moment, there is his need to burn things he wishes to forget, and there is his second sight, of which both Siggi and Jepsen are afraid. Even the way his external figure fills space as a solitary, grotesquely Gothic image is worthy to be painted: "Up there, significantly outlined against the empty horizon, he swung himself into the saddle again, sailed off, a solitary sloop under his taut, billowing almost bursting cape, along the top of the dyke to Bleekenwarf, always to Bleekenwarf, always mindful of his orders'' (pp. 12, 10). He is the compulsive, sullen messenger of the gods on his bicycle, isolated in his demonic shut-upness, his silent guilt. The powers he relates to and who give him his orders are abstract powers reaching him by way of the telephone, at which he stands at attention screaming "Polizeiposten Rugbüll" into the receiver as unheard voices issue their commandments.

Jepsen refuses to realize that his natural allegiance lies with his family and with his community. Brodersen, the one-armed, uniformed but humane mailman, another messenger on a bicycle, asks him repeatedly to desist from persecuting Nansen; but Jepsen can only respond with a lecture on duty. The community realizes that Jepsen is not just obeying the law but is after Nansen. At the end, the community literally backs away from him and turns towards Nansen during the Volkssturm's ridiculous attempt to resist the advancing British army. As they move away, Jepsen feels betrayed in the same manner in which he feels betrayed by his children. On a larger historical scale this sense of betrayal is reflected in Germany's reaction when her former ally, Italy, declares war on her. The voice over the radio rationalizes, "Only now, no longer hampered by consideration for an unreliable ally, could we display all our virtues" (pp. 300, 251). The traitors are rejected as having always been unworthy, and the unhappy Jepsen, like Germany, is not able to see a fault in himself. He broods in a silent and sullen posture of guilt that cannot be brought into the light of speech, unable to free itself in the confession of fault because there is no awareness of fault.

Jepsen is an unhappy consciousness who remains unaware that the law of love and the law of the state provoke conflict within him. He can never fulfill either law and must always violate both. The law of the Führer demands absolute surrender, and the law "love one another" is equally unfulfillable. Those whom he loves somehow come in conflict with political law, and he is forced to choose. While the written law gives comfort through definition and pattern for action, it does not make Jepsen happy as he tries to follow it. That law is issued by superiors who act willfully and destructively in a world far removed from Rugbüll. Franti-cally, he tries to keep the forces of life—family love, friendship, and artistic creation—within the confines of a law that says "thou shalt not" and demands that darkness prevail (pp. 214, 178). His aggressions toward Nansen are those of sterility and emptiness against life. His inner hollowness, a protective measure, reverberates for Siggi with a sense of wrong and guilt that threatens to inflict punishment. In his sullen, inner directedness, Jepsen becomes a mockery of the German ideal of *Innerlichkeit* (inwardness), hateful to Siggi: "I hate that way of sitting, that masterful attitude of his, and I am afraid of that silence which sets out to be full of meaning; I hate that solemn taciturnity, that gaze roaming the distance and that gesture that is so hard to describe; and I am afraid, yes afraid, of our habit of listening as though to an inward voice and making do without words" (pp. 129, 106). This inwardness leads to Jepsen's ability to have second sight, an ability revealed when he predicts the slide sequence concerning a naval attack. He is himself frightened of what seems to him a useless and irrational gift that he cannot control. After the irrational has emerged in this way, he sits with his friends in the local inn, "entirely withdrawn into a brooding sense of guilt that he couldn't or wouldn't explain to himself" (pp. 163, 135).

If the content of Nansen's paintings springs into the perceiver's consciousness with demonic suddenness, Jepsen's sudden appearances are so predictable that they become tedious; the Kierkegaardian definition of demonic tediousness, the opposite of demonic suddenness, partly applies to the repetitive compulsiveness of Jepsen: "Tediousness, the impression of being extinct, is in fact a continuity in nothingness . . . . The vacuous or the tedious characterize in turn shut-upness . . . ."[12] Again, this shut-upness is not peaceful self-containment but an expression of the fear of expanding and life-affirming good. Keeping in mind that it is Siggi who is portraying his father, with whom he shares many characteristics, Jepsen is a being whose core is empty and does not want to be filled. The civilizing forces of law and order have become so rigid in him, so much the illusory form of the Apollonian self, that there is no life within him. Even light becomes negative in his case. He turns it off, blacks it out, or lights fires that repress or erase memory and incrimination, as when he burns his papers just before he is arrested or when he burns the painter's sketchbook. When Siggi begins to have second sight, he takes upon himself the power of his father as he sees flames encroach upon dangerous paintings. Like his father, he has begun to look so deeply into things that his true sight is impaired. With this he also takes on the sickness of his father. Only in the process of writing himself free of his memories does Siggi overcome the sickness which imprisoned him; and he learns to see like Nansen, namely, to perceive images clearly and sharply through his own personality, to create his world in terms of a mutual swapping between inner and outer reality.

B. Nansen and the Mythology of "Blood and Soil"

Whenever Siggi's point of view is in control, and that is almost
throughout the novel, Nansen appears in a better light than Jepsen, for
Siggi wants to love Nansen and be faithful to him even after the painter
has rejected him. There are, however, two crows fighting for the piece of
gut. Nansen, too, becomes guilty in terms of Siggi's problem, but Siggi
does not want to admit this. Hilke, as she browses through her brother's
notebooks, reminds him that their father "used to tell us stories, sometimes" and that the painter "didn't talk for days at a time" (pp. 549,
461–62). The ambiguity of Nansen is most clearly revealed in Mackenroth's report, whose often political content contrasts with the loving and
personal portrait Siggi wishes to project. The fate of Nansen under the
Nazis is quite similar to that of the expressionist painter Emil Nolde (born
Emil Hansen). Mackenroth points out that Nansen joined the NSDAP
two years after Hitler became a member and that he at first welcomed the
events of 1933. A year later, however, he turned down an appointment to
the directorship of the State Academy with the following telegram:
"Gratefully acknowledge honor stop Suffering from color allergy stop
Brown diagnosed as cause of trouble stop With humble regrets Nansen,
painter" (pp. 199, 165). He resigns from the Party in 1935 and begins to
use colors in opposition in his paintings, proving "once and for all that
great art also takes its revenge on the world by immortalizing the things
the world despises" (pp. 199, 165). Nansen immortalizes the pride of
narrowness which the Nazis advocated and which characterizes most
people in Nansen's environment. His art is a parody of Nazi esthetics, a
militant and demonic irony towards the mythology of "blood and soil."
Nansen loves the landscape he paints, and he has an affinity for archetypal images. But these images become grotesque when he discovers that the
mentality of which they are a part is proud, narrow, and repressive. The
Nazis prohibit his paintings and the process of painting them because they
consider the images sick and *artfremd* (having no kinship with the racial
community), even though they are actually *arttreu,* reflective of the
community.

Through parody, Nansen maintains the ties that originally bound him
in sympathy to the Nazis. Nansen's sudden revelations of demonic
images, whose colors are politically aggressive, are, of course, sick and
must be prohibited. Gudrun Jepsen, whose priestly voice always decides
between the healthy and unhealthy, presents the official definition as to
why Nansen's work is *artfremd:*

Sometimes I think Max ought to be glad about the ban. I mean, if you just look and see the sort of people he paints—those green faces, those mongol eyes, those lumpy bodies. There is something strange about it all—there must be something ill about that kind of painting. Now you don't see a German face in any of his pictures. In the old days—oh yes, you did then. But now. You can't help thinking it's a kind of fever, it's all done in some fever . . . . Just look at the sort of mouths his people have. Black and crooked, and they are always shrieking and stammering, those mouths never produced a sensible word, anyway, no German word. [pp. 218, 181]

She and others do not realize what a nemesis these paintings represent, a reflection of xenophobic people in their pride of narrowness and portrayed through images that are abhorrent to them. As Siggi realizes, "The all-out narrowmindedness into which people are lured by local patriotism *[Heimatsinn]* probably finds its completest expression in people's notion that they are called upon to give an expert answer to all questions: arrogance born of narrowness" (pp. 163, 134).

Siggi-Lenz satirizes the blood and soil fixation of these provincial minds in his description of the evenings of the Glüserup Folklore Society *(Heimatverein)* held under the auspices of his maternal grandfather, Arne Schessel, an avid collector of prehistoric Germanic items and artifacts. Such gatherings were actually widespread during the Nazi period and served to promulgate an ethnic identity with blood and soil and race consciousness. Siggi, however, remembers primarily the symbolic atmosphere of these gatherings: "If I concentrate and submerge myself in the past, I come to the conclusion that, where those meetings of our association are concerned, what is imprinted on my memory is above all semi-darkness, the core of light from the projector, the dazed insects, the noises from the stable next door, and the whispering, I should like to say the good-tempered expectancy of the audience, all of whom received written invitations, in winter more frequently than in summer, to attend those meetings that took place on Külkenwarf, the place the Schessels call their ancestral home" (pp. 144, 118). Schessel's collection of the great Germanic heritage includes stone scrapers, axe heads, urns and bangles of the middle bronze age. The main attraction, however, is "the wrinkled, shrunken, leathery corpse of a girl who had been strangled with a noose—of course, made of reindeer hide—a noose she still wore around her neck as a somewhat bizarre ornament" (pp. 144–45, 119). These mementos from a brutish and violent past are sentimentalized in the present. Nansen's art has no part in the easy myths that are perpetuated in semidarkness and in a *Kaffeeklatsch* atmosphere.

The depth with which Nansen characterizes the vacuousness and demonic tediousness of his country folk is not revealed in his own personality; at least Siggi does not give him such depth. Except for his conflict with Jepsen, Nansen is very much part of the community. His first appearance in the novel is a revelation in almost Heideggerian terms in that the essence of being is in its existence: "Da stand der Maler Ludwig Nansen" (There stood the painter Ludwig Nansen) (p. 31). His appearance is that of a local eccentric, a magician who wears an odd-shaped, huge, grey blue coat with pockets so large that he could have children disappear into them. When he paints, he talks to his alter ego, Balthasar, "who wore, in those pictures in which he was imprisoned, a bristling purple dusted fox pelt and who had slanting eyes and a crazy beard of bubbly boiling orange dropping sparks" (pp. 33, 27). This ludicrously demonic muse represents dangerous depths which the painter in ordinary life never reveals and actually seems to avoid consciously (pp. 402, 336). In his self-portrait after the war, the face is split into grey red and yellow grey and reveals his lack of self-knowledge, or perhaps the impossibility of such knowledge: "Here there is simply too much missing. It hasn't been seen, and so it hasn't been mastered" (pp. 402, 336). Finally, there is nothing about a man but what he invents about himself: "In order to get your own likeness you have to invent yourself, over and over again, with every glance, whatever is invented turns into reality" (pp. 401, 335). Nansen and Siggi, however, also shape and invent others. Siggi sees Nansen as demonic, but also as a kind person who adopts children, who saved Jepsen, who shelters Klaas. Jepsen, however, is invented primarily as the "Polizeiposten." Yet in the end, before the reality of his arrest, Siggi dreams that both Nansen and Jepsen capture him in the net of the past; they both had made him into a juvenile delinquent.

In his final appearance, the painter is a caricature. He appears at the exhibition in the costume of a German patriarch, not as he is in his provincial environment, but as he invents himself as if he were in agreement with a blood and soil *Weltanschauung*. Surprised, he agrees with the high-blown phrases of the critics that his art has "expressive pathos" and "elemental powers," as though he were becoming aware of these powers for the first time. This is quite possible, for Nansen insists that art is filled with potentialities that the artist may not be aware of himself. His paintings have a far greater depth than he consciously put into them, or perhaps the perceiver gives them that depth. In an open society his paintings have lost the power to enrage the perceiver. They are now acceptable in a world that cancels out one vision with another, in a world where the unconventional becomes convention. The young, like Klaas and his friends, see in the paintings nothing but theatrics and call Nansen an *Anstreicher,* the very term that has been applied to Hitler in the two senses of house painter and trickster. Siggi objects angrily to such a definition. His life is tied to Nansen's works, and he feels that he is the only one who can really understand them. The irony is that Nansen does not know he has at least one ideal viewer.

At the end of the narrative, the antagonists are in similar circumstances. Jepsen's life continues in smug self-righteousness. His children have left him, but he does not seem to mind. Nansen, too, has lost his family and, no longer able to provoke society, lives as a lonely eccentric. Siggi, the *Mitwisser,* wants to keep faith, but his loyalty or neurotic bondage to Rugbüll would at best be met with indifference. For neither Jepsen nor Nansen are able to understand him. He does not even have an ideal audience of one. He has reached as good a state of consciousness as can be achieved at the age of twenty-one, but his penance has alleviated no pain. It has failed in the conventional pedagogic and therapeutic sense, for he realizes in the end what he knew in the beginning: time heals nothing. He has gained some knowledge and raised many unanswered questions in the process of writing, a process that gave him the momentary illusion of discovery and meaning; but, in the final analysis, Siggi's autobiography does not bridge isolation. He concludes by imagining how he and the director of the reformatory will face each other during their final interview: "He will make a gesture and we shall both sit down, shall sit facing one another without stirring, each of us thoroughly pleased with himself because he feels that he has won." A cognitive block, a state of satisfied shut-upness, is reached as the little demons come to rest.

4

Günter Grass's *Dog Years:* The Dark Side of Utopia

Günter Grass's poem "The Scarecrows" provides a lyrical leitmotif for the metaphors of evil in his novel *Dog Years:*

> I don't know if old jackets and old pants
> when, with spoons in cans,
> they ring rusty and tinny in the wind,
> ring in the scarecrows' insurrection.[1]

As opportunistic and stuffed, hollow men, Grass's scarecrows stand in a wasteland garden; and although they behave as the wind behaves, their hollowness could be given the significance of spiritual yearning, making old jackets and old pants truly human and not merely an inflated human image. Yet how can a poet, who feels that all ladders of aspiration and all grand mythologies have been lost, create that meaningful world towards which the emptiness of the scarecrow vaguely yearns? Grass turns to the remnants and refuse of the world without and within and projects through his twisted and grotesque images the desire for a world of reason and light: "And every prayer beseeches the cable of the lift to remain whole, in order that light, daylight, once again the sun-drenched May. . . ."[2]

Unfortunately, those who believe that they possess the vision of utopia usually neglect to ponder the dark side of utopia. For a balanced view, both progressive aspiration and conservatively reflective skepticism are necessary, as Grass tells us in his autobiographical work *From the Diary of a Snail.* In it he attempts to answer the questions of his children, who stayed with their mother in Berlin while he campaigned for Willy Brandt in 1969. During this campaign for a politician whom he generally associated with progress, Grass also worked on a lecture about Dürer's

"Melencolia" and discovered that melancholy is no longer an aristocratic or intellectual expression of *Weltschmerz* but is today found anywhere in our pluralistic and democratic society: "Often, on the road, during jams on the Autobahn, besieged by exhaust fumes in my slowly forward jerking waiting space, laned-in as though forever and engulfed in the creeping progress of rush hour traffic, I saw her sitting sullenly at the steering wheel: Melencolia with a driver's license."[3]

Progress at a snail's pace, retarded further by the broodings of melancholy over the absurdity of human struggle, is hardly acceptable to those who want to glory in the vision of utopia, that world of plenty achieved without historical guilt. Grass, however, prefers the pace of "two steps forward, one step back" to the "rapid forward thrust across the graves"; for while the former may be slow and often mistaken, it is bloodless.[4] Moreover, those who think that they have achieved utopia always lock Melencolia—the mutterers and malcontents—behind bars. Alone, melancholy projects images of frustrated and constipated egocentricity, but as a counterforce to utopian optimism it becomes a reality principle that forces the optimist to come to terms with the reality of negation. Therefore, the best attitude is one that combines melancholy and optimism; it is the optimist who has sat "on the empty snail shell and experienced the dark side of utopia" who can evaluate progress (*Diary*, pp. 368, 310). *Dog Years* is a message from this dark side, specifically, the utopias of Nazism, West German consumer democracy, and, to a lesser extent, East German socialism. These utopias prove to be hollow, and their inhabitants, to use an image from the novel, are scarecrows in a plundered garden.

Because Grass has so often been accused of negation, of giving the reader no affirmative vision, I will precede my discussion of *Dog Years* with a review of those of Grass's political, ethical, and esthetic beliefs that are relevant to *Dog Years*, a novel which Grass himself called not only his best work but also his most political novel.[5] The student of Grass's life and work will not find a definite ideology or intellectual system, but, rather, certain attitudes. The word *attitude* is appropriate because it implies a posture meant to reveal a mental state or emotion rather than systematic thought. Even the formal problems of *Dog Years*, caused in part by the novelist's attempt to communicate "the many levels of meaning in our time,"[6] reveal an attitude towards certain fictional forms rather than the conventional fulfillment of them.

I.
Günter Grass: The Melancholy Activist and Mythmaking Poet in Spite of Himself

In his book on pessimistic philosophies of history, Christoph Eykman defines the disintegration of historical consciousness in modern times and cites Grass's *Dog Years* as a prime example of this process: "History in the two great novels of Grass is presented primarily as political-military history whose effect on the life of the little man cannot be defined but is, on the other hand, sporadic and in no way all embracing. History reveals itself as a colorful conglomerate of dislocated, isolated events. The eras may change, but wars, catastrophes and new beginnings recur mechanically. Only fashion changes."[7] For Grass, history does not have a beginning, middle, and end; it does not have a destiny. Instead, it is repetitive circularity expressed in the image of generations of dogs biting each other's tails, hardly an image of peaceful containment, but, rather, an expression of an aggressively monotonous round. Nevertheless, Grass always had a keen interest in history, not only because of the quaint or brutal absurdities of history, but also because, pedagogue that he is, he wants to stem the tide of forgetfulness.

Grass objects to the mythmaking of the historical consciousness which either enters the historical moment with preconceived notions of what constitutes the purpose of history or comforts itself *post festum* by inventing mythical patterns to explain historical events. The mythologies of history give a grand and ordered view of the chaos of historical time and are always offered at the expense of the suffering of history's victims. Thus, Hegel may have admired Napoleon as the embodiment of the world spirit storming over graves, but Grass prefers to be the world spirit on a hollow snail shell. He is resigned to the fact, however, that the artist who asks himself "What is real?" cannot recapture the human agony in history, and he should not mythologize that agony in order to give it meaning.[8] Nevertheless, as we will see, Grass the artist cannot avoid becoming a mythmaker of sorts. For, as his iconoclastic attitude shatters historical continuity into single words such as *Kristallnacht* or *Himmelfahrtskommando* (night of crystal; suicide mission), these words as shards of history become mythical nuclei which, after they have passed from the language, will require extensive footnotes. Thus, they become abstractions rather than evocations of a specific historical reality. Grass's iconoclastic, mechanical, and grotesque concept of history is, however, never merely a gesture of negation but is always accompanied by ethical motivations.

Nowhere is Grass's conflict over the absurdity of history and the need for historical consciousness more clearly revealed than in his attitude towards Auschwitz and the "final solution." During the opening in May 1970 of an exhibition of works by Auschwitz inmates, Grass spoke on the topic "of the difficulties of a father in explaining Auschwitz to his children." He said:

> Adorno's word that poetry could not be written after Auschwitz has provoked so many misunderstandings that we have to interpret it: poems, written after Auschwitz, must suffer to be measured by Auschwitz. At most, I hesitate here, listen after the word Auschwitz and try to measure the echo effect of the word Auschwitz. We know its most trivial resonance: Auschwitz again! still Auschwitz! Will that never stop? Doesn't it want to stop? I hope: no. I also contradict that nobly stated echo: The answer to Auschwitz could only be silence, may only be shame and muteness. Auschwitz, however, was no mystery which demands distanced reserve and introverted reflection, but reality and thus something made by man which can be investigated. [9]

Diary of a Snail is to a large extent an attempt to tell his children about the difficulty of talking about Auschwitz. In *Diary* as well as in *Dog Years*, Grass is at best doomed to talk around the subject rather than get to its essence.

If the dull round of history could be broken at all, it would be by means of the continued consciousness of humankind concerning the suffering of the victims of history. Such consciousness, however, is unlikely since victims and persecutors prefer the comforts of repression. *Dog Years* is an impressive example of "getting used to it" *(Gewöhnung)* by sublimating the memory of fault and guilt. Memory, however, must be cultivated so that the symbols of the day, leitmotifs, as Grass calls them, do not become murder motives, and that murder motives are not again displaced into leitmotifs. Consciousness about history may well lead to melancholic wallowing in guilt, but awareness of guilt can be constructively channeled: "Repentance as a social state of mind would then be the corresponding utopia; it presupposes melancholy rooted in insight" *(Diary,* pp. 359, 302). This statement is the crux of Grass's ethical attitude as an activist and an artist. He admits that it is derived from the great Western religious and philosophical systems which both form and fail us. Nevertheless, Grass, the disappointed idealist turned satirist, considers love and reason the two forces that could bring about an ideal state. [10] It is the repeated failure of reason and Christian love which is the bitter and dark lament of *Dog Years,* where original sin is the failure of brotherly love.

As a political activist, Grass is primarily influenced by the rationalism of social democracy: "It is my conviction that after the failure of modified state socialism of the communist variety there only remains modern social democracy."[11] In his political activities and speeches he projects a persona quite different from that of his novels: he is a character in, rather than the author of, a situation. By being politically active, Grass tried to avoid the perennial charge made against German intellectuals and artists: inwardness and withdrawal from human reality. He claims that he relates easily to ordinary people, that he likes "to delineate the *Mief* [familial smells] of their petit bourgeois dreams. . . . I come from a petit bourgeois background and I participate in that *Mief.*"[12] When Grass becomes politically engagé, he is an intellectual who goes slumming and is his own object lesson: involvement permits him no reflection and leads inevitably to disappointment, sitting on the empty snail shell and reflecting about human turns on the dark side of utopia.

Yet Grass waxes utopian on the issue of rediscovering the lost homeland; he even goes so far as to suggest that one solution for the preservation of the culture of the past lies in the building of cities with names like New Danzig or New Breslau. "Let us be founders of cities! Let us have pioneer spirit, " he proclaims in Whitmanesque tones, unaware of the artificiality of that spirit.[13] And so, Günter Grass, who wants to demythologize history, has his own vision of New Jerusalems, has dreams that are unrealizable. An ironic mythical vision emerges in his great Danzig trilogy of the *Tin Drum, Cat and Mouse,* and *Dog Years.* Danzig is lamented as the lost city of childhood, but it is also the geographically defined city of Danzig-Langfuhr, the microcosm where anything that happens in Germany can also happen. Danzig, too, becomes then a ground of deprivation and a nightmare for its middle class men and women.

Danzig is a city of "once upon a time" in Grass's novels, especially in *Dog Years:* "There once was a city—in addition to the suburbs of Ohra, Schidlitz, Oliva, Emmaus, Praust, Sankt Albrecht, Schellmühl, and the seaport suburb of Neufahrwasser, it had a suburb named Langfuhr" (pp. 374, 316–17). Two characteristics of Grass's style are evident in this brief passage: his tendency to evoke a magic reality by listing and sounding names, in this way keeping such names alive in the historical present, and his creation of a seemingly hermetically closed microcosm within the macrocosm of an historical era, thereby reducing the notions of

Reich to a provincial town and magnifying provincialism to universal proportions. The historical situation of Danzig provided Grass with circumstances that lent themselves especially well to mythmaking.[14] Within its concentrated space the evils and consequences of Nazism spent themselves; these included Stutthof, the concentration camp, over whose mound of sand, human ashes, and bones the Poles built a stone pyramid after the war. Today the old city of Danzig is rebuilt, a stage trapping for nostalgic German tourists. But the Vistula, lined with grotesquely shaped willow trees, still runs its sluggish course at the outskirts of the city. As Grass attempts to keep the past alive in the presentness of the literary work, a similar unreality descends on the city as seen from the perspective of an adult who recalls his childhood, describing a former reality with catalogues of suburbs and streets that are mere fanciful names, only words for the reader who is not a native Danziger.

Grass's mythmaking process is defined in the first book of *Dog Years* by the narrator who offers a set of terms that become a paradigm for mythmaking in literature and history, in esthetics and ethics (acts). The terms are *Spieltrieb und Pedanterie* (man's urge to play and his urge to instruct), leitmotif and murder motive, and ornament and apocalypse. The implications of the middle set are the most far-reaching for the novel. The two halves of each pair are not in dialectical opposition but can intertwine and even fuse: "The urge to play and pedantry neither dictate nor contradict each other" (pp. 7, 11). When the narrator of the first book suggests that his name, Brauxel, can be spelled Brauchsel, he alludes to the Weichsel (Vistula), the ironically idyllic river of childhood and the demonic river of history; for Auschwitz was built near the source of the Vistula, and the ashes from the crematoria were often dumped into the river. Hence, in his part of the novel Amsel-Brauchsel writes, "Amazing how many things are becoming to the Vistula, how many things color a river like the Vistula: sunset, blood, mud, ashes. Actually the wind ought to have them. Orders are not always carried out; rivers that set out for heaven empty into the Vistula" (pp. 11, 14). History, however, insures that "rivers that set out for hell empty into the Vistula" (pp. 605, 507). The playful element in art becomes inevitably involved with ethical questions (pedantry) posed by history. Thus, a literary image may at the outset be an unconscious and playful coalescence of letters, objects, or patterns which are progressively englobed with allegorical-ethical connotations until a mythic structure evolves that is enacted and judged in the time scheme of the novel, an artifice that nevertheless affirms the concept of man as *homo ludens*.

Albrecht Goetze points out in his Marxist analysis of *Dog Years* that Grass uses the double meaning of *Leitmotif* to expand the reader's consciousness within and about the novel. A leitmotif originates in the unconscious and emotional realms and can become the motivating force of human action: "If a leitmotif becomes an unquestioned suggestive motivation for action and thought, then it functions like a leader in an animal team whom the herd follows without contradiction or thought. The leitmotif becomes the Führer to whom one gives one's self. 'Führer command, we follow'—the propagandists of fascism formulated suggestively."[15] From the beginning, the leitmotifs condition the response of the reader and suspend disbelief over the fictional world that is about to unfold. The river, the dog, the scarecrow, and the knife of the beginning of the novel appear again at the end. In childhood, these images were associated with play and fantasy. In the second book they become the murder motives of history. In the third they expand and shrink into the demonically decorative apocalypse of Brauxel's mine.

The radical of Grass's paradigm is the desire for form out of the chaos of history. Grass describes the need to give shape by alluding to the struggle of the crafty Ulysses with the many forms of Proteus until the latter finally assumed a fixed shape and revealed a needed truth.[16] Moreover, the artist does not only approach a content externally; he has to get into it like a shaman getting into the skin of an animal. Grass believes that a writer is "from book to book the sum of his characters, including the SS men who appear therein; and, if he wants to or not, he must be able to love these figures not in a literary, cool, distant way; he must get into them; he cannot disguise himself and call them disgustedly 'the others.'"[17] The literary participation in *Mief* must be done with love, a word that seems surprising in this context but is quite plausible and necessary in terms of esthetics and ethics. Grass is unwilling to purge himself of his sense of guilt by inventing fictional scapegoats. His characters are expressions of a guilty humanity whose guilt Grass shares.

The emphasis on, the sharing of, and, at the same time, the satirizing of the familial smells of the petit bourgeoisie remind the reader of the real origins of the Nazis and effectively destroy the megalomania of Nazi mythmaking. Instead of showing the SS man as the sadistic blond beast, Grass asks us to look at local grocery store owners, frustrated actors, and contented beer drinkers with large posteriors. As in Lenz's *German Lesson,* but with more militantly satiric aggressiveness, the large awe and fear-inspiring attitudes of the Nazis are compressed and repressed into demonic shut-upness. This balled and bottled-up demonic power, this fierce agressiveness in vacuous and usually bored individuals, is just as dangerous as the obvious power display of a Nuremberg Party Rally, the latter being nothing but the sublime theatrical gestures of the pride of narrowness. Grass robs evil of its sublimity, its hot-air hyperboles, and thus deflates pride; but this does not mean that he really demythologizes. Instead, he is the mythmaker of the banality of evil, the petty evil of every man that leads just as effectively to murder.

Another characteristic of Grass the mythmaker is his astonishing ability to *invent* in the classical meaning of the word. The exuberant pouring forth of stories, anecdotes, digressions, and catalogues puts Grass into the tradition of Rabelais and Sterne. A novel written in this fashion creates the illusion of unhesitating extroversion, of a voluminous sharing of momentary insights, images, and memories. It is all the more surprising, therefore, to discover that the verbal outpourings are really a means for repression. Nowhere in *Dog Years* does guilt, realized through the logos of speech, lead to a social state of mind; nowhere is the melancholy of the narrators rooted in genuine insight. Here they differ from the persona of the author. As the characters remain locked in a deeply ironic world, no better society emerges at the end. No prize is given for the quest through historical time; no guilt feelings are genuinely transformed after voluminous confessions, detailed analyses, and dissections. This pessimism is intensified by the morphology of the linguistic universe of the novel, so locked up that its anatomy of Germany and Germans only reaches melancholy conclusions and remains on the dark side of utopia, a dark side where nothing is certain and where no way is seen to cross over into "the other kingdom."

II.
Dog Years: **The Dark Side of Utopia**

In its basic pattern, *Dog Years* is an ironic comedy concerning the failure of friendship. Part one describes the youthful friendship between Walter Matern and Eddi Amsel, whose father was Jewish. The rift of this friendship is told in part two as Matern becomes an SA man and, with a group of eight fellow Nazis, beats up Amsel. Part three shows how Matern tried to avenge Amsel and how he was eventually reunited with him. Two problems, however, arise immediately. The first is that the structure of the novel can be inverted. The second is an artistic problem, for Grass grafted the narrators onto the structure of the novel after the work, at first entitled *Potato Peels,* was nearly finished.[18] Although certain narrative inconsistencies are evident in the reading of the novel, I

will assume that Grass did intend specific narrative points of view,
namely, third person point of view in books one and three and first person
point of view in book two. All three narrators are trickster figures
motivated by guilt. There is Brauxel-Amsel, the victim, who avoids
discussing his share of the guilt by concentrating on and limiting himself
to the relating of childhood memories. As witness, Harry Liebenau can
afford to comment ironically and intellectually about guilt feelings or
transpose them, when they get too uncomfortable, into a fairy-tale
sphere. Finally, Walter Matern, the persecutor-avenger, desires consciousness and confession of guilt but continues to project guilt onto
others.

The fictional framework that prompts the writing of the three books is
the following: The mine owner Brauxel commissions Harry Liebenau
and Walter Matern to write their memories of Eddi Amsel. Harry's
account will deal with the Hitler years, Matern's with the postwar era.
The three authors write simultaneously in West Germany during the
winter of 1961–62 while snow is falling on the Berlin Wall, built in that
year. Rumor has it that the world will end on 4 February 1962, and,
therefore, the confessional manuscripts must be finished by that date (pp.
131, 118). In spite of difficulties, they do arrive punctually on the
apocalyptic date, which comes and goes as other such dates.

Amsel-Brauchsel is the *architectus* of the novel: "He is in charge of
the mine and of the author's consortium; it is he who pays out the
advances, sets the delivery dates, and will read the proofs" (pp. 132,
118). His powers are even more awesome when the reader learns that
Amsel is the moving force behind the economic miracle of postwar
Germany. He is ubiquitous and never really disappears, even when
persecuted, for he merely slips into another shape. Because he is also the
god who has been wronged and demands expiation, he orders his co-
authors to concentrate only on him; but both fail to do this. Harry is
concerned with his private amours and Matern with his vendettas to
assuage his guilt. Amsel himself lacks the courage of insight into guilt.
So, in the final analysis, his power is limited where he needs it most.
Eventually, Amsel will arrange the three parts with his early shifts at the
bottom, with Harry's love letters in the middle, and with Matern's
Materniads on top (pp. 132, 118). The novel will then begin with the
present and recede into the past until the point is reached where the two
boys Eddi and Walter are with the dog Senta on a dike along the Vistula.
This is where the novel begins, whose trickster narrators and whose
cosmos as an elegiac, grotesque fairy tale reveal the novel's metaphors of
evil.

A. The Narrators of *Dog Years:* **Tricksters in the Posture of Subordination**

The mythological tradition of the trickster combines a variety of traits subsumed under the concept of trickster as principle of disorder and as culture hero. In primitive mythology he is, as Norman O. Brown points out, "surrounded by unsublimated and undisguised anality," which may express itself in creating a world out of excrement.[19] As Brown shows, the figure of Hermes is already in classical antiquity produced by sublimation-negation of anality and becomes a god of beguilement, of the dead, and of commerce.[20] The Christian tradition splits the tricky culture god into the Savior Christ and the Seducer Satan, the latter being once again associated with anality and filthy lucre. But, as Brown argues, "His anality is not cathected with libido or magic life, as in the magic-dirt complex, but is seen as death. The whole evolution from Trickster to Devil and on to the pseudo-secular demonic of capitalism shows the progressive triumph of the death instinct."[21] In *Dog Years* characters and cosmos are displacements of the demonic trickster and the world he creates. Symbols of anality abound from city sewers to Hitler's bunker, to Amsel's scarecrow mine. Matern seeks God and finds excrement, and he plays filthy sexual tricks with the women of his former SA companions. Harry Liebenau, witness and memorabilia collector, is "a shitter with a file card memory" (pp. 568, 477), from which he trickily extracts items on suitable occasions. Amsel, however, is the greatest trickster; he is exile and culture bringer. As Amsel (blackbird) and Haseloff (running hare), he even possesses the animal qualities of the primitive trickster. He is also the crafty creator of a scarecrow culture which ostracizes him and which he blesses with the questionable rewards of business and money. In spite of his dubious qualities, he retains the childlike and endearing qualities of the trickster, as when he pretends only to be a good-natured fat fellow who wants so much to be part of it all that he dons an SA uniform, collects money for the Party, and distributes "his little jokes among the populace" (pp. 238, 206).

Displaced into historical time, the trickster loses much of his power and has to assume the posture of subordination. The greatest trickster of the time covered in *Dog Years* is not one of the characters but, rather, is the *Anstreicher* (house painter, trickster) Hitler, who remains invisible in the novel. It was he who tricked everybody into believing that he was the unmoved mover until the armies of his enemies forced him to retreat into the bowels of the earth, from where only his ghostly voice can be heard.

The human being who takes upon himself the power of an immovable deity forces everyone into a posture of subordination, an infantile posture. Thus, in a world that is in bondage, the individual pretends and takes on disguises traditionally associated with the trickster, but without the divine power of that spirit. In his many disguises, in his adjustments and readjustments according to whims of time, the individual is in danger of losing his selfhood to mere survival. Yet times are such that the person who insists on identity will be destroyed, as the example of the teacher Brunies shows. In the final analysis, the disguises of the ironic trickster fool not only others but himself as well. He becomes the scarecrow who, with each change of costume, overlays and represses the past and the memories of which he should be conscious.

All three characters become phenotypes, distinguished by visible and external rather than internal traits. Scarecrows through which the wind blows, they do not have a self; rather, they have an inflated ego which Jung defined in the following manner: "An inflated consciousness is always egocentric and conscious of nothing but its own presence. It is incapable of learning from the past, incapable of understanding contemporary events, and incapable of drawing right conclusions about the future. It is hypnotized by itself and therefore cannot be argued with. It inevitably dooms itself to calamities that must strike it dead. Paradoxically enough, inflation is a regression of consciousness into unconsciousness. This always happens when consciousness takes too many unconscious contents upon itself and loses the faculty of discrimination, the *sine qua non* of all consciousness."[22] We find that the three narrators of *Dog Years* appear hyperconscious and self-aware but are really deceiving themselves and others. In the end, they remain caught in their unconsciousness and are unable, in spite of their desire, to find the creative word that would transform the dark side of utopia into the light of "sun-drenched May."

1. Eddi Amsel, "the most agile hero" (pp. 33, 32) and narrator of the early shifts

Throughout the novel, Amsel is marked as the devil as trickster, an association generated by his status as outcast, by his ability to take on the many shapes of his scarecrow selves, and by his skill to turn waste products and guilt (*Schuld,* i.e., guilt and debt) into money. It is through this skill that he creates a world that is not utopian but is sullenly content. Amsel is an outcast because his father was a baptized Jew who died in

World War I a few months before Eddi was born in 1917. Eddi and his father are outcasts trying to survive in a hostile world and, if possible, gain power over those who reject them, thus achieving the illusion of belonging to the community. Eddi's father did this by converting, marrying a Christian girl, and by reading Weininger's *Sex and Character,* whose chapter on the Jews made such an impression on him that he tried to contradict it throughout his life, leaving the book for his son as if it were the family Bible. Eddi, also an outcast and scarecrow, will gain his power through money. Existentially, his life must always be inauthentic. Unable to define himself as an exile and nonconformist—as, for instance, his teacher Brunies does—Eddi is able to change costumes, join the Reich during the time of the "keen laws," and entertain German troops with his ballets. As a phenotype, he prefers surfaces and displaces "in depth search" by building his scarecrow mine. Repression of pain and guilt allows him to cope but imprisons him in the vicious cycle of dog years.

Amsel authors the "early shifts" of the first book of *Dog Years* and thereby avoids talking about the far more complicated and implicating years of the Nazi era. Literally, *Frühschicht* refers to the early shifts in Amsel's mine; he thus writes in the morning about the morning of his life. There are thirty-two *Frühschichten* and one unnumbered last shift. As a leitmotif, the number 32 refers also to the teeth Amsel loses when he is beaten up by a group of SA men, to the thirty-two stalls in his mine, and to the thirty-two years of this century that preceded the Nazi takeover of power. It is in 1933 that history begins for the Nazis and for the characters in the novel. It is in the last shift that Amsel begins to make extensive references to dates; time becomes chronological. The word *Schicht* with its meanings of order, level, and layer makes Amsel's book *Frühgeschichte,* the early story or prehistory on whose level of experience the primary leitmotifs are established.

Since Amsel does not like history, he relegates the Nazi era to the witness-narrator Harry Liebenau and chooses instead to write about his childhood friendship with the Catholic miller's son Walter Matern. True, it was in childhood that the fat little Amsel first experienced the pain of alienation; but he can meliorate that pain through elegiac nostalgia for the time when he and Walter went into the scarecrow business, when they both went to school, and when they explored the city sewer and the murky dark of the German forest. Amsel writes about himself in terms of the child that he was; he writes in the preterit and in the third person, meaning that he looks askance at himself.

As outcast—fat boy, Jew, and artist—Amsel possesses this ability from the beginning, and it allows him to cope with pain and rejection: "Displayed each day ludicrously round and freckle-faced to the eyes of two villages, he became a whipping boy. . . . but through the tears which, as everyone knows, confer a blurred but uncommonly precise vision, his greenish-gray, fat-encased little eyes never ceased to observe, to appraise, and to analyze typical movements. Two or three days after one of these beatings . . . the very same torture scene would be produced in the form of a single many-armed scarecrow between the dunes or directly on the beach, licked by the sea" (pp. 42, 41). Art enables Amsel to exorcise pain and actually win the friendship of Matern after the latter sees his image in one of the scarecrows. Art has a pedagogic effect on Matern, and he, who was the first to utter the crucial word *Itzig* (sheeny), becomes Amsel's friend. However, that friendship very soon becomes corrupted by money, for Amsel increases his scarecrow production, starts selling his products, and makes Matern the business manager who carries the money bag and is mocked by the children: " 'Flunky, flunky!' blasphemed the children when Walter Matern flunkied for his friend Eddi Amsel." They are blood brothers who cannot do without each other. But, like God and the devil, it becomes unclear which is which—they are in a state of perpetual tension (pp. 73, 68).

The character of Amsel pervades, of course, the whole novel, but already during the early years he refers to the philosophy he later studied, namely, Otto Weininger's. On her death bed, Amsel's mother communicates to him the family secret and warns him: "Your very own father was one of the circumcised as they say. I only hope they don't catch you now the laws are so strict" (pp. 38, 38). Amsel begins to study Weininger, whose influential book went through many editions and who admitted his Jewishness in order to enhance his credibility by presenting an "inside view." Quite accurately, Weininger defines the anti-Semite as one who first of all hates that in himself which has been defined as Jewish: "He intends to separate himself from it by re-locating it [Jewishness] solely in his fellow men, and thus deems himself free from it momentarily. Like love, hate is a projection phenomenon: man hates only that person who reminds him of himself."[23] The qualities discussed by Weininger as Jewish can apply to many people, but Amsel views them as defining himself as a Jew and tries to live counter to that definition. As he learns to sing like a Christian, as he participates in sports as befits any upright German, he exchanges one stereotype for another, hoping that the new stereotype will make him acceptable. As life becomes more complicated for him in the next two books, ironies increase; but the greatest irony of all is that he fits in many ways the stereotype of the Jew as the Nazis concocted it. Grass, however, makes sure that the other two narrators have "Jewish" characteristics of which Amsel remains unaware. In his verbal agility, Harry Liebenau possesses "the sterile Jewish intellect," while Matern's degenerate sexuality could have provided *Der Stürmer* with many a salacious headline.

Amsel admits that "Weininger has grafted quite a few ideas onto the present writer. The scarecrow is created in the image of man" (pp. 38, 38). The ideas fashionable in the cycle of dog years are grafted onto human beings and deprive them of becoming truly human. Amsel is both a scarecrow created in man's image as well as a bird, as his name indicates. Several times he calls himself "der Federführende," he who guides the quill and he who wears feathers, Amsel the bird. He emphasizes that his name is not Jewish like Adler (eagle); but the reader, in recalling the black feathers and yellow beak of the Amsel-bird, is reminded that the Nazis associated black and yellow with the Jews: the yellow Star of David with the black letters of "Jude" written across it. Throughout the novel, birds are associated with individuality, with freedom, and with libidinal forces that may turn freedom into license. Birds are also insistent witnesses that cannot be scared away. They see the attack on Amsel and tenaciously draw attention to the mound of bones from Stutthof. Harry points out that Amsel saw all birds as individuals; a flock of sparrows were to him "individualists that had camouflaged themselves as a mass society. And to his eyes blackbirds were never, not even in snow-covered gardens, identically black and yellow billed" (pp. 217, 189). The bird, like Amsel's giant dickey bird scarecrow, has destructive as well as life-giving qualities, while the chaotic though rigid scarecrow is the repressive "thou shalt not" that keeps the birds from licentiously plundering the garden. When the human being becomes defined through the fragmented tatters of slogans and political gesturings, his freedom as a person is denied and repressed; and, when it does emerge, it does so as destructive license. When Eddi makes mechanized scarecrows and has them parade before him, it is difficult to decide whether he is satirizing the Nazis or wishing to be part of them—perhaps he desires both. The real life SA men with Matern among them only see, however, the insult of the satire and respond by physically attacking Amsel.

After the attack, Amsel has to change appearance or die. He moves unscathed through the war years as a young and slim ballet impresario. While Matern and Harry allegorize the mound of bones from Stutthof,

Amsel is silent about it even though he knows that the bones of his teacher Brunies are among them. He has nothing to say about those who were defined as scarecrows and were *vogelfrei* (outlawed; lit., bird free), metamorphosed into scarecrows of skin and bones. Able to avoid such a fate, Amsel represses the consciousness of evil as much as do persecutor and bystander. Yet he desires the moment of genuine consciousness; for otherwise he would not create the scarecrow mine as an allegory of humanity, and he would not hire the author collective to write about these dog years. Both attempts to provoke consciousness fail since the scarecrows are also products to be sold and since Harry and Matern are paid to write about Amsel. As he creates a world through money after the war, he deludes himself that Germany has become clean again, as if its outward prosperity were a sign for inward virtue. Those who hurt him are now in his debt, not morally but financially. Amsel's money multiplies as do Harry's verbal outpourings and Matern's sexual escapades. But those outpourings merely repress, divert, and pervert; they do not liberate.

The words that could bring light to the dark side of utopia are not spoken, for neither Amsel nor Matern can say, ''I have wronged you, forgive me, let us love one another.'' As a result the two friends are suspended between living and dying, as the last section of the novel makes so clear. ''If I cannot have love, I will have money'' seems to be the motto of that world where everybody remains isolated. The Amsel bird is a scared bird, a human being who learns fear early and uses his intelligence to discover the means to control both threat and fear by turning himself and others into scarecrows, by behaving as the wind behaves until the self is nothing but a costume puffed by the wind.

2. Harry Liebenau, the file card memory

In the third book of *Dog Years,* when Harry has caught up with Matern, an exasperated Matern reflects:

> That shithead with his file-card memory. Wherever he goes stands sits, always shuffling cards. Nothing he hasn't got the dope on: Proust and Henry Miller; Dylan Thomas and Karl Kraus; quotations from Adorno and sales figures; collector of details and tracker down of references; objective onlooker and layer-bare of cores; archive hound and connoisseur of environments; knows who thinks left and who has written right; writes asthmatic stuff about the difficulty of writing; flashbacker and time juggler; caller-into-question and wise guy; but no writer's congress can dispense with his gift of formulation, his urge to recapitulate his memory. [pp. 568, 477]

Harry's first person narrative concerns the past he witnessed as a child and adolescent; it is the Nazi period chronicled by a person who could in good conscience say that he was innocent. Yet, as in the case of Siggi Jepsen, the child as witness does somehow get implicated by what he sees. Unlike Siggi, however, Harry does not raise guilt to painful consciousness, for Harry can glibly talk about everything, especially the guilt of others.

Harry's narrative is mainly in the form of letters to his unresponsive beloved, his cousin Tulla, a demonic but honest little person whose grotesqueness springs largely again from deprivation. To Harry, the letters are merely an artifice, but they do recall the convention of intimacy found in the epistolary novel and, by means of contrast, point out that Harry is really incapable of true intimacy. He cannot make contact literally because Tulla has disappeared from his life when he writes the letters. The first set of letters recollects Harry's early years of growing up near Danzig where the Nazis become more and more visible. The adopted daughter of Brunies, fat little Jenny and future ballerina, begins to play a major role in Harry's life. The dog Harras is of great importance during those years, for Harras fathers Prince, a puppy the Danzigers give to Hitler. Prince will become the Führerhund, the dog of the Führer or the lead dog that will make history.

Harry becomes aware of Amsel and Matern when Jenny Brunies begins to take piano lessons in Harry's neighborhood. Amsel, who befriends her, comes along and often talks to and sketches Harras, whom he calls Pluto, the god of the underworld and of riches. Amsel again becomes implicated in guilt as far as Matern is concerned, for he encourages Matern, who has drifted into acting and communism, to join the SA so that he, Amsel, can get uniforms for his scarecrows. The crucial event of Harry's childhood years happens in the snowy winter of 1936–37 when Matern and his companions beat up Amsel, knock out all of his teeth, and roll him into a snowman. Nearby, Tulla rolls the fat little Jenny also into a snowman. Harry rushes back and forth between these two scenes of aggression, but he does not interfere. It is here that Harry becomes guilty, a guilt witnessed only by the crows flying overhead. He never admits this guilt, and he can mollify it with the knowledge that a slender Amsel and a strip of a ballerina emerged from both snowmen. He and Tulla demonstrate a similar unemphathetic silence when Matern, guilt-ridden and displacing aggression, poisons their beloved Harras. Harry will later use his knowledge as a witness to exercise power over and astonish Matern with his scenario for the great public discussion about Matern's and Germany's guilt.

As witness-observer, Harry literally stands between Amsel and Matern; his love letters will always be in the middle no matter how Amsel arranges the narratives. He, like the dog, will always ''stand central.'' He is the uncommitted man, less because of opportunism than because he refuses to choose. If he were not a child and adolescent during the Nazi years, he would fail seriously as a moral being. As a child, he is also representative of the average German reduced to a childlike posture of subordination in an authoritarian state. He escapes into the realm of familial affairs partially because he has developed the askance view of the trickster who basically knows very well what is happening. For example, when he recalls the ''big day'' on which he was supposed to visit the Führer and his dog, he admonishes himself: ''At the time I feared that I might look upon the Führer through eyes blinded by tears, and today I have to make an effort to prevent the tears from blurring anything which was then angular, uniformed, beflagged, sun-lit, world-shatteringly important, sweatdrenched and real'' (pp. 300, 257). While the adjectives evoke the Party rallies with the rhythm of boots aimlessly marching in Hitler weather under the colors black, white, and red, the compound adjective *schweissdurchsuppt* (sweatdrenched; lit., souped through with sweat) undercuts the propaganda picture and prevents Harry-Grass, as well as the German reader, from getting that nostalgic knot in his throat. Moreover, Harry never saw the Führer on that day but merely saw a dog that might have been Prince. More memorable than anything else on that day is Brunies's nonverbal no: ''One flag pole was empty, cast doubt upon all the occupied flagpoles, and belonged to Dr. Brunies'' (pp. 301, 257).

Historical reality finally reached out for Harry ''with two fingers and put me into a life-size tank as an ammunition loader'' (pp. 139, 125). When the discomforts of history press too closely, Harry, now an adolescent, escapes into fantasy as he did during the attack on Amsel and Jenny. In trickster fashion, he switches to the third person in the *Schlussmärchen,* the final fairy tale that makes historical reality into once-upon-a-time, a reversal of Amsel's last early shift. Images of disintegration and death dominate the *Schlussmärchen,* which is nevertheless a masterful example of Harry's verbal acrobatics. The young intellectuals of the town allegorize Stutthof's mound of bones through Heideggerian jargon even after Tulla brings a skull from it as indisputable evidence. Tulla, bored and promiscuous, gets pregnant and thus offers Harry the opportunity to pretend that he is the father. She miscarries during an outing and, in a grotesquely pathetic scene, she and Harry bury the embryo. In the first book of *Dog Years,* the child was a promise when Brunies was discovered in a forest clearing with the abandoned Jenny in his arms; now that promise is denied.

The disintegrating world of the *Schlussmärchen,* again a parody of the "they lived happily ever after" of fairy tales, closes with three farewells. Jenny breaks off her relationship with Harry after her toes have been crushed during a bomb attack; she will never dance again. Tulla becomes a streetcar conductor and gives Harry his farewell ride through Danzig as he is on his way to the army. At the end the narrative shifts to Berlin where the Führerhund Prince, with his canine instinct for survival, escapes the Führerbunker. Hectic commands to recapture the dog are issued from below, and the energies of the German army expend themselves to find the dog. But the dog, along with thousands of refugees, flees West in search of a new master and a new time.

In the third book, Harry remains the precocious child and threshold intellectual who metamorphoses everything through words. Since he never grows up, it is appropriate that he becomes a director of radio programs for children. But, albeit phenotypically, Harry has to compulsively reenact the two traumatic events of his childhood and adolescence: his witnessing of the cruelty against Amsel and Jenny, and the end of the war. The latter is indicated mainly by the date on which he plans to stage the great public discussion of Matern's guilt—8 May 1957. The scenario will be nothing but a stage setting wherein he can project his own guilt on Matern while at the same time demonstrating his dangerous talent for new radio forms (pp. 564, 474). As discussion leader he will try to trap Matern and avoid his own involvement as a witness. Since no one knows that Harry was a witness, he appears omnipotent in his knowledge about the day when he fell from child-like innocence to the childish innocence of the trickster. His sense of play, his *Spieltrieb,* overshadows his pedantry, the urge to instruct. After this he has fulfilled his function as middleman and disappears from the novel. He can mockingly indict himself: "For Harry merely cogitated in his head what others actually did . . . . A melancholic, who liked honey cake . . . a young man of inaction . . . . A hypersensitive boy . . . a fetishist . . . a visionary, a uniformed high school student . . . he succeeded in burying a real mound made of human bones under medieval allegories" (pp. 375, 317–18). Even in guilt he playfully inflates himself with well-rounded phrases which Matern punctures with his blunt definition: "He'd have done fine as a Gestapo dick" (pp. 568, 478).

3. Walter Matern, the guilty quester who seeks and avoids atonement

The windmiller's son Matern plays the role of persecutor in the triad of victim, witness, and persecutor both in his relationship to Amsel and in his futile revenge campaign after the war. His friendship with Amsel is always at best a channeling of guilt feelings for having been foremost among Amsel's child tormentors. During the years of their friendship, Amsel is generally dominant, and this dominance cumulates aggressions that Matern releases periodically, never with such vehemence, however, as on that fateful winter day when he "gangs up" on Amsel. From that time on, Matern commits diversionary offences for which he is punished —he pilfers the SA cash reserves, he poisons Harras, he gets drunk and insults the Führer. But since the real offence is never punished, he cannot atone. Moreover, after the war he projects his guilt on his SA companions and thinks he is punishing them through the diversionary tactic of seducing their women, usually in the most ridiculous fashion. Amsel and Matern share the problem of finding the right word that would heal. Amsel represses his pain by creating a world from out of the symbols of corruption and refuse; Matern represses his wrath by grinding his teeth. As the *Knirscher,* the teeth grinder, he deprives his friend of teeth; but he is also *zerknirscht,* crushed with remorse and a general sense of melancholy.

As such he is, however, no more than a parody of murky German inwardness. Like Amsel and Harry, he is a man of surfaces, best revealed in his choice of profession, acting. Instead of building scarecrows or inventing fairy tales, Matern the trickster puts on masks. None of them is perhaps more symbolic of the trickster role than the hide of the reindeer that disguises him during Jenny's Christmas ballet, and none is more viciously real than the one that covers his face when he beats up Amsel. As he is well aware, the mask is not confined to the stage but is part of the chaos and rigidity of historical time and hides a hollow inside: "Behold me: bald-headed inside and out. An empty closet full of uniforms of every color. I was red, put on brown, wore black, dyed myself red. Spit on me: clothing for every kind of weather, adjustable suspenders, bounce-back man walks on leaden soles, bald on top, hollow within, bedecked with remnants . . . ." (pp. 514, 434)

Because he insulted the Führer, Matern finds himself as an anti-Fascist in a detention camp after the war. The world looks bleak, and he can hardly remember his friend; when he looks for God he finds excrement. His mind "has a spoon but no memory" as he scratches his empty tin like a scarecrow. In truth, Matern wants no memory, but the world demands that he remember. The demand may be no greater than that made by a British questionnaire; or it may take the form of a large black dog which keeps at his heels. The dog is none other than the Führerhund, Prince, as Matern learns when the dog howls at the sight of Hitler's image on a stack of posters. Matern accepts the dog, the hound of guilt whom he calls Pluto, without recalling that Amsel once used that name for Harras. The greatest demand on his memory is made by one named Brauchsel who wants Matern to write about the past (pp. 431, 365); Matern, however, wants to write in the present tense. Third person and present tense distinguish the Materniads from the other two books, except at the very end where Matern switches to a conscious first person for only a brief moment. The present tense insists on surfaces and thus refuses to come to terms with the past; any banal object can, however, create reverberations with the past. Writing in the present is a trap since every direction leads to a dead end and a turnabout. As Matern realizes, "Jeder Feldweg ist ein Holzweg" (Every path in the woods leads to the place where the trees have been cut), the *Kahlschlag* or illusory *tabula rasa* that many intellectuals imagined after the war (pp. 473, 400). In terms of Matern's guilt this means that every road he takes on his quest will lead to a blank spot where he has to turn around to start anew, for he always avoids the genuine center of his quest, his own guilt. His revenge spree, therefore, begins and ends with former SA man Sawatzki and his wife, now on the road to economic prosperity. Even his descent into Brauchsel's mine is a cul-de-sac, for when he arrives at the bottom, he finds no narrow passage that will lead him through the center of gravity into a new world. Rather, he simply turns around and takes the lift up. The Materniads are a shifting and shunting of the excrements of guilt, relieved only momentarily through grotesque acts of aggression.

Matern's revenge campaign, his infection with venereal disease which he spreads throughout Germany, and his eventual cure of the disease are typical examples of Grass's grotesque displacements of aggression, punishment, and atonement. Driven by pain, Matern rides through the land like an apocalyptic horseman but actually is only looking for a wall-socket. Then he finds one: "Matern, to put it plainly, pisses into the socket and obtains—thanks to the unbroken stream of water—a power-ful, electric, skyhighsending, and salutary shock; for as soon as he can stand up again, pale and trembling under hair aghast, all the honey drains. The milk of vengeance curdles . . . . Cured but unredeemed, master and dog leave the withered Lüneberg Heath. From this moment on the clap is on the decline in Germany. Every pestilence purifies. Every plague has its day. Every joy is the last'' (pp. 472, 399). Pedantry is not omitted in this playful invention, for the shock is merely a physical shock and not a shock of recognition; it is no gift of grace, no Damascus experience. Matern has cured only the symptoms but not the cause of his condition, sprung from a failure to love.

A bored and tired Matern is eventually discovered by a media representative who recognizes that Matern's appealingly primitive and animalistic voice would be appropriate for a *Kinderschreck,* a bogeyman for children who really only rattles a spoon in his tin. In mask after mask Matern's voice once more inflates the self by means of theatrical stereotypes in which the leitmotifs and murder motives of ambition and oppression expand to global proportion, only to implode again to the beginning when the trickster first puts on the animal skin. Nevertheless, the reader's sympathies remain with Matern, for he finally decides to be voiceless after Harry gives him the script of the great public discussion, which is to appear as a spontaneous event. Grass interpolates this play within the novel in such a way that the reader is left unsure whether the discussion took place or not.

The scenario opens with the question as to whether Matern will be *diskussionsfreudig* (eager to discuss), a neologism that reminds the reader how *deckfreudig* (eager to copulate) the pure-bred Harras was when he fertilized the bitch that was to whelp the Führer dog, Prince. As Nazi racial theory encouraged breeding among "pure Aryans," so the pseudoreligious ritual of the discussion now uses the past and the guilty individual for maximum external effectiveness rather than for insight. *Spieltrieb* dominates pedantry as public exposure of the self becomes as dehumanizing as copulation for the sake of political doctrine. Matern attempts, therefore, to hide himself behind generalities. After admitting that he was born on 20 April, the day "Hitler, the greatest criminal of all times, was whelped," he assures himself that "all people have something in common with Hitler" (pp. 588–89, 494). As the discussion drives home to the "Jewish question" and Matern's guilt regarding it, he exasperatedly establishes the connection between himself and the dog years: "What guarded the miller's mill, what watched over the carpenter's shop, what in guise of favorite dog rubbed against the boots of the Reichsautobahn builder, attached itself to me, an anti-fascist. Have you followed the parable? Don't the accursed dog years balance for you in the seven digited number?" (pp. 608, 510) But Matern cannot take flight into statistics of the murdered; he has to answer the question "Do you love the

Jews, as you love animals, or don't you love the Jews?'' Since he has already admitted that he poisoned Harras, the question and the answer are ambiguous. The dog, different and yet always the same, ''stands central'' in the paradigms Hitler-dog-Jews and Amsel-dog-Matern. The generalization ''All people have something in common with Hitler'' parallels Matern's evasion ''We have all of us gravely wronged the Jews.'' Finally, his aggression breaks through as he verbally reenacts his hostility towards Amsel: ''The Itzich got beaten up. Ei, Wei, shoilem boil'em. He got it square in the puss'' (pp. 611, 512). Now the discussion shows that besides the fixed point ''black German shepherd'' there is the number 32, the teeth that Amsel lost, the first years of this century. The discussion concludes and the reader learns in the opening of the next Materniad that it never took place; for Matern reads this final broadcasting script in the canteen of the Radio Building. Matern has not said anything; he has proved not to be *diskussionsfreudig*. Everything has been said for him in a script that is disturbing because it predicted phenotypal reaction so accurately.

Matern attempts to leave dog and guilt behind him only to encounter both again in Berlin where he meets Amsel and the dog. The dog leaves Matern after he has passed through Amsel's scarecrow mine, but not because Matern has finally gained insight. He does not see himself, as he once did, in Amsel's scarecrows. The point of conversion does not take place since Matern gets used to hell and even seems to enjoy it. When the two friends finally sit in their bathtubs, they achieve a moment of Lethe —aggressions and guilt are not recognized; they simply fade away. Although Matern shifts to the first person as if self-integration has finally been reached, the two brothers remain separate: ''I hear Eddi splashing next door. Now I too step into my bath. The water soaks me clean. Eddi whistles something indeterminate. I try to whistle something similar. But it's difficult. Each of us bathes by himself.'' The series of brief sentences piles irony upon irony. There is mutal nakedness, not the disguise of the scarecrow, but the vulnerable common humanity. Yet the friends do not see each other. They do not emerge from the bath to behold themselves as they really are; the dog years separate them in spite of the ritual of cleansing. Eddi whistles indeterminately, and Matern cannot get in tune. At the very end there is the muted effort at harmony which tries to overcome the dark side of utopia through this infantile setting, through this gesture of becoming a child again. This world of make-believe shapes the dog years of the novel as a whole into its vicious cycle of repetition-compulsion by characters who cannot cope with the world they have made.

B. The Cosmos of *Dog Years*—An Elegiac Grotesque Fairy Tale

As Amsel, Matern, and the dog Pluto sit reunited in Jenny's bar, Amsel urges, "More stories. More stories. Keep going! As long as we are telling stories, we are alive. As long as stories keep coming, with or without a point, dog stories, rat stories, flood stories, recipe stories, stories full of lies and school book stories, as long as stories have power to entertain us, no hell can take us in. Your turn Walter. Tell stories as long as you love your life" (pp. 640, 536). Amsel is well aware that stories divert murder motives, his own and others, and he will even pay to keep stories coming. Stories *unterhalten,* a word that means to entertain and to converse casually; but it also means to support and maintain and, finally, to hold under or, in our context, to repress. The story tellers maintain and support each other; but since their talk is merely *Spieltrieb,* it represses what should be the true concern of the story tellers. Harry, the greatest escapist, used the word *Schlussmärchen,* but Amsel uses the word *Geschichte* with its dual meanings of history and fiction. As memory shapes experience through nostalgia, the desire to return home again, *Geschichte* becomes a fairy tale and is regressive because the adult should become conscious of the pain history brought. The characters in *Dog Years,* however, do not wish to really grow up: they believe that they can control the world through the verbal magic of the fairy tale.

We saw how people in the extreme situation of the camp world needed a myth, a story that would sustain them; but that need was a progressive projection of utopian longings for a better world. The fairy tale world of *Dog Years,* however, is regressive as it seeks to escape the past by making it ahistorical and therefore amoral. History as "once upon a time" frees us from taking an ethical attitude toward it. In fairy tales, obstructing characters can be shoved into ovens, forced to dance in red hot shoes, or rolled down the hill in a barrel spiked with nails; while the children turn peacefully homeward, and prince and princess live happily ever after. In *Dog Years,* the fairy tale is the creation of adults who refuse insight. It is the magic for repressing guilt, but there is a catch. As memory is made timeless in the story it becomes eternally present. The directness and precision of fairy tale images stimulate reverberations that can return the adult to the very same disturbing thoughts he sought to escape. Grass's fairy tales are always in tension with historical reality; as adult fairy tales they are consciously elegiac and grotesque, qualities appropriate to the dark side of utopia. A seemingly harmless reverie by Amsel illustrates this clearly: "No dear Walter, no matter how you rumble against your great Fatherland—I, however, love the Germans.

Alas, how mysterious they are and filled with God-pleasing forgetfulness. They cook their little pea soup on blue gas flames and think nothing of it. Besides, no other than this land can boast such brown and velvety gravies'' (pp. 646, 540). Here the supermen of the fatherland have shrunk to one of Grass's favorite images, the wicked cooks. The gas chamber has contracted into blue gas flames and the excremental brown of the Nazis into a gravy so easily stirred up and swallowed. Amsel's ''ach'' (alas) expresses both a yearning for German *Gemütlichkeit* and the regret over adamant forgetfulness. Here the lower middle class kitchen is a metaphor of evil that encapsules the holocaust and masquerades with a veneer of God-pleasing innocence.

The elegiac tone is reiterated in the exile's complaint about the lost home, the lost innocence of friendship; but the grotesque image keeps the elegy from becoming sentimental by encrusting it with something material and mechanical, something that is repetitive and compulsive. By undercutting the elegiac emotion with the grotesque, by superimposing upon it what Bergson has called the sudden anesthesia of the heart, the critical intelligence is roused. Grass's novel is a ''deflection of life towards the mechanical'' (Bergson). As such, the grotesque is the reality principle of a guilty world. Yet at the core of this unnatural human cosmos there is the vague yearning that the material and the hollowness it encloses may be transformed. Three fairy tale motifs express that yearning: the desire of the scarecrow to be transformed through love; the make-believe world which prevents this desire from being realized; the quest and escape into the dark and deep.

One reviewer criticized *Dog Years* because ''Amsel and Matern as well as other figures in *Dog Years* are in the final analysis marionettes. Besides, the background itself has often something of a stage setting.''[24] Precisely, the characters of this patchwork world are all somehow encrusted by the mechanical, and even the most original and independent individual, namely, Brunies, becomes predictable in his addiction to sweets. His routine gesture of popping malted bon bons or vitamin tablets into his mouth and pushing them from cheek to cheek will eventually lead to his doom. Another noncomformist, Tulla, brushes a strand of hair from her eye ''with a mechanical movement that Haseloff's figure could not have done more mechanically'' (pp. 347, 295). The rigidity of the mechanical gesture numbs empathetic responses to the world, and the emptiness behind the gesture seems to be the preferred state of being, a protection. As phenomena, rigidity and emptiness always reverberate for the perceiver with a yearning for transcendence, for the spell-breaking moment when the costumed puppets come alive, fulfilling the familiar desire with which the creative imagination of a child surrounds a favorite toy.

In *Dog Years,* hints at a transcendent reality are hardly comforting. God is either *der liebe Gott* of childhood who benignly muses over the perversities and brutalities of history, or he is the tinker who builds mechanisms into people and is very likely a scarecrow himself. He is rather like the trickster Eddi Amsel who, while entertaining German troops, creates a ballet which expresses the metaphysics of *Dog Years* in fairy tale images. Jenny writes Harry that the ballet is called "The Scarecrows," but also "The Gardener's Daughter" and "The Revolt of the Scarecrows" (pp. 401–4, 338–41). A wicked gardener's garden is plundered by birds with whom the gardener's daughter partially allies herself. Her father advertises for a scarecrow, but the first applicant abducts the daughter to his subterranean kingdom, where a great wind-mill grinds out the fashions of history. The daughter is able to avoid a wedding by dancing everyone to sleep except for the twelve-legged hound of hell (Senta, Harras, Prince-Pluto). When she returns to the garden, she is rejected by her father and, finally, is tumultuously carried off by the combined forces of birds and scarecrows. The gardener remains alone in his wasteland, and, teased by birds, he changes into a scarecrow during a macabre solo that Amsel had planned to dance himself.

Jenny, the elegiac, graceful anima of the ballet, writes Harry that she "has learned a lot from the mechanical figure," (pp. 347, 294), for Haseloff's ballet takes "positions lovely enough to give you religion" (pp. 346, 294). Although her letters are clever and witty, Jenny is really incapable of serious thought and unaware of any parabolic meanings of the ballet. Grass points out in his essay on the ballerina that the effects of spiritual weightlessness are caused by tormented flesh forced into silver slippers. The classical ballerina should be an ordinary girl, a mere vessel for the spirituality that she unconsciously projects.[25] She is comparable to the marionette. Kleist, whose influence Grass admits, pointed out in his essay on the marionette that the spiritual is reflected through the physical, for instance, through the angular position of an elbow. As the spiritual becomes darkened and submerged in the physical, the physical turns all the more splendidly physical. Kleist argues that, since we have lost paradise, we must go roundabout to see if we cannot recapture it through its opposite, the totally physical. Grace(fulness), Kleist con-cludes, appears at its fullest in that body which either has no consciousness at all or total consciousness, the marionette or the god. The ballerina is suspended between the two. Empty as she might be, she mimics through her rigid yet elegant movements the mystic's desire and fulfillment in the one and all.

This is what the ballet allegorizes or what the perceiver would like the scarecrows to signify. Mechanically graceful, the gardener's daughter falls in love with the scarecrow who leaps into and out of the garden with a grand jeté. The example of the Heideggerian "Werden im Sprung," which Grass satirizes in another part of the novel (pp. 363, 308), is the leap that makes the dreamer fly, the leap associated with faith, the leap that inevitably reaffirms the pull of gravity. The lovers leap, not into freedom, but into the Orcus of history. In the fairy-tale world the ballerina can dance the chaos of history to sleep, but historical reality will crush her feet and all their tiptoe yearning. The scarecrows revolt by abducting the gardener's daughter; for if they cannot have her through love, they will have her by force. The motivation is similar to Amsel's hiring of the author collective. It is left open in the ballet whether the beautiful will transform the grotesque world or whether it will also become grotesque. The evidence of the novel points to the latter. The lonely gardener-god and scarecrow maker becomes a scarecrow himself in the pathetic loneliness of his ravaged garden. Nasty and repressive from the beginning, he becomes the empty mechanism pretending to be alive, the god-man-scarecrow.

Any putting on of costume is, of course, a metamorphosis of sorts in that it hides or reveals the being beneath. Metamorphosis can become the means of escape for an individual caught in a situation so intolerable that he has to break through into another dimension of existence. The irony is that the shaman's mantle, the metaphor, always advertises the psychological problem that prevented the individual from dealing with the intolerable. Thus, metamorphosis is both an escape from and a revelation of character. Usually, metamorphosis does not lead to insight —the butterfly does not remember the caterpillar. It is therefore quite different from the kind of change *(trasumanar)* that Dante experiences as he ascends the various levels of paradise. The damned in hell, metamorphosed as they are into various shapes, live without insight and hence without the possibility of redemption; their punishment is just, however, because the shape they have for eternity is the shape they always wanted. The state of the characters in *Dog Years* is similar in that they attain the state that was always in them and that they deserve.

The most obvious and startling metamorphosis in *Dog Years* is the transformation of the fat Amsel and the plump, teddy-coated Jenny into a slim young man and a graceful ballerina. The event is, however, no more fantastic than the metamorphosis of human beings into living skeletons or, as Grass repeatedly hints, the human being into soap. In *Dog Years,* the child's perception meliorates a traumatically cruel event by transforming the victims into snowmen from whence they emerge as more desirable. It is the child's version of the adult argument that suffering brings spiritual insight and wisdom, for child and adult want suffering to have meaning so that the guilt of the witness who did not cry out is assuaged. This is furthered when the victims themselves seem not too deeply affected. After the thaw, Amsel does not look for "hell's victory," or "death's sting," or God; he simply looks for his teeth (pp. 262, 226). Similarly, Jenny explains her tiredness to Harry by casually saying, "You see, I was inside a snowman" (pp. 265, 229). Suffering does not necessarily lead to insight, and the sufferer usually simulates a state of normalcy as quickly as possible.

Language tends to be the greatest power of metamorphosis that adults possess. Here, philosophical terminology takes the place of snowmen and transforms the *Knochenberg* of Stutthof into an allegory that pretends to affirm life by repressing the reality of death and murder. Yet magic is more difficult for the adult who faces the wasteland of history, as does Harry in the *Schlussmärchen*. For the adults, Stutthof is first of all a word that has a life of its own; it is an amorphous bogey to keep others in check: "You got a yen for Stutthof?—'If you don't keep that trap of yours shut, you'll end up in Stutthof.' A sinister word had moved into apartment houses, went upstairs and downstairs, sat at kitchen tables, was supposed to be a joke, and some actually laughed: 'They're making soap in Stutthof now, it makes you want to stop washing'" (pp. 324, 277). The reality of the mound of bones draws attention to itself because the crows flock to its stench, a stench that hangs like a bell over the area and can be tasted in one's mouth (pp. 369, 313). Nevertheless, the characters attempt to repress this reality in spite of its impingement on primary senses: "Nobody spoke of the pile of bones. But everybody saw smelled tasted it" (pp. 369, 312). Only Tulla callously insists that the mound is of bones and comes from Stutthof. She offers proof, but the young philosophers evade it with "the most we can say is that here Being has come into concealment" or "there lies the essence ground of all history."

Grass is not implying that Heideggerian verbal constructs contain no truth, but, rather, that the *Spieltrieb* that necessarily underlies them controls the truth or pedagogic content. Grass, too, plays with language as he tries to call things by their name. The pontificating young man is right: the essence of history does implode into a pile of bones where being comes into concealment. But such grandiose and sublime words repress the stench and taste of death as well as the agony of every muscle and sinew of the victim's body. All power of language, conciseness of images, and abstract loftiness fail to come to terms with the *Knochenberg* in an ethical sense. The reader is apt to admire once again the inventive skill of Grass and not Grass's ethical concerns. In the final analysis, Grass, like Harry, succeeds in burying "a real mound made of human bones under medieval allegories. The pile of bones, which in reality cried out to high heaven between Troyl and Kaisershafen, was mentioned in his diary as a place of sacrifice, erected in order that purity might come to be in the luminous, which transluminates purity and so fosters light" (pp. 375–76, 318). Harry succeeds so well in repressing that memory that at the time of his writing he has to check his diary. What makes this use of metaphors different from the metaphors used by the person who is a victim of the extreme situation is that the latter uses metaphors to make the incomprehensible somewhat understandable to those who did not experience it. Conventional metaphors become a device to communicate with one's fellow humans rather than a means of repression. Philosophical and poetic language often strives for the purity of essence, but Grass realizes that such striving will always be alloyed by the excremental brown of the Nazis, as Harry's elegiac, grotesque paean to the lack of purity reveals:

> No closing of the circle is pure. For if the circle is pure, then the snow is pure, the virgin is, the pigs are, Jesus Christ, Marx and Engels, white ashes, all sorrows, laughter, to the left roaring, to the right silence, ideas immaculate, wafers no longer bleeders and geniuses without efflux, all angles pure angles, piously compasses would describe circles: pure and human, dirty, salty, diabolical, Christian and Marxist, laughing and roaring, ruminant, silent, holy, round pure angular. And the bones, white mounds that were recently heaped up, would grow immaculately without crows: pyramids of glory. But the crows, which are not pure, were creaking unoiled, even yesterday: nothing is pure, no circle, no bone. And piles of bones, heaped up for the sake of purity, will melt cook boil in order that soap, pure and cheap; but even soap cannot wash pure. [pp. 357, 303]

When the human being as scarecrow can no longer find the means to dress up reality, there remains only the escape into the dark and deep; but the scarecrow's underworld in the ballet or in Amsel's mine is merely a reflector of the Orcus of history. The underworld is above ground on the dark side of utopia. The dark and deep is externalized in this novel where no character ever has a nightmare, for a nightmare might reveal inner depths that are inadmissible to the scarecrow phenotype. In childhood, the exploration of the dark and deep may be an exciting venture into independence, as when Amsel and Matern investigate the Danzig sewers or come upon a clearing in the dark and spooky German forest. For the adult, the deep and dark is an escape from responsibility. Hitler escapes into his bunker; Amsel into his mine. Thus, the adventurous places of childhood expand to include historical reality and, finally, the interpretation of history.

Grass mocks the tradition of German romanticism and its fascination with mythical descents into the realm of the mothers, of night, and of death by associating the bowels of the earth with the excremental and its stench of mortality. Amsel-Brauxel's memory of boyhood sewer explorations is stimulated in the present after his morning purge: ''Who is standing here contemplating his excrement? A thoughtful anxious man in search of the past . . . Brauxel, the present writer, raises his eyes and pulls the chain; while contemplating he has remembered a situation'' (pp. 89, 81). Amsel remembers not only the sewer but also Matern's aggressions against him which the latter had simply repressed after their friendship began. When the boys finally come upon a skeleton beneath the church of Sankt Trinitatis, Matern falls into a wordless teeth-grinding reverie, while Amsel reaches for the skull thinking it would do well on top of a scarecrow. Matern considers this *Spieltrieb* impious, kicks Amsel into the dust, and utters the fateful word *Itzig*. After that he raises the skull in a Hamlet posture, while Amsel relieves himself, purges his own aggressions, and can again be friends with Matern. All this is a very probable boyhood adventure but also establishes leitmotifs: there is Amsel's propensity to see everything as useful (Brauchsel) for his art; there is Matern's teeth grinding, violence, and habit of repressing guilt through philosophical ponderousness.

We have seen that Amsel's narrative is dominated by fairy tale fantasies, while history is reserved for the last early shift. Just before that, in the thirty-second early shift, he evokes the deep, dark German forest: ''Hoo, how dark it is in the German forest!'' (pp. 110–18, 122–31) Here the spooks of German folk mythology fly in abandon, scaring no one but children. Here the teacher Brunies sits like Rumpelstiltskin over the fire, making caramel bonbons. Gypsies are in the woods, not yet destined for the gas chamber, and they abandon the baby Jenny for Brunies. Because this is still childhood, the center of the woods reveals a sunlit clearing where the teacher finds the gift of a child: "The scrag, schoolie, brain buster, teacher, Oswald Brunies, stood under the sun with the screaming child and didn't know how to hold it . . . neither Dr. Brunies with the strident little bundle nor the picture-book meadow showed surprise when again something miraculous happened: from the south, from Poland, storks came flying over the meadow with measured wingbeat. Two of them described ceremonious loops and dropped, first one, then the other, into the blackened and disheveled nest on the cracked chimney" (pp. 131, 118). In spite of the ironies, which keep the passage from becoming sentimental, this is the most positive image in the entire novel. In the center of the woods an awkward but loving man accepts the abandoned child. Until she is crippled by history, Jenny's beauty and grace associate her with the miraculous origins possible in fairy tales; the storks may well have brought her. A stork's nest atop a house is a sign of blessing and peace for that house, and here the birds bring that blessing even to a cracked chimney. But all of this is a picture-book vision of light; in reality, storks do not bring babies, gypsies will be gassed, and chimneys are the only means of escape for the dead. The idyllic scene actually emphasizes the grimness of the novel, especially as far as the potential of love and life is concerned. In book two, Tulla, who wants a child, miscarries her embryo in a grotesquely pathetic scene; in book three, Walli is the offspring of the sexual degeneracy of Sawatzki-Inge-Walter. On the dark side of utopia the promise of the child remains unfulfilled.

The great powers that rule the world with their questionable aims are never seen in the three novels under discussion. Hitler, the greatest power in *Dog Years,* is also an absent god. His image appears on pictures and posters that are cherished like holy pictures, but he is never seen in the glory of personal appearance; only his dog can be seen. As Harry's voice takes on omniscient and oracular tones in the *Schlussmärchen,* as the fairy tale of Hitler comes to an end, the Führer is nothing but a ghostly voice underground. The real smells of mouldy dampness and excrement in the sewers of Danzig are gone; instead, logorrhea, a continuous flow of words, at once inflated and repressive, issues from the bunker. The scene again has an aura of theatricality for which Grass has been criticized. It seems to me, however, that the cabaret-like atmosphere of the end has been prepared by the leitmotifs of the novel and by the theatricality practiced by the Nazis themselves in their elaborate stage settings, projecting the triumph of their will. Since Grass cannot communicate individual suffering in Stutthof, he cannot give a mimesis of the suffering of the Germans during the fiery collapse of Berlin; one agony cancels out the other. The Knochenberg parallels the allegorical Führerbunker from which the dog Prince escapes from the dog that brought Germany to the dogs. In the final analysis, Grass's playful description is no more inappropriate than the description the historian gives of the end of the Third Reich. In Alan Bullock's treatment of this subject, for instance, we find the same concentration on the person of Hitler, whose tragic posturings and language are an unintentional parody of existential Angst. Bullock quotes Hitler as saying, "Now nothing remains. Nothing is spared to me. No allegiances are kept, no honour lived up to, no disappointments that I have not had, no betrayals that I have not experienced—and now this above all else. Nothing remains."[26] How easy it is to burlesque such rhetoric of the totally egocentric orator, whose turns of phrase reveal in the end the emptiness they always possessed!

Following a dog's common sense, Prince runs away, a betrayal that the Führer cannot tolerate; Hitler, therefore, sets in motion what is left of the German army to recapture the nothingness of the dog. A frantic outpouring of meaningless energy results, and the historically conscious reader is reminded of the futile stand for "final victory." In light of these historical absurdities, it is not strange that the German army is set in motion to recapture Hitler's dog. The code names for the dog are nothingness and transcendence, as the following "Führerexlocation" shows: "The question of the dog is a metaphysical question, calling the entire German nation into question" (pp. 421, 355). The voice intones hectically that "Berlin remains German. Vienna will be German again. And the dog will never be negated." Again there is much pedantry in this *Spieltrieb;* for Hitler the dog left a dog as heritage to his nation, a dog that becomes in an ironic sense *der Hund des Herrn,* the *canis domini* that hounds our guilt, and specifically in terms of the novel, Matern's guilt. Hitler disappears underground, but the Orcus rages above under an indifferent sky. As Götterdämmerung and "radio silence settle over the government quarter of the Reichskapital," the new time is already beginning as the refugees pour west, "all eager to start out fresh with living, saving, letter writing . . . eager to forget the mounds of bones and the mass graves, the flag poles and party books, the debts and the guilt," eager to continue the dog years in another place and time.

The final underground journey is Walter Matern's quest through Amsel's scarecrow mine. In this last *Schlussmärchen* of the novel the fantasy element has taken over to such an extent that the reader is not sure if the characters are alive or dead. They sing in the fiery oven of Jenny's bar and then take a walk through Berlin, during which Matern once again throws the pocketknife into the river while Amsel again promises him a new one, just as they did in the beginning. Impotent with "human rage, which always looks for words and finally finds one," Matern says for the last time, "Itzig." Like Goethe's Faust, he says a fateful word at the end. After uttering it, Matern, like Faust, sinks to the ground and submits himself to Amsel's power. Amsel calls a taxi and drives with Matern and Pluto to the airport, for "anyone wishing to travel below ground will do well to take a start in the air: ergo, British-European Airways to Hanover-Langenfeld" (pp. 648, 542). The journey underground could be an education for Matern, but he is no pupil, just as Amsel is no teacher as Virgil was to Dante. Both simply confirm their damnation, their paralysis in the *status quo*. All the levels of the scarecrow mine reflect aspects of Matern's character and experiences and make him therewith into an everyman: sport, religion, military service, the virtues of democracy and the nuclear family, sexual potency and impotence, social and metaphysical philosophy, history and the means of coping with history through opportunism, profiteering, and inner emigration. Only the ever changing fashions of the times distinguish one epoch from the other. Compulsively and repetitively he mutters, "This is hell." But hell is not only above ground, as Amsel reminds him; it is also within himself. Unable to make analogies and see relationships, the whole experience is wasted on him. He may take the lift up at the end, but he remains spiritually at the bottom of the cave.

This fantasy receives its full meaning only when it is compared to the tradition of journeys to the underworld, the realm of the dead or the damned.[27] Underground travelers such as Hercules, Aeneas, Christ, or Dante may or may not be conscious of the experience after it occurred, but it always strengthens and defines them. Matern, who did not learn anything in this world, will not learn anything in the grotesque, artificial world Amsel has constructed to teach his friend. History and art fail to enlighten the human being. Yet in keeping with the tradition, hell punishes the sinner according to his crime. Therefore, Amsel's hell is shallow and mechanical, proper to the surface-self of the phenotype. There are no profound demons that mock the creative premises of a just and omnipotent creator; here evil is banal. Moreover, this allegorical hell is not only playful and pedagogical; it is also profitable, for Amsel sends his products all over the world. In his mine "materials are made ready for the manufacturing process" (pp. 656, 548), a phrase reminiscent of the jargon of concentration camps where human beings reduced to scarecrows were processed. The mine's gate also displays paradoxical slogans "Glück auf" similar to Auschwitz's "Arbeit macht frei" when the true slogan should be, as Matern suggests, "Abandon all hope ye who enter here." At the bottom of this pit, the thirty-second level, there is no paralyzed three-headed demon, impotently beating his wings in frantic parody of divine breath, but merely a tidy and organized mail order service where address labels are put on boxes filled with scarecrows. There is no secret at the center, no horror in the pit, either on the personal or historical level. The scarecrow has been made in the image of man and is thus less frightening than man himself because it is less powerful.

Eddi Amsel built this hell and has his private joke with mankind, a joke no one seems to get. The crucial leitmotifs *Itzig* and 32 have been defined, but they belong to the dark side of utopia. The liberating, creative, and loving word has not been found in all these pages; hence, Amsel and Matern will not make the laborious ascent up Mount Purgatory, assisting each other with reason and affection until the earthly paradise is reached.

5

To the Last Syllable of Recorded Time: The Dull, Violent World of Uwe Johnson's *Jahrestage*

"The place where I come from no longer exists," says Gesine Cresspahl, the narrative consciousness of Uwe Johnson's *Jahrestage, Days of the Year,* or *Anniversaries.*[1] She is referring to the fictional town of Jerichow in the province of Mecklenburg, the point of origin for her awareness and memory. As in the cases of Siggi in *The German Lesson* and the author collective of *Dog Years,* her thoughts return to the provincial microcosm with mixed feelings of desire and rejection. Desire arises because it was there that the possibilities of love existed, whose denial is made bearable in the present by mythical screens and memory filters as well as by hopeful projections. Nevertheless, Gesine knows that the denial of love is the origin of the guilt-generating chain of betrayals that bind each day of her present. The childhood world was not a paradise; rather, it was the time and place where the child was initiated into the betrayal of love, a betrayal that may be repeated in adult life both in the private and familial as well as in the political sphere. Deprivations urge wish projections which inevitably become catastrophic as the individual tries to realize them. The adult cannot escape the orginal landscape of betrayal, no matter how far he or she may move. Siggi maintains his close ties to Rugbüll; the narrators of *Dog Years* are forced by historical circumstances to leave Danzig-Langfuhr, but they spread their guilt, their leitmotifs, and murder motives throughout West Germany. Gesine Cresspahl, in search of the morally neutral Switzerland where she would be free of guilt, moves from East Germany to West Germany and finally ends up in New York, only to discover that, as the geographical boundaries expanded, guilt likewise expanded to global proportions. The human desire to escape the condition of guilt remains, and for this reason Gesine wants to return in the summer of 1968 to the Eastern bloc country of Czechoslovakia in order to "do something there," presumably to work for the dream of a socially just and free society. It remains to be seen if such work can be done without betrayal and guilt.

More than the other two novels, Johnson's *Jahrestage* is an anatomy of the melancholy of our condition. Gesine's narrative seems on the surface cool, understated, and detached. She does not indulge in apocalyptically decorative allegories and allusions; instead she turns to the reasonable and dignified voice of the *New York Times,* which records the daily dull round of violence and betrayal in private, public, and global events, demanding only that they must be "fit to print." As present and future readers of the novel work themselves through that dull violent year, 1967–68 may seem to have been an exciting time when the Vietnam War was contended and defended, when racial and political unrest disturbed the aims of law and order, when Martin Luther King and Robert F. Kennedy were shot, when "speed" killed, and when the Czechoslovakian dream of a socialist democracy came to a halt on 20 August, the date Johnson assigns to the end of the fourth volume. Gesine's dream will be lost in historical ambiguities, will be banished to the dark side of utopia. Secretive and ambiguous, Gesine never states her political intentions clearly. Expressing her commitment through declarative utterance, the challenge and the boast are not for her. She speaks with many tongues, literally because she is a foreign correspondent in a New York bank and also because she is an ironic self, consciously ironic and ironic in terms of her repressions and desires, of which she may or may not be aware. Like her creator, Johnson, Gesine Cresspahl is caught in a plurality of possible lives.

I.
Speculations about Uwe Johnson

Uwe Johnson, a year younger than Gesine, was born in Pommerania in 1934 as a child whose birth the Nazis might have interpreted as his parents' trust in Germany's future. In his understated manner, he gives the following account of his father, who joined the Party in 1936: "My parents were not farmers but children of farmers. It is true that my father never quite escaped his country background. He was an employee of an animal protection office. He watched over the quality of milk and gave advice regarding the breeding of animals. My father died in 1947 or 1948, we are not sure of the exact date. After the war, he was confined and died in a labor camp in White Russia."[2] In 1944, Johnson drew upon himself the attention of a National Socialist Commission scouting for future SS material. He was sent to a National Socialist boarding school, but what he learned there did not affect him traumatically or permanently: "The Führer stood in the center of my parents' life, not my life. I was too young to be permanently influenced. Vacations were my main interest in that boarding school."[3] Like the main character of his first novel, Jakob Abs, he fled Pommerania at the end of the war and went to Mecklenburg where he finished his secondary schooling in 1952. He joined the Free German Youth and believed for a while in the ideology of East German communism.

The years 1952–56 were taken up with studies of German letters and literature at the universities of Rostock and Leipzig. When East Germany experienced an intellectual thaw in 1956, Johnson wrote an examination about the problem of truth in contemporary literature. Hans Mayer, his teacher, noticed at once that "this was a personal and political disagreement with the Ulbricht state and its literary theories." Caught in a delicate situation, Mayer did not evaluate the work but offered the candidate an opportunity to justify himself in an oral examination; the examination, however, ended after a few minutes when Johnson said that the whole thing was pointless and walked out. He was able to conclude his studies eventually, but this particular event indicated the beginning of his argument with the German Democratic Republic.[4] At that time he was already working on *Ingrid Babendererde,* a piece of fiction rejected by the Aufbau Verlag for political reasons and by Suhrkamp for artistic reasons. The latter, however, brought out Johnson's next book, *Speculations about Jakob* (1959). When that novel was published, Johnson moved to West Berlin but maintained contact with friends in the East. Johnson had been in the United States for three months when the Berlin Wall was built and largely severed his contact with the East. However, he insists that he did not flee to the West, a phrase much too melodramatic for him: "I calmly moved, in one hand the typewriter, in the other the briefcase."[5] Mark Boulby points out that Johnson "discloses a skeptical attitude to the political realities of West Germany."[6] In 1966 he left for his second and two-year stay in New York. During that time he gathered the material for the New York life of Gesine Cresspahl. Like Gesine, he lived in an apartment on Riverside Drive with his family; and, like her, he has, in spite of difficulties, an affinity for the English language through which he can express things at times better than in German.[7]

Usually not very communicative, Johnson defines his Germanness and its consequences in no uncertain terms: "I am German. I feel as a

German. German is the language with which I grew up, without which I cannot work. Since I want to work in this profession, I must stay most of the time in Germany. I cannot disassociate myself from the German past or the German present. To every foreigner I am a German. Our daughter grew up in New York with Jewish children—we were always the Germans. German history is an inescapable factor to me. For every person, for every fictional character, it is one of the most important questions.''[8] Johnson's preoccupation with the concentrationary universe is more evident in his fictional characters than in his personal utterances. He seems to be on the side of those who wish to be silent about it, not because they want to repress and forget, but because they fear the arrogance associated with those who did not experience it and yet talk about it: ''Actually, we should all have remained silent after 1945 . . . . This is a land with an ignominy that cannot be forgiven. The only thing that could justify talking and writing about Berlin is just this division, this border, this distance. And this because I think—though it is, of course, an excuse—that this border through Germany is perhaps representative of the difference in the two life styles that are offered today and of the urgency of the alternative which one presents to the other. That could be of interest to the world and gives us the right to say: we are here, we are worthy of notice. But nothing else.''[9] East and West German attitudes towards the concentration camps are poignantly expressed in *Speculations about Jakob* when the adult Gesine reflects in 1956 on her thirteen-year-old self asking Jakob, ''Is it true, Jakob, about the camps? . . . I am thirteen years old every moment before Jakob's broad motionless face and his half closed eyes and hear him say Yes that is true. With that one cannot live, it is useless, how could it be accounted for.''[10] Here are two attitudes towards history, one a regressive awareness and guilty fascination towards the past, the other a progressive refusal to let one's self be hindered by the crimes of the past. One attitude reflects towards the past; the other projects into the future. The first retards action because past mistakes may be repeated; the second leads to action, nonreflective action in which the mistakes of the past are likely to be repeated with variations. In *Jahrestage,* the adult Gesine Cresspahl will be conscious of both attitudes and will attempt to synthesize them.

The choice between the two life styles is a subject that concerns all of Johnson's novels. Presumably, the ideal society would be one that combines individual freedom and socialist community, but Johnson reveals no program as to how this is to be achieved. He has been called the author of the divided Germany because he was the first to occupy himself intensively with this problem. He sees division as a condition and exemplifies it by living in Berlin; yet he lives on the western side because only there can his books be published. Like his fictional characters, he is secretive when asked to define his political allegiance, an attitude unacceptable to the East. In *Speculations,* Jakob has to die once his attitudes have fluctuated. When he returns east, he is run over by a train on a foggy morning. Gesine, who chose to go west and is perhaps involved in espionage and counterespionage, is caught in private and public ambiguities for which a pluralistic society has no concern.

Johnson admits no political or religious affiliations; however, both politics and, to a lesser extent, religion are major influences for the form and content of his works. He prefers to define himself as a very private person: "I am satisfied with passion in private life. By writing I want to find out the truth. Through my characters and stories, I try to get closer to real life." Johnson is the artist as trickster when he defines the ends and means of his art. Thus, he insists that Gesine decides what will be important for her biography.[11] Among his more reliable comments are the following remarks: "I do not think that it is the task of literature to offer reproaches to history *[Geschichte]*. Rather, the task of literature is to tell a story *[Geschichte],* in my case this would mean not to tell it in such a way which would lead the reader into illusion, but which would show him how this story-history *[Geschichte]* really is."[12] The convoluted phraseology of this statement reveals the trickster artist whose views of the creative process are, however, so simple that the reader-critic is again puzzled. Johnson claims that when he thinks of a story he accumulates it piecemeal fashion and does not write anything down until the whole has been thought out. Thinking and writing take about a year each. Unlike Grass, Johnson does not claim that his characters have a share in his personal self. He insists, "My characters are independent persons from myself."[13] Nevertheless, the reader will eventually be able to see Johnson's work as a great confessional statement of a man caught in ambiguities and consciously struggling to maintain an image of human decency.

Such a view of Johnson's work will be especially justified since his novels are until now a unified statement about the alternatives of East and West. In a sense, *Jahrestage* is a culmination of that vision in terms of geography, chronology, characterization, theme, and style. Gesine Cresspahl—the adoptive sister, friend, and beloved of Jakob in *Speculations*—lives in New York where she maintains contact with various other characters of Johnson's fictions. The ties between Europe and America remain intricate and are enhanced by technological communications so that Gesine's expanded world is also a global village. Further intricacies are developed through the interrelationships of the private self with public events in the past, present, and future. Gesine's chronicle records three types of events: the past, as she lived it, as it was told to her, and as she interprets it; the daily record of the *New York Times,* "the blind mirror of the day," which records the seemingly haphazard dull round of daily violence as history is on the run, eventually involving Gesine's private life through the Czechoslovakian experiment in democracy; the daily record of Gesine's life at the bank, her relationship with her daughter Marie, her friendship with D. E., her hopes for the future. All three chronicles interrelate and reveal to the reader a consciousness caught between past and future in the hairbreadth moment of the present.

As I am beginning my analysis of the German edition of *Jahrestage,* the fourth and final volume of the novel has not yet appeared, a frustrating and challenging problem for the critic who likes the tidiness of beginnings, middles, and ends. But the open-endedness adds a reality dimension; for the critic, like the character on whose consciousness she is focusing, has to grope towards an intimation of what the final vision might be. I am confronted with a blind spot that demands at least an intellectual leap of faith. But whatever the end of *Jahrestage* will be, it will not be unambiguous.

In my discussion of this multivolume novel, an anachronism in an age of instant information, I will first turn to the problem of point of view and its relation to psychological and historical consciousness. Secondly, I will examine those events in Gesine's past and present that make her consciousness a screen against painful memories and a protection for the tentative and hopeful projections she nurtures for the future. The point of view of *Jahrestage* is the essence of the novel's irony; for Gesine defines consciousness as rational awareness and reasoning ability, even though she has to admit that both are made ambiguous by the amorphous and connotative influences of unconscious association. As her consciousness evokes, reflects on, evaluates, judges, and chooses among the events of past and present, it is surrounded by the collective power of historical events and undermined from within by the cumulative power of private, often repressed, memories. Yet in spite of its fragility, her consciousness possesses that quality of a tragic excellence that our tradition admires: it separates and individuates itself, stands exposed in the world where it presumes and provokes its own defeat by the very forces it seeks to influence and control—personal memory and history.

II.

Point of View in *Jahrestage:* Psychological and Historical Consciousness

Gesine's rational goal for writing her chronicle is to become aware of repetition-compulsion and thereby control it. Also, she wants to help her daughter Marie understand the past and protect her from repeating it. This rational intent is undercut in many ways. The principle of repetition and repression is inherent in the process of recollecting and recording. Gesine selects and chooses; but she often remains unaware of the analogous moments between present and past of which the reader is aware. Furthermore, she seeks to justify herself to Marie so that Marie will have a loving and nonaccusatory memory of her mother, a memory Gesine does not have of her own mother. But Marie lives in New York in 1968, and what she hears "is a presentation of possibilities against which she feels herself immune, and in another sense it's just stories to her" (3. 7. p. 833). Marie's insecure presumptuousness actually prepares her to succumb to the pattern of repetition-compulsion.

Gesine often comes very close to probing the wound of primal pain that led to the construction of protective and abstract screens. She is in the grip of a guilty past whose dead voices communicate to her (11. 9. p. 278), and she exemplifies a psychological consciousness that is self-contained and leads, not to a substantial transformation, but only to displacements. Her Eden is the yearning for a secular, communal paradise; it is not an inner state of being. Her Apollonian surface, her cool and understated manner, is as deceptive to others as it is protective to her. She hides her pain, which emerges at times of physical tiredness: "In the fall of 1956 [when Jakob died] they treated me like a child, like a madwoman in Jerichow. As if I didn't understand their situation. Sometimes I am so tired that I speak as disorganized as I think. I don't think it is orderly the way I think. The place where I am from no longer exists" (11. 29. p. 386). Historical consciousness is preferable to psychological consciousness because it lends itself more readily to rational ordering and is less painful. Her dream of an adult and free community is the projection of the archaic need to return to the place of origin and shelter, a place that Gesine hardly ever approximated. The point of view of the chronicle is, therefore, in its technical and philosophical aspects an expression of the special problems of the narrator.

The reader senses that Gesine holds a deep interest for Johnson, almost as if she were a sister-self rather than a narrative voice. An egalitarian relationship exists between author and narrator which especially comes to the fore when Johnson appears in the novel as a lecturer at the American Jewish Congress. In trying to explain current German politics, Johnson fails as miserably as Gesine in her attempts to justify painful memories. Such memories are spoken in snatches by the victims: "My mother. Teresienstadt. My whole family. Treblinka. My children. Birkenau. My life. Auschwitz. My sister. Bergen-Belsen . . . ." (p. 256) In the back of the room, Gesine watches Johnson's floundering, and he challenges her: "By the way, who's narrating here, Gesine?" She replies, "Both of us. You can hear it, Johnson." In many difficult moments, she will ask the "comrade writer" *(Genosse Schriftsteller)* to lend her the appropriate words. When thus dramatized, Johnson is as helplessly authentic as Gesine; but, at the same time, the "author's second self," as Wayne Booth calls it in *The Rhetoric of Fiction,* is distant from the novel and fully in control.

The cooperation with the writer as character is one reason for the third person point of view which is maintained even when Gesine would be incapable of it, for instance, in the recollection of her mother's suicide and funeral when Gesine escapes into a severe attack of the flu. While the *I* can emerge at any moment, even in the middle of a sentence, *Jahrestage* is not written in the first person. The third person center of consciousness permits Gesine detachment and objectivity. As she writes about herself as an object, she avoids using the chronicle as a therapeutic outpouring of her private pathologies. But the objectification is also an alienation, an internal alienation between the adult that she is and "the child that I was." The adult views the child as a separate being, a very quiet child whose observant but prereflective consciousness "took in" the world, an attitude often maintained by the adult woman in an alien world. However, the adult woman also has to respond verbally to experience and create a world through words. In that alienating world, she sees herself taking the subway, entering the bank, and taking the elevator to her office, where she sits at her typewriter and creates an ironic distance between what she is and what she wants to be.

She believes she can live consciously by reading the *New York Times,* but this is an illusion. The reader does not participate in history; history is made for her or him through an underhanded game wherein one power undermines another. The *New York Times* participates in that game by dropping hints for its favorites, hints that remain undetected by the naive reader. Furthermore, Gesine chooses certain items from the *Times* for her chronicle because she wants to avoid more relevant items and because she knows that "quotations are reliable in a narrative" (10. 27. p. 229). Gesine admits her unreliability: "And I don't trust what I know because it has not always revealed itself in my memory; then, it suddenly appears as a notion. Perhaps memory creates some such sentence that Jakob said, or perhaps said, could have said. When that sentence is finished and present, memory builds the others around it, mixing even the voices of quite different people. I am afraid of that. All of a sudden I converse about a conversation in my thoughts which I did not participate in, and the only true thing in it is the remembrance of his intonation, the way Jakob talked" (11. 29. p. 387). Unreliability is also increased in that much of what she tells about the past is second hand. Marie often criticizes her mother with comments like "You can't know that," and she inquires why Gesine always presents the past from her father's and never from her mother's point of view, an inability to empathize that makes Gesine feel guilty and aggressive. Marie says, "You fill in the missing links and yet I believe you." Gesine admits, "I have never promised the truth" (2. 1. p. 670).

Just as Marie will be clued in by letters that are written to be read in the future, so the reader, too, will have to do much critical detective work in order to decipher the private and secretive Gesine. On occasion the reader is surprised that an eleven-year-old child should be interested in and understand the intricacies of provincial politics or the ambiguities in the marriage of her grandparents, especially since she is growing up in a fatherless home. At one point Marie assures her mother, "I often feel that I understand something" (3. 7. p. 833), a feeling that the reader, too, experiences at the more obscure parts of the novel. Gesine knows that Marie maintains her attention because she is truly a captive audience: "It is difficult for me to endure your stupefied and attentive face that you put on when you don't understand something. You nod, and one can see that you continually repeat in your thoughts what you have heard, as if it could be better comprehended that way. You consider that courtesy, but it is nothing more than the remains of your fear from the year 1960 when you realized that you could not exchange me for another parent . . . ." (2. 7. p. 688) Since Marie is neglecting her German, she will eventually understand little of her mother's chronicled communications, just as the novel will have to be heavily footnoted for future readers.

The narrator's language is a language that has been uprooted. Gesine's past is perceived through German, while her present is defined through English translated into German. Her sense of mission for a better future grows as her skill in a new language, Czechoslovakian, increases. As she reads and translates the language of the *New York Times* into German, she makes the news part of her self. Problems of translation, beyond the awkwardness of translating contemporary slang, become overwhelming, even more so if the novel should be translated into French or Italian; for then the effect of Gesine's often Anglicized German would be lost. The relationship of English and German locks the novel into its own peculiar linguistic universe. As Marie loses contact and feeling for her mother's language, she will not learn from her mother's chronicle but will, as Gesine foresees, fall into the same patterns of repetition-compulsion. The tragic sense of *Jahrestage* lies to a great extent in the inability of a historically and politically conscious self to really prevent anything with that consciousness.

Every public and private event that Gesine chooses to include in her chronicle receives a symbolic dimension, no matter how much it may first appear to have been selected at random. Words and syntax become the containers for progressive and regressive connotations agglutinated to images and events. Emphasis on the progressive connotations furthers a life-affirming, active shaping of the future by repressing the past; emphasis on regressive connotations leads to self-awareness through reflections over the pathology and guilt of the past. Awareness of the origins of pain and guilt causes anxiety and an inability to commit one's self in word or deed for fear of reenacting, as a displaced variable, the primal experience of fault. Gesine experiences existential nausea over the eternal repetitions in personal and political life, but she represses her insights and decides in spite of everything to "start something" that would further her dream of social community.

At one point, Gesine unintentionally defines her relation to history as process by using the mechanistic metaphors of winch and pawl. After reading the East German cliché "The wheel of history cannot be turned back," she comments sardonically, "History as a winch that wraps up the past, irrevocably towards eternity. Forward!" (5. 25. p. 1222) Progress depends on forgetfulness as one layer of rope covers the preceding one as the winch turns *(Seiltrommel)*, but the metaphor also signals, through the material (rope) and the motion of the winch, that history will always take the same pattern. Gesine complies with and resists that motion, as her explanation of the etymology of her name shows. For personal and political reasons Gesine rejects a Christian interpretation of her name and argues that the name is a combination of *cross* and *pall* (pawl): "Yes, the pawl in the cogwheel which prevents the backward slip of the winder, and, to be sure a rough, crude, coarse one . . . ." (6. 1. p. 1253) Gesine defines herself by means of a metaphor that resists the pressure of the past, but the metaphor also implies that if the wheel should slip back, be regressive, the pawl would move contrary to the wheel and not in conformity with it. Gesine's ideal concept of communism would consider East Germany's communism regressive.

Metaphorically, the pawl is aware that the forward movement has a built-in tendency to become regressive, and the crudeness of Gesine's pawl hints that it will prove insufficient to prevent such slippage. Finally, backward and forward movement retrace the same eternal round, the cycle that starts as the child tries to control the adult world through imitation. Thus, the child begins to destroy the potential for a life different from that of the parents who also perpetuate the schemes that imprison them, even when such schemes are devised to better the human condition: "How often will hope still build a foundation of nothing but rational building blocks and then define space with irrational walls in which disappointment will eventually find comfortable quarters. Why doesn't repetition make fireproof—children entertain themselves with repetition because they don't succeed in it completely. The new is not yet the same" (3. 25. p. 913). As the child grows it realizes that "the unconsciously engrooved norm saves [spart] time, but repetitions also eat away [spart] at consciousness until the latter starves." Such spiritual deprivation has physical origins, as in Gesine's mother withholding food from her child or the Russian occupation forcing starvation upon Jerichow. Abstract concepts like socialism, capitalism, and order are accepted by the child for "the sake of the father, to please him; out of fear of school and society which threaten with ostracism in case of disobedience" (p. 914). Nevertheless, the adult continues to build the house of dreams with nothing but rational foundations; herein lies the mistake, for the building blocks do not take into account the whole human being who will be confined behind walls of unreason, behind which he or she takes sullen refuge. Reason defines but neglects connotations which take revenge by pouring amorphously into the receptacles of reason.

The microcosm or microbe of a single word can cause this process. On 27 October, Gesine reads in the *New York Times* that Princeton University conducted an experiment in which nonsense syllables, word associations, and electric shocks established the relationship between memory and pain. Gesine begins to play her own game by asking Johnson to give her ten nonsense words, the first three being from the Wilhelm Busch series "Plisch und Plum," which contains a satire on Englishmen and Jews: "Plisch, Plum, Schmulchen, Schievelbeiner, Roosevelt, Churchill, bolschewistisch, Weltjudentum, Untermensch, Intelligenzbestie.

These words Gesine knew at the age of ten, but they were as unreal to her as DAX or CEF: 'The words came out of picture books, newspapers, adult slips of the tongue. They were toys'" (p. 321). Strange connotations began to attach themselves to these words: "Overnight the picture book [Wilhelm Busch] had been locked away. One talked with shyness and premonition about *the* Jew . . . . The words did not take root in the actual life of the town. They weren't words, just receptacles, resounding ones, for contents which did not belong to them, but which were intertwined and crawled as an undefined mass between the walls of the letters, expanding, agglutinating themselves, softly, wobbly, not graspable" (p. 231). The rigidity of words and their formless connotations become metaphors of evil as they are applied to living persons whose reality corresponds in no way with the symbolic suggestiveness of the word. Linguistic fantasies lead to holocaust and war. The electric shock, accompanied by a set of words such as *defamation of a minority, genocide,* or *victim,* is administrated by a photograph of Bergen-Belsen and formulates the realization of guilt in the adult Gesine: "I am the child of a father who knew about the systematic murder of the Jews" (p. 232). In New York, "the emigrant Cresspahl stepped furtively and quickly out of a luncheonette when she realized that the language of the owners was Yiddish" (p. 233). Nothing is forgotten; Busch's verses drift uninvited into her consciousness, and the word *Roosevelt* is always accompanied with the corrective that "he wasn't really the head of world Jewry." The shock is not constructive; it stimulates the desire for forgetfulness, for the winch that winds up history by explaining that concentration camps were a manifestation of the end of monopolistic capitalism.

Historical consciousness is always motivated by private desires and fears and hence is unreliable. Intellectually, Gesine is fully aware that the construction of systematic causality is an attempt to give meaning and assuage pain and guilt (9. 8. pp. 63–64). Yet, like her father, Gesine emigrates, and, like him, she will return as informed about conditions in the Eastern bloc countries as he was about Nazi Germany. Cresspahl sacrificed his political integrity for his love for Lisbeth, and the novel intimates that Gesine might sacrifice her daughter in some way to her political dream. No matter how conscious she may be of that pattern in retrospect, she cannot see it now. An outstanding example of her own unconsciousness and critical consciousness of others is her reaction to the memoirs of Svetlana Stalina, whose mother also committed suicide. She responds to the serialization in the *New York Times* by sarcastically accusing Svetlana of "having comprehended nothing about the twentieth century but her own private circumstances, an incurable daughter who, as ever a dependent child, wants to exonerate her father from the non-emotional definition of the history books'' (9. 11. p. 76). Gesine does not realize that she too apologizes for her father's political past because, unlike her mother, he was affectionate towards her. Furthermore, like Svetlana, Gesine is a refugee from authoritarian socialism; she, too, betrays. Finally, there emerges in the novel the impossibility of consciousness, in spite of all attempts to gather material, to explore the past, to define the nature of consciousness itself. Genuine consciousness would involve a coalescence of ambiguity on all levels and a simultaneous awareness of these levels, a feat desired but unachieveable by human intelligence and imagination.

III.
Anniversaries and Daily Round in the Cosmos of *Jahrestage*

The structure of *Jahrestage* has a surface rationality defined by the building blocks of each entry as it is ordered and fixed by the icon of a number. The linear effect of the numbered days of the year is an illusion of progression, for each day is or has the potential of becoming an anniversary that will always come round again. The content of the entries alternates between recollecting the past and recording the present, the majority of entries being triggered by news items from the *New York Times* which universalize the particular. The rhythm of the chronicle, as it relates time past and time present, generally pulsates between the chaos of hopeful or anxious connotations and epiphanic vignettes, whose precise images reverberate directly or analogously with Edenic and demonic connotations.

Those parts of the narrative that Gesine does not understand completely or represses partially are dominated by the chaos of connotations. The past of her parents, lived at a time when secrecy and subtlety were paramount to survival, has been garnered second hand or is recollected by an adult who tries to make sense out of the intimations experienced by herself as a child. Gesine's plans for the future, especially her plans "to start something" in Prague during August of 1968, are similarly imprecise. By not revealing them, she attempts to maintain their uncorrupted potential, whereas direct statement would raise questions as to ends and means within the confines of historical time. The chaos of connotation of the past is associated primarily with an evil time, a time that is to be overcome when a better future is created out of the chaos of present connotations. Herein she is repeating the desire of her father to do the same. Moreover, all present connotations are detours from Gesine's original fall, her experience of death and lack of love, which she ritualistically repeats or perceives in the daily round she seeks to transcend. Such transcendence will, of course, be impossible because she is bound in a secular cycle of time. Her fall was already the consequence of the guilt of her parents, and her hopes for the future are being corrupted by the guilty world of money, the bank, on which she depends for her livelihood. It saps her of life's energy, though she consciously resists the transient and material gratifications of capitalism. Gesine is inevitably manipulated and watched by powers that leave her bewildered even as she tries to manipulate them.

In my discussion of the cosmos of *Jahrestage,* I will first concentrate on Gesine's past and its metaphors of evil, as generated by the chaos of connotations and projected by the points of her memory. Secondly, I will turn to her present life in New York, a world of objective correlatives for loss and desire, guilt and redemption.

A. Origins of Deprivation and Guilt: The Past and Its Metaphors of Evil

Gesine Cresspahl is the only child of the cabinetmaker Heinrich Cresspahl (1888) and Lisbeth Papenbrock, the youngest daughter of Albrecht Papenbrock, the "king" of Jerichow who profited by exploiting the indebted landed aristocracy as well as the poor. Failure to love and betrayal on the personal and ideological levels are the sins of both parents. Their failures and the resulting sense of loss lead to reenactments in variable situations as well as to the desire to overcome the scene of deprivation. Cresspahl attempts this by always seeking to stake out a life that would allow him to live in harmony and without guilt; Lisbeth finally escapes her guilt through suicide.

The reliving of life-affirming or life-destroying experience is already evident in the repetitive use of names. Gesine is named after the first love of Cresspahl, his master's daughter, and Lisbeth is a variant of the independent Elizabeth Trowbridge who helped Cresspahl establish himself in Richmond and who bore, unknown to him, his son. Both will be killed by an air raid. A few hours before Lisbeth kills herself, she witnesses and reacts against a raid on a Jewish shopkeeper, whose daughter Marie is shot during the incident. It is implied that Lisbeth dies to atone for the death of Marie. Marie Cresspahl will, of course, be exposed to the turbulent political situation in Czechoslovakia in 1968. Private life and history continually cross each other, and in Gesine's memories of her childhood we can see how the child slowly becomes aware of the time and place that enclose its microcosm.

Cresspahl had planned to stay in England when he came to Germany in 1931 to settle his affairs. It was then that he saw Lisbeth, whose age, social status, and education were so disparate from his. With her he wanted to relive a young love; but after their marriage and after settling in Richmond, the attempt at an idyll fails. While Cresspahl feels at home, Lisbeth is homesick, blames Cresspahl for her unhappiness, and feels guilty because Christian love and the sacrament of marriage demand that she should forgive. In their mutual silence the couple become distant from each other (27. 9. p. 124). At the end of January, after Hitler has become chancellor, Lisbeth returns to Jerichow in an advanced stage of pregnancy, while Cresspahl manages to convince himself that she went with his approval (19. 10. pp. 193–94).

When Cresspahl comes to Jerichow on 2 March 1933 to be present at the birth, he arrives into the new Reich. The Nazis are everywhere, and their torchlight procession goes past Papenbrock's house on Gesine's birthday. Cresspahl tries to escape once more and returns to Richmond without asking Lisbeth to follow him: ''From the outside Cresspahl could watch for eight months how the Nazis set up their state'' (ll. 24. p. 348). He reads about the Enabling Act of 24 March which established the perfect dictatorship and ''removed the distress of people and Reich'' by October. Cresspahl's opinions about the Nazis were confirmed in every respect (p. 365). He even knows about the concentration camps. Gesine assumes that he had his advantages while living in England but became guilty nevertheless: ''It was just that Cresspahl wanted to let injustice slip past him in England in order not to become guilty. Wasn't that selfish? Could one leave one's country just to live in security?'' (11. 25. p. 365) Gesine's present poses similar problems, and she will eventually return close to her place of origin, though ostensibly for ideological rather than private reasons.

By the end of 1933, Cresspahl decides to stay in Jerichow. His New Year wishes concern his relationship with Lisbeth and the political life of Germany. He wants ''security for his family from economic need, political danger, fire and lightning. And, therefore, in the beginning of July 1934, he went to the town hall and had Friedrich Jansen give him an application form for the Nazi Party'' (12. 6. p. 418). He deludes himself that he is at home in Jerichow, but the community always suspects that he is a British spy, which he does become after he starts work on the military airport near Jerichow. Cresspahl and Gesine can rationalize his party membership as well as his income from the war effort since he is a spy. To Marie such treason is unjustifiable even when one disagrees with the policies of one's country (3. 2. p. 809); but Gesine, who knows that espionage is dull, assures her that "treason is boring, Marie" (3. 12. p. 862).

Because of her religion, to which Cresspahl and the Nazis object, Lisbeth, too, is subversive. Failing to obey the laws of family, state, and religion, she develops a scrupulous conscience. As Ricoeur defines it, "Scrupulousness is the advanced point of the experience of fault, the recapitulation, in the subtle and delicate conscience, of defilement, sin, and guilt; but it is at this advance-post that the whole of that experience is on the point of capsizing."[14] Her impasse through guilt leads to a denial of life. She finally commits suicide on 9 November during the pogroms of the infamous Kristallnacht. Gesine and her father are out of town as Lisbeth witnesses the anti-Semitic vandalism of Tannebaum's shop. No longer able to contain herself as a passive bystander, she slaps the mayor of Jerichow as he is humiliating the Jew. After Marie Tannebaum's death, she kills herself by setting fire to Cresspahl's workshop and tying herself up in the tool shed, where she suffocates from smoke inhalation. By trying to make it look like murder, she almost accrues another, posthumous guilt.

The record of Lisbeth's death and burial is given between 18–22 February 1968 while Gesine, suffering from the flu, talks irrationally in her fever, a clear example of repression through disease. The style, however, is clear and precise as usual, for Johnson takes over as narrator. Pastor Brüshaver goes against the law of religion by giving Lisbeth a Christian burial and against the law of the state by stating his reasons why Lisbeth killed herself:

> It was a matter between Lisbeth and her God that she expected more of Him than He was willing to give. She was free to die or to live, and even if it would have been better to have left death to Him, she offered herself for another life, self-murder for the murder of a child [Marie Tannebaum]. If that was an error, it would not be discovered in Jerichow.
>
> On the other hand, it was very much the concern of the inhabitants of Jerichow that Lisbeth Cresspahl had died. They were part of the life she could not bear. Now came the accounting which was the basis for judgment against Brüshaver. He began with Voss who was lashed to death in Rande, he did not forget the crippling of Methfessel in

the concentration camp nor the death of his own son in the war against the Spanish government, then he got to Wednesday night before Tannebaum's shop. Indifference. Passive acceptance. Greed. Betrayal. Also, the egotism of a pastor who only saw the persecution of his own church, who remained silent contrary to his mission, while under his eyes a member of the community was able to seek her own inevitable, graceless death. Where all refused to accept God's perpetual offer for new life, one human being alone could no longer trust in it. [2. 21. pp. 760–61]

A few hours after his sermon, Brüshaver is arrested and sent to a concentration camp. He is unaware that Lisbeth had neglected her own child.

Gesine interprets her mother's suicide as the final gesture of depriving Gesine of love. As a small child, Gesine did not talk much, "but she had her eyes wide open" (12. 19. p. 475). To be deprived of love leads to the deduction that one is unlovable, and since there must be a reason for this lack of quality, one must somehow be at fault. The small Gesine experienced a fall in her state of prereflective consciousness, a fall that the adult tries to avoid recalling; when she has to recall, because of Marie's insistence, she concentrates on the imagery associated with the fall while rationalizing its possible meaning. The fall occurred during the rain barrel or "water butt" incident in 1937 when Gesine, wanting to play with the old cat lying inside the kitchen window, climbed up the rain barrel and fell head first into it. Lisbeth watched passively while Cresspahl pulled out his daughter just in time, gave her a memorable spanking, and no longer entrusted her into Lisbeth's care (1. 19. p. 615). Gesine begins her account by emphasizing "the fat, long grasses, juicy flowering weeds" surrounding a barrel filled with "the purest water in nature." Throughout the novel, the regenerative powers of water are secondary to their oneiric attraction wherein consciousness and thought are dissolved.

Her next diversionary tactic is the cat in the window: "The child often stood outside, head bent back, looked up to the cat and talked with her, and the cat looked at me, as if she knew a secret and yet would not tell it to me" (p. 617). The point of view shifts from third to first person in a single sentence as the narrator sees herself as object in the past, a past image still relevant to her present "I." Cats are an important leitmotif in *Jahrestage*. They are associated with memory, with the unknown future, with repression and personal secrecy, with death as well as with sudden moments of consciousness when "the cat is let out of the bag." The old cat of her

childhood was a real animal, but she also becomes the Cheshire cat of the
adult Gesine's uneasy dreams. Marie, however, insists that Gesine come
to the point, and Gesine manages to rationalize her mother's passivity and
thus make the memory livable, although Marie actually says the crucial
words:

—She wanted to kill you!
—She wanted to give me away, Marie.
—She must have hated you.
—It wouldn't have taken long. The drowning.
—But she wanted to be rid of you!
—"He who loves his child," Marie, he . . . . She would have known
that the child was secure, far from guilt and becoming guilty. And of
all of them, she would have made the greatest sacrifice.
—You want to say she loved you.
—That I want to say. [1. 20. pp. 618–19]

Gesine becomes her "father's daughter," especially after Cresspahl
discovers that the child is starved by Lisbeth and forced to take little "cat-
like" bites from the lunch bread of the apprentices (2. 8. p. 693).

The experience of deprivation combined with the longing for home is
so traumatic that the child cannot be happy, even when she is with her
mother's sister's family, the Paepckes. The summers with the Paepckes
and the Schlegelhof experience after the war are the two pastoral settings
of her childhood memories. Love and food abound: "Great picnic bas-
kets full with bread and cake and hard boiled eggs and milk and fruit were
carried with us when we went swimming in the Oder. At Paepcke's the
children got continually something to eat . . . . At Paepcke's a child
would sit drawing or cutting material, and Hilde never passed by without
praising the work, not by flattering, but with questions. At Paepcke's the
children learned who they were" (3. 8. p. 840). This free community of
love was possible during the war. But the Paepckes were not escapists;
they were "informed hearts" continually conscious of the pressures of
the outside world, pressures that might be exerted from Nazi neighbors
whose children celebrated Germanic Easter festivals. Alexander and
Hilde are aware of the illusion they have created, and Alexander advises
Gesine to keep in mind that "there is nothing that cannot, in a certain
artistic light, appear charming for the moment, and even right. But it's all
illusion—remember that, Gesine" (p. 839). She will remember and apply
the warning to any idyllic moment in her present; she can afford to do this
because her true Eden is a projection to be realized somewhere in the
future.

During her experience on the cooperative farm called Schlegelhof, she cannot afford to heed the warning. On the surface, the Schlegelhof seems no illusion; it does not pretend to be an Eden but is a temporarily healing world where love has been replaced by kind authority which distributes labor fairly and constructively. Here is a rational community where plenty of food is provided; yet that food is garnered painfully as the stubbles cut into the feet of Gesine and her friend Hanna. Their friendship, too, is ambiguous, for both girls have transferred love from familial feelings to secretly nurtured erotic yearnings for the indifferent Jakob. It is summer 1946, a time when the Russians deprive Jerichow of food and incarcerate Cresspahl in the concentration camp Fünfeichen. As an adolescent, Gesine cannot reflect upon either deprivation, and as an adult she still rationalizes the conduct of the Soviet occupation forces. For to see it for what it was would mean to admit the corruption of the socialist dream in historical time.

Thus, Gesine insists that, in spite of everything, she felt gratitude as a child towards the Commandant K. A. Pontij, for ''he had taken away the corpses'' which the British forced the population of Jerichow to accept (5. 5. p. 1111). The British insisted on the pathology and fault of the German past; the Russians repressed the knowledge of past fault but perpetuated the causes of fault in the present. The Jerichowers had to accept as theirs corpses which had been inmates of Neuengamme who had been evacuated onto ships that were then bombarded by the British. Hundreds of corpses floated along the shores and drifted up onto the beaches. The British forced the local population to gather the dead, load them on trucks, and drive them through the towns: ''It wasn't easy to recognize the freight for what it was. It was damaged by gun shot wounds, burns shrinkage, bomb splinters, beatings. It could be recognized by the discolored, tattered, twisted apparel of striped cloth. Human pieces were often incomplete. Parts were missing, or torsoless parts were lying on the truck's platform; one time nothing more than a piece from a head. Too many fish had eaten away at it. The British gathered the people of Jerichow in the market square. In the middle lay the first load of the dead. The Commandant gave the Germans their dead. He made them their own . . . those who would not accept the dead, would not eat'' (5. 5. pp. 1114–15). Gesine, who was even more affected by a picture of Bergen-Belsen, concludes, ''We ate fish from the Baltic Sea. Until today, the Germans eat fish from the Baltic Sea. Almost ten thousand prisoners are still at the bottom of the sea'' (p. 1116). The childhood experience of death by water which would have obliterated conscious-

ness of a loveless world has now been transferred to a historical event of
such fault that the generative powers of water and fish become in the
narrator's verbal construct the incorporation, the eating of the knowledge
of fault and death.

Gesine specifically implies that the Germans unconsciously incorporate that knowledge. Detached, she "watches them" eat the fish that fed
on the dead as she herself continues to rationalize the suffering of the
father who once saved her from death by water. As an adolescent, she
could not afford to imagine his fate: "Where he was remained a secret.
As if he were dead" (5. 6. p. 1254). Since his suffering implicates her
utopian dreams, she rationalizes it as a bureaucratic mistake. Cresspahl
himself never learned the true reasons for his imprisonment. As always,
he attempted to stake out a new life on rational foundations; and as he was
just about to succeed, Pontij responded with nonrational motivations that
landed Cresspahl in the excremental world of Fünfeichen, largely run by
German *kapos* who demonstrated their efficiency to the Russians. Here,
Cresspahl entertained the Russians with goose-stepping and shouting: "I
am an old Nazi pig and want to carry shit." After an escape attempt in
1947, he is mercilessly beaten and resigns himself as an old-timer:
"Fünfeichen had become the world. Outside life did not enter . . . . One
could plan death, voluntarily through hunger, voluntarily on the fence.
Fünfeichen offered lots of ontologies. To be sure, Cresspahl would have
preferred trial and judgment" (6. 4. pp. 1297–98).

At the end of the third volume, Gesine's recollections of the past hover
between hope and anxiety. For Cresspahl the future holds possibilities of
death or freedom; for Gesine it holds the loss or gift of Jakob's love. Time
will eventually fulfill all possibilities. The memories of idyll and trauma
in the summer of 1946 as well as in the deeper past have become
condensed points, anniversaries whose reverberations influence the
seemingly shapeless flux of the day to day present. Here, dream and
nightmare are dispersed into the light of common day or coalesce momentarily into fleeting epiphanic images. For this reason, Gesine's
chronicle of the present seems more fragmented than that of the past. Her
collage of letters, notes, telephone calls, and tape recordings captures the
drift of her life in New York. But by 19 June 1968, Gesine's life has
propelled itself from the harmless 20 August 1967 to the catastrophic 20
August 1968. Among the many news items she reads, one anchors itself
so firmly in her consciousness that she decides to become a participant in
and not merely a reader about history. The catch is that, as a reader of the
New York Times, "the consciousness of the day" (9. 9. p. 68), Gesine

can live consciously (10. 22. p. 210) through reflection; but when her desire for the redeemed life in historical time urges her to leave her apartment and her office in the bank, she becomes a blind participant in historical time.

B. Gesine's Present: Objective Correlatives of Guilt and the Desire for Redemption

The news item that generates the plot of Gesine's present is casually summarized in the second entry of her chronicle: ''The corpse of the American, who did not return to his hotel in Prague last Wednesday evening, was found in the Vltava. Mr. Jordan, 59, was a co-worker of the Jewish auxiliary JOINT. He had left to buy a newspaper.'' An item among many, this news clip becomes iconic for Gesine, for the Dubcek experiment in socialism and democracy, and for the novel as a whole. The death of the murdered Jew in Prague raises anxieties and hopes, anxieties because of possibly renewed anti-Semitic aggression, and hope because a supposedly closed society publicizes this murder. Much later, after Gesine has begun to subversively work towards her dream, she expresses her tentative hopes in a letter that Marie is to read in 1976: ''Dorogaja Maria, it could be a beginning. I could freely work for it. I sit here alone at the table with your picture cut-outs from the *Times,* alone with the lamp and the breath of your sleep which is louder than my pen, and alone with a silly trust in this year. I wrote this to you so that you may understand, late enough, what I will perhaps begin this year, at the age of 35, oh dear, for the last time. So that you won't have to guess as I had to'' (2. 7. p. 690). The murdered Jew becomes for her a symbol of hope. Yet her dream remains undefined—''what I will perhaps begin this year''— for an unfinished dream retains possibilities: ''As long as I don't think it through, it doesn't exist'' (10. 22. p. 210). She also posits no program in order to avoid laying the rational foundations upon which the irrational, connotative, and imprisoning walls would be erected. Her only preparation is the study of Czechoslovakian, the language of the future, for a new language always appears at first uncorrupted by time.

But even without the rigidity of reason, Gesine cannot avoid the chaos of connotations. She unconsciously prepares for the catastrophic realization of her dream by casually provoking the attention of those powers that have an interest in her allegiance. She is watched with interest by the Eastern bloc and by the bank, two powers that appear only superficially irreconcilable. Both are founded on economic concepts, both are international, and both lure the human being with the dream of security and freedom while all the while depriving him or her of life-giving energies. Both powers are always present and envelop Gesine's existence, but she establishes her inciting and conscious contact with them by means of two letters. The first she writes herself to East Germany; the second she translates for the vice president of the bank, de Rosny.

During her holiday on the New Jersey coast, she realizes that blacks would be unwelcome at the resort, and this realization stimulates her memory and prompts her to write to East Germany: "As a former citizen of Jerichow and as a once regular visitor to Rande, I am politely asking you to inform me about how many summer guests of Jewish faith were in Rande in the year 1933" (8. 20. p. 8). The veiled, anti-Semitic and propaganda-laden reply informs her that she is still a citizen of the German Democratic Republic and that, in spite of her defection, she has the duty not to harm the state (11. 28. pp. 382–85). The power of the bank distinguishes itself through elusive indirection and enlists allegiance, not by threats, but by the incentive rewards of personal interest and promotion. After meeting de Rosny for the first time on 12 September, she translates a letter for him in the intimacy of his Waldorf Astoria suite, "a letter from Prague, in Polish French, about night spots, sixteen milli-meter films, a girl named Maria Sofia, about state credit based on dollars"; the latter and most important item is lost in trivia that appears as if "it was fun. It was odd. It was overtime without pay" (9. 13. pp. 84–85). From the beginning of her fateful year, both powers watch her keenly as she gets inevitably involved in subterfuge and betrayal. As she speeds towards the destruction of her dream, the imagery of the novel darkens. While the first two volumes had concluded with affectionate references to Marie and Jakob, the third volume closes with ominous foreboding: "In the evening a thunderstorm hangs over the river. The lightning makes silhouettes of the park, sometimes it brightens the other shore with chequered white. A few, very short flashes, hardly percep-tible, etch sharp cracks into the brain. As children, sitting under a grain rick in a thunderstorm, we thought: somebody sees us. We are all observed."

The power that watches over this world of loveless and dull violence is the collective interest of human power and not a transcendent being. At one point Gesine defines her idea of God by bursting out, "The God, who invented the atom bomb, also shoots the sparrows off the roof" (2. 24. p. 775). This inversion of the loving father, who cares for the fall of the sparrow, turns all longing for an oneiric home into illusion. The illusion persists also because Gesine is afraid to commit herself to a personal love, for that has always led to deprivation. She indulges in daydreams of home, especially in her apartment on Riverside Drive; but it, too, reminds her of the precariousness of all idylls: "In winter one can see through the bare branches of the Palisades of New Jersey, and the breadth of the river, the hazy air does soften the architectural wasteland on the other side into a mirage of an unspoilt landscape, into intimations of openness and distance" (8. 26. p. 28). European handcrafted furniture fills her apartment where she secludes herself on Sundays to read about the violent world outside, but she unconsciously recollects her uncle's admonition, "It is a deception and feels like home" (10. 1. p. 134). In the park below, patrol cars stop and dark-skinned women care for the children of their "pink-skinned" employers. Beneath, connecting the ironic idyll with the larger world, flows the Hudson: "We have the river. Beneath the open sky, the river rolls toward the nearby sea and offers slowly moving boats, fog horns at night, and green, grey, blue colors mixing with those of the park—vacation prospects. But the river is so poisoned by industry that people are not permitted to bathe in it. The river gathers the light of the sky and the dirt which colors the sunsets dangerously. The smell of the river follows us to Riverside Drive" (5. 19. pp. 1190–91).

While her futuristic daylight dreams are life-affirming, death, the ultimate deprivation, motivates her longings. Death is the core of deprivation within her and defines the periphery of her daylight consciousness. There are the assassinations of Martin Luther King and Robert F. Kennedy, the Vietnam War and the familial murders of the Mafia, and the daily toll of individual acts of violence recorded by the *New York Times*. Death is also analogically displaced in the image of the slum, a wandering "jelly fish in society" that pours itself chaotically into houses that were once respectable. Applying to herself the language of the society page, Gesine records, "Mrs. Cresspahl and her daughter went slumming this afternoon, and children were in the streets in our slum areas. Among them those who had to use the street to relieve themselves" (3. 9. p. 847). Again, it is childhood where deprivation is felt most. Yet while the excremental environment of the slum can be repressed by consciousness, there is a small, hard creature which becomes a metaphor of evil to reason and light: it is the ubiquitous cockroach which resists all efforts of hygienic liquidation (3. 5. pp. 822–27).

This little impurity appears in the most unlikely places and destroys reason's tidy definition of the world. Small but innumerable, it provokes phobia because it is a demonic reflection of ourselves. The cockroach is the "odious vermin" that nature suffers to crawl upon the surface of the earth, a ubiquitous emblem of human stain and guilt. Very old insects, cockroaches "can comprehend, they are intelligent, they can learn. It is not quite clear why they live their five months, since their sole purpose is to give themselves to the future, but they are here. They live with poor and rich . . . it is possible that they will be on the moon before man. They are a cunning crowd" (p. 826). The connotations of this discourse create montage effects in the reader's perception. The cockroach mocks attempts at surface purity and cleanliness as it suddenly emerges and then quickly disappears into cracks one did not know existed in one's kitchen floor. The insect is internationally classified into the American, the oriental, and, most frequently, the German cockroach. Gesine finally gets used to the shame of it and can conspire with the women in the park about the latest sprays; for, most of all, one desires the death of this useless creature, gets used to killing it, and invents ingenious ways of doing so. Gesine, usually so conscious of words and their connotations, remains unaware of how similar her verbal aggressiveness is to that employed by the Nazis against the Jews. Marie, who at first pitied the insects, reacts when reminded with intensity of her former emotion and "hits all the harder and goes after the beasts with the spray can, cursing without being contradicted." If the slum is the wandering chaos, slowly crawling through the city, the cockroach is an image of evil that, like a word or fragment of memory, suddenly and persistently appears uncalled for to the consciousness as a reminder of the fallen world.

One can read about the chaos of violence, one can visit the chaotic world of the slum, and one can liquidate the rigidly persistent cockroach or chase it back into the cracks in the floor. But it is harder to cope with the powers of which the smaller violences are symbolic: the rigidity of East German righteousness and the amorphous power of the world of money. In civilized form, the god of this world does not project itself as atom bomb inventor or sparrow shooter, not even as filthy lucre, but rather as credit extender. For four years Gesine has worked in the cunningly made world of de Rosny's bank, a world that seems separate from her political dream. Yet both she and her dream are dependent on the abstraction of money. The bank is the world of clocked time, of work and money, and most important, of power. It provides life by giving the means for living in a material world, but it also is the cause of debt and guilt. By working for what is the archetype of the capitalistic system, Gesine joins an ambiguous community and must necessarily betray whatever utopian visions she may have as she is successful in dealing with time and money. To the individual as well as to nations, the bank extends credit but expects its due. In *Jahrestage* the bank world has its own cosmology, which is only partially understood by Gesine who, while promoted close to the top, is not at the top and thus cannot comprehend the machinations of the essence in the inner sanctum of finance. The rational world of money serves and is served by the *homo economicus,* both of which are a negation of the sacred. As Norman O. Brown writes, "The money complex is the demonic; and the demonic is God's ape; the money complex is therefore the heir to and the substitute for the religious complex, and an attempt to find God in things."[15] It comes as no surprise that there are many religious metaphors associated with de Rosny's bank.

The trickster de Rosny is not a god in the bank world but a mediator, the beloved son of god. The bank president as god remains unseen as a *deus absconditus,* and only his voice is heard over the loudspeaker of the cafeteria in the basement of the bank. When he chooses to manifest himself in order to observe Gesine, he does so inconspicuously at the end of the second volume when de Rosny asks Gesine and Marie to go with him to a baseball game at Shea Stadium. This is only the pretext, for Arthur, the black chauffeur, is sent "during the game to get a god named Rutherford from the Regency Hotel and bring him to a conference in the stadium." Until he arrives, de Rosny displays childish delight in the game as he explains it to Marie. "Then comes Arthur with the god Rutherford, a white haired upright old man who does not even glance at the playfield, a golfer" (p. 1007). The name Rutherford has been carefully chosen by Johnson. Gesine defined God as the one "who invented the atom bomb [and] shoots also the sparrows off the roof." The physicist Ernest Rutherford not only discovered the atomic nucleus but also knocked a nucleus of hydrogen, a proton, out of the nucleus of nitrogen, starting a chain of events which led, among other things, to man's release of atomic energy. The name Rutherford, then, belongs to that team which can be defined as a first cause, the human cause of man's power over life and death. Like the banker, the physicist with his mysterious formulas can play at being a powerful god. As Gesine serves the world of money, so D. E., the man who loves her, serves the world of science, both, of course, being wedded in an inextricable knot of compromise and guilt in historical time.

Shea Stadium, where Gesine is surveyed as a prospective initiate, is a displacement of the mystic rose of Dante's blessed saints. Airplanes fly overhead with messages from the sponsors of the world of getting and spending like the angels that ministered to the saints "like a swarm of

bees,'' flying "ceaselessly to the many-petaled rose/and ceaselessly
returned into that light/in which their ceaseless love has its repose
(*Paradiso* XXXI, 7–12). At Shea Stadium, the urban blessed insist that
they "demonstrate festive excitement, yell, and toot. Fifty-thousand
want that there be joy.'' Here, de Rosny has an especially designated
place in the bowl, his throne; when he sits in it, "the man of the world is
transformed into a little boy,'' into a parody of the "Lest ye become as
little children ye cannot enter the kingdom of heaven.'' De Rosny can
even select who shall be saved. He has plans for Willy Mays with whom
he has never spoken but for whom he will reserve a place in the money
cosmos: "When he can no longer play—He'll get a post at our branch
office in San Francisco'' (4. 18. pp. 1003–7).

As the beloved son of this world, de Rosny did not have to work for his
money: "His parents had given it to him, to him only, and he had
breathed through money's nourishing protective shell since he knew his
first name'' (4. 25. p. 1051). This name no one knows since de Rosny
does not want to be defined or touched personally; he would, as Gesine
points out, have his suit chemically cleaned if someone slapped him on
the back. Money provides him with a womb-like security so well projected by his limousine, which "is a shell for a private first class
compartment, a cabin upholstered all around with four seats, telephone,
reading light, writing board. This cabin is separated from the outside
world by a darkly tinted glass'' (9. 12. p. 79). Seeing through a glass
darkly, he is kept out of touch with the real grime of New York. Trickster
that he is, he is a helpful guide, a dangerous imp, and a builder of
civilization. Intentionally charming and boyish, he comes from the West,
the manifest destiny of the United States. While he builds his bank, he
does not want to be its president, for such a role would confine him too
rigidly. He prefers to fly from country to country in a multiplicity of roles
that personify the ability of money to multiply itself. Change and impermanence are attractive rather than troubling to him. For like the god
who is self-contained and yet expands himself into his creation, so the
beloved son of money is in his protective shell; and yet he spends himself
into the world. What he creates is, of course, artificial and reflects him in
its impermanence (4. 25. p. 1056).

Gesine, his fellow albeit less powerful trickster, has moved upward in
the many-storied bank, a vertical and material aspiration of this world.
Although her secret self rejoices over small violations of decorum and
routine, her days at the bank are abstract and meaningless, without
personality (p. 61). Only her dream keeps her involved with this kind of

world, for she has developed that characteristic split of the alienated person. Beginning with her mechanical smile in the morning, which she "polishes to extravagance," to her behavior during a stockholder's meeting, she moves through her day with ironic distance. Neither does she participate in the consumer society that furthers the ends of the bank. Shopping sprees and television are no temptations for her. She watches the world askance, unable to share with it the dream she holds dear. Her political secret isolates her from everybody and eventually indicts her because she must inevitably betray people who are on the whole decent human beings. There is no "moral Switzerland" to which she can emigrate.

"Guilt is never to be doubted."

The principle that shapes the form and content of *Jahrestage* is the principle of repetition-compulsion with all its comforts and discomforts, its security and nightmare. Time in this novel is, therefore, circular rather than linear; the days do not drop off into nothingness as from a digital clock but recur on the face of the annual clock from 20 August 1967 to 20 August 1968. The numbered dates are iconic, recurring with predictable rationality even though the content of each day will vary. But the dates always bring back the day of her mother's death; the summer of 1945 under Russian occupation will lead to the summer of 1968 when Czechoslovakia will be invaded by the nations of the Warsaw Pact. Gesine, the pawl in the cogwheel of history, is very conscious of the tenacious conservatism in human life and its history; but she counters that conservatism with her dream of community and freedom, of social concern for others combined with the need for personal authenticity. If it could be realized, it would truly be a progressive dream through which the repetition-compulsion towards the nightmare of history could be abolished. Gesine's dream is that of an adult who remembers the pain of childhood, for the dream combines the nurturing and protective environment so necessary for a child with the pleasure felt by the adult over his or her individuated consciousness.

To fulfill her dream, Gesine does not join a socialist group in New York but plans to return to a country close to her point of origin, a country beginning to struggle towards the dream. Her desire is, therefore, archaic. She must go back where all the repetitive compulsion began. Freud defined this archaic goal as death, the desire to return to the material: "Those instincts are therefore bound to give a deceptive appearance of being forces tending towards change and progress, whilst in fact they are merely seeking to reach an ancient goal by paths alike old and new . . . the instinct to return to the inanimate state.''[16] It is the moment of unconsciousness that Gesine loves when she dives with a "curious header" into the pool. But death cannot be a conscious goal; it has to be displaced into some rational and desirable goal because, as Freud also pointed out, we are secretly convinced of our immortality as long as we are conscious.

Although the fourth volume has not yet appeared as I write these concluding remarks, I am obviously not risking much when I say that Gesine will not fulfill her dream. Aside from historical hindsight, the work would not permit such a fulfillment. Gesine claims to have made consciousness a way of life, and yet she remains as unconscious as any of us. What she does not want to admit to herself is that her mother did not love her, that she watched her fall into the rain barrel as if Gesine were a female Isaac to her god, and that she was not joyful when a kinder father rescued her. History continued to repeat the pain of deprivation; it imprisoned her father and killed Jakob, the only man she loved. As a result of such repetition she developed a fear of love. She writes to Marie, "When I get involved with a human being his death would pain me again. Therefore, I cannot get involved with somebody." Checking herself, she adds, "This does not include a child named Marie Cresspahl." This fear of commitment to human love is one reason for her repeated rejection of D. E.'s proposals; however, she talks to him again about marriage when she returns from Europe. D. E. would make an excellent father for Marie, and he, sensing that she may fear losing the child to him, promises that Marie will always be hers. Yet her relation to Marie is tensed with the fear of developing too strong an attachment, a cathexis, and for this reason she pretends that their relation is more like a friendship than like a mother-daughter relation. As she keeps on the surface of this middle ground of compromise, she controls the fear of separation. But she also cannot get involved in life; she cannot make the commitment until August 1968 when she will attempt to reconcile her divided self.

The memory of her childhood pain hurts so much that she can recount the events of that time but not the feelings that accompanied them. These cannot be raised into the consciousness of speech, and thus, suffering remains unrelieved. She will reenact the past in the present, and in search for a never possessed reality she will take Marie to Prague and create the possibility of sacrificing her daughter to her beliefs in a manner different from and yet similar to Lisbeth's desire to sacrifice the child Gesine. She will become guilty either towards her child or towards her dream. In spite of her stated political motives, Gesine is blind to her true motives—her need for love which can never be fulfilled because human beings are subject to death. She projects, therefore, this need in terms of the apparently rational secular paradise, forgetting that earthly Edens are in history and time and thereby subject to those who do not desire freedom and community but, rather, sheer power. As Gesine and her future move relentlessly towards each other, the reader knows what will happen historically, but Gesine's fate remains in suspension. She may die; she may commit suicide like her mother or be imprisoned like her father. She may lose Marie in the summer of 1968. She may decide to escape into definite commitment and work either for socialism as it is or for the bank, but such choices would be a betrayal of her character. She could also betray her dream by withdrawing from all public involvement and accept D. E.'s offer of marriage. In that case *Jahrestage* would be an ironic comedy.

The ultimate irony and pessimism of this novel are finally centered in the realization that Gesine's consciousness can be nothing but illusory and that she betrays herself by believing in it. Unable to reexperience her primal pain and overcome it, she is doomed to recapitulate it in ritualistic acts that perpetuate her guilt. In all this she is so thoroughly human. She is a reflector for us even as we look at her from the elevated position of readers. In her first reference to the *New York Times,* she objectively records a report about a murdered Jew in Prague, and on this objective, hence "rational" event she founds her hope for the future. The murdered Jew will not be redeemed in time as Gesine hopes, and she herself, through the law of repetition-compulsion of which she is rationally aware, will become, in one way or another, a victim to her desire for redemption.

Part Three

Confronting and Turning Away from
the Audience: Documentary Theater and
Lyric Poetry

6

Rituals of Judgment: Hochhuth's *The Deputy* and Weiss's *The Investigation*

For ye shall hear how our Heaven King
Calleth Everyman to his reckoning.
Give audience and hear what he doth say.
  Anonymous, *Everyman*

. . . the play's the thing
Wherein I'll catch the conscience of the king.
  Shakespeare, *Hamlet*

At the core of Rolf Hochhuth's *The Deputy* and Peter Weiss's *The Investigation* lies the desire that the iniquity of the unspeakable situation should find its nemesis in an epiphany of the law. Twentieth century atrocities, however, have undermined the surface comfort of the law court ritual and have revealed its inherent ironies. The possibility of reforming or exorcizing the criminal has become remote. Moreover, the reflective consciousness is aware that the radical evil of the delinquent may well serve to repress the scrupulous, if not guilty, conscience of the judge and the polis. The hope for an epiphany of law and justice, the final cause of a trial, has faded and been largely replaced by the therapeutic process of the trial as a demonstration or show aiming to raise the consciousness and conscience of the world rather than of the criminal.

The idea of the trial as therapeutic and didactic show has been discussed by Hannah Arendt and Yosal Rogat in their analyses of the Eichmann trial, a case where criminal guilt was self-evident. Rogat writes, "The trial was aimed at reminding the world of what was done to the Jews. We were all to be put on guard against any kind of re-enactment . . . . But Israel was not simply anxious to affect the consciousness of the age by forcing the world to think about the relevant events; it cared about *how* it affected it, about *what* it taught.''[1] In reading the accounts of the Eichmann trial (1961) or the Frankfurt Auschwitz trials (1964–65), we are struck by how little the criminal becomes aware of guilt; instead, the judicial process is the trial of recollecting suffering as the witness has the day in court. Thus, a trial has largely become a show, but the archetypal pattern of drama, both in tragedy and comedy, also evolves from a problem of law and the ritual of the trial, be it experiential or judicial.

Theatrical trappings provide rehearsal, scenario, and disguise for crime in historical reality, but in the case of the concentration camps that reality was of such magnitude that a theatrical imitation is a mere metaphor of evil and not a heightening of it. This puts any such drama, and specifically documentary drama, into the ironic mode. However, documentary drama about the Second World War, no matter how it is overwhelmed by the facts of document and reportage, is also a parody of two earlier, ''life-affirming'' forms of documentary drama, namely, the political theater of Erwin Piscator in the 1920s and early 1930s, and, even more profoundly, the mystery and morality play of the Middle Ages. This parody is crucial, for while it negates it also projects by contrast, however tentatively, the secret yearning for a transcendent judge who contains all anguish and makes justice possible, and for a utopian polis where the ritual of judgment is unnecessary because the mystery of iniquity has been exorcized. Because the parody of optimistic documentary drama is so formative for the metaphors of evil in Hochhuth's *The Deputy* and Weiss's *The Investigation,* I will first briefly review that tradition and its displacement into irony before turning to the plays themselves.

I.
Documentary Drama: Its Modern and Contemporary Origins and Its Medieval Roots

Erwin Piscator, the communist director of the Volksbühne in Berlin and exile during the Nazi period, optimistically welcomed Hochhuth's *The Deputy* as a means to change the history of humankind through consciousness rather than through force. In spite of the ironies and ambiguities permeating *The Deputy* and *The Investigation,* Piscator staged both plays as a forum for his vision. In the pre-Nazi era that vision consisted of three steps that would hopefully lead to revolutionary action:

Kenntnis (knowledge), *Erkenntnis* (insight and recognition), *Bekenntnis* (the pledging of one's self towards a political program and action).[2] By using all technical means available to him at the time and by forging his actors into a collective, Piscator made the theatrical event into a communal event. A successful evening at his Volksbühne would have to include an audience willing to pledge itself to political action, willing to become part of the thousands that filled the theater and saw their "own fate in this great demonstration."[3]

Today, such enthusiasm seems pathetic and ironic, for we cannot fail to recall that at the same time another group staged its own theatrics, its *Versammlungen* and *Kundgebungen,* its demonstrations and mass meetings. In the postwar era, the third step in Piscator's stages of political consciousness is less a *Bekenntnis* in the sense of a commitment to an ideology than it is a *Bekenntnis* in the sense of *bekennen* (confessing). Lost, too, is the romance that goes along with a political faith that envisions itself unfurling the flag on the barricades; the two playwrights to be discussed will emphasize instead the mediocrity of the makers of history and the smallness of the rooms in which the destiny of peoples is decided. As a communist, Piscator saw himself as part of a community in which the Russian revolution was still an affirmative process. But what about a Marxist playwright like Peter Weiss who knows about the corruptibility of communism in history? He also expresses a faith, at least in theory, while in practice a play such as *The Investigation* is, in spite of certain political aims, an interpenetration of ironies.

Weiss's "Notes towards a Documentary Theater" are observations aiming at a definition of a model for that kind of theater. Weiss uses no specific examples for his theories, for such examples would immediately give rise to questions. His "Notes" are divided into three basic topics: documentary material, its artistic interpretation, and its polemical aim. Documentary material does not imply a mimesis of life; instead, it is the information the playwright has gathered about life through reports, statistics, governmental decrees, newspapers, and media reports. This plurality of sources is then ordered by the dramatist: "Documentary theater refuses to invent, it takes authentic material and projects it from the stage, unchanged in content, but integrated in form."[4] This has two results for the creative process and its end: the playwright does not have to use depth psychology to motivate his characters, and he can write about places, persons, and conditions with which he is by no means familiar. Summarizing the virtues of this kind of theater, Weiss comments in his "Notes": "The strength of documentary theater lies in its ability to forge from the fragments of reality an applicable pattern, a model of actual events . . . . Through the technique of editing, precise particularities are lifted from the chaotic matter of external reality. By confronting contrasting details, it draws attention to an existing conflict for which it offers, by collecting evidence, a possible solution, an appeal, a question.'' On the one hand Weiss insists that a documentary drama has an authentic artistic pattern; on the other hand he feels that playwright, play, actors, and directors should be in a state of continual and organic revolution, which can, however, only happen if all share a common faith. While documentary drama relies on a "rich archive of facts [and] is able to make scientific investigations," it should never serve to point out the absurdity of human existence: "Documentary theater presents the alternative that reality, no matter how obscurely it reveals itself, can be explained in every particular." Nevertheless, Weiss's *The Investigation* retains a kinship with the notion of absurdity and is far more complex and ironic than Weiss's theory or Piscator's hopeful revolutionary rituals.

The documentary playwright studies the recorded word of the courtroom, archive, or mass media and is comparable to the medieval preacher who studied the sacred text and made it comprehensible to his audience through sermon and spectacle, through precept and example. When seen through the filter of secular documents, the unspeakable situation is interpreted in secular terms, primarily in terms of the dialectics of power and in terms of money, the symbol of *homo economicus*. Factual reports and rational explanations prove, however, insufficient to the reflective creative imagination overwhelmed by a sense of evil, against which it protects itself by defining it as incomprehensible. It attempts to explain that incomprehensibility by relying on the familiar Christian ideas of sin in this world and punishment in hell and by displacing both into the ironic mode. But the reality of historical evil has such power that the hopeful message of Christianity as well as communism is at best muted if not silenced. The titles of Hochhuth's and Weiss's plays already indicate their kinship to medieval drama: the first is subtitled a Christian tragedy *(Trauerspiel)*, while the second is an oratorium in eleven cantos.

The Christian mystery and morality plays are documentary drama in that their images were culled from the Scriptures and projected, to transfer Weiss's words, an alternative to the reality known to sinful humankind. The radicals of the mystery and morality plays combined insight and the mystery of integration. In the Easter ritual, the three Marys come to the tomb of Christ, find it empty, and are informed by the angel that he has risen. The resurrected Christ was judged according to political law, through which the divine law triumphed and fulfilled itself in the resurrection. The mystery play emphasizes that which surpasses understanding, while morality plays, such as *Everyman,* instruct humankind to follow the divine commandments in historical time so that we may eventually be integrated into the mystery of divine love. Since suffering is only a stage in the process of one's destiny, tragedy is impossible. As the young Jesuit in *The Deputy* asserts, "In Him all anguish is contained," a belief mocked by the persecutors' jeering remarks about sending their victims home to Abraham's bosom.

The potential for the ironic mode is already contained in the mystery and morality play, for the empty tomb stimulates a negative metaphysics about the possibility that it always has been empty. The morality play may also lead to the realization that, in spite of all preachings and good intentions, humankind simply goes on sinning. The emphasis on everyman, on the great democratizer death, and on the last judgment common to all puts the morality play into the low mimetic mode, which in its proletarian plainness is much more appropriate to documentary drama than the heroic gesture of high mimetic tragedy.

While the Christian view of history begins and ends in transcendence, the human being's conduct in historical time is also of great concern to Christianity. Erich Auerbach clearly defined the interrelation of history and eschatology in medieval drama: "Everything in the dramatic play which grew out of the liturgy during the Middle Ages is part of one—and always the same context: of one great drama whose beginning is God's creation of the world, whose climax is Christ's Incarnation and Passion, and whose expected conclusion will be Christ's second coming and the Last Judgment . . . . In principle, this great drama contains everything that occurs in world history. In it all the heights and depths of human conduct and all the heights and depths of stylistic expression find their morally or aesthetically established right to exist; and hence there is no basis for a separation of the sublime from the low and everyday, for they are indissolubly connected in Christ's very life and suffering. . . . To be sure the entire course of world history is not presented each time . . . . But the whole is always born in mind and figuratively represented."[5]

In documentary drama the Christian's pilgrimage becomes the anti-quest, and the only judge to whom the playwright can appeal is the audience, who are themselves caught in the bondage of history. There are no deputies of Christ in history, and a Father Fontana, who so consciously tries to imitate Christ, cannot harrow the hell of Auschwitz; he can only participate in the dance of death that ends in the crematorium. Since the audience is the only judge, the dead cannot expect a last and just judgment. Moreover, those who should be judged actually are rewarded by the world, as is the case with Baron Rutta in Hochhuth's play and with the accused in *The Investigation,* whose orchestrated laughter is the final triumph over their victims. In the ironic world of documentary theater, Everyman is rewarded for his greed and presumption and does not even experience that night of the soul that finds itself lost in a dark wood.

One who was thus lost, namely, Dante, combines the mystery and morality tradition in his *Divine Comedy* and influences Hochhuth and Weiss both structurally and thematically. The confrontation scene between Fontana and Pius XII, which immediately precedes the Auschwitz act, projects themes and images of the vestibule of hell where the uncommitted follow only those causes that serve their advantage. In the last scene of the final act, Fontana emerges from the pit. But he can only go as far as the guardhouse of Auschwitz, for the historical pit has no center of gravity whence one passes through to the shores of Mount Purgatory. In the final analysis, Hochhuth's play asks a theological question, namely, how deeply must God be provoked before he reveals himself and answers. Since he does not answer, he does not exist. A healing vision is not possible in *The Deputy.* Peter Weiss, who has written extensively about Dante, sees the healing vision of history in socialism. Several commentators have pointed out that *The Investigation, An Oratorium* is not only a passion play about everyman but is also modelled structurally around Dante's concept of the mystic number 33, each of its eleven cantos being divided into three sections.[6] This number, I might add, is ironically displaced, for 33 is also the number of the year that Hitler came to power. The testimony presented in *The Investigation* follows Dante's pattern of narrowing circles as it moves from the periphery of Auschwitz, the ramp, to the center of the camp experience, the gas chambers and the fiery ovens.

As Auerbach points out, the matter of Christian drama was great, but it could be conveyed through a plain and low style, even through farce. In the quest of Everyman, the grotesque and its ironies have always been a counterpoint to the sublime, as the gargoyle is the counterpoint to the virgin or the transcendent god. Dante praised in his "de vulgari eloquentia" the language of ordinary men and wrote his poem in his native Italian. For the ironic writer, however, the illustrious vernacular has degenerated to the rigid language of cliché, the defense mechanism against evil. Language failed Dante in his moments of deepest pain and joy, but the Eichmänner of today can talk about the final solution while bowling or eating ham sandwiches. Farce and parody are, therefore, not flaws in these plays but an integral part of their didactic message.

Hochhuth's *The Deputy* and Weiss's *The Investigation* are documentary plays that project rituals of judgment about the perpetrators and collaborators in the unspeakable situation of the concentration camp. Neither play demands a political or religious pledge of faith from the audience as the theater of Piscator or the drama of the Middle Ages would demand it. At best, the plays have the more muted aim of insight into how the individual is inevitably implicated in history. The matter of both plays is large: *The Deputy* attempts to project the guilt of the world from the stage, while *The Investigation* contracts that guilt into the narrow space of a secular courtroom from which universal meanings again aureate. Both playwrights see themselves as teachers and consciousness raisers, but the final irony of their choice of mode is that it allows them to repress and disguise their personal sense of guilt by the very reliance on historical fact and documentary material.

II.
Rolf Hochhuth's *The Deputy:* A Christian Tragedy

In an interview, Hochhuth pointed out, "The total collapse of Germany was a great shock to me. I considered it my responsibility to study the shameful history of the Third Reich. Again and again I thought 'what would you yourself have done if you had been old enough to act.'"[7] He does not believe, however, that Germans alone have been chosen to bear the mark of Cain but argues that there is a hierarchy of guilt which includes religious institutions. Hochhuth's own Protestant faith was shaken by the events at Auschwitz and Hiroshima. How deeply he was affected is borne out by the theological question raised in the final act of *The Deputy:* "Auschwitz, or where are you God?"

The Deputy, which he finished at the age of thirty, was inspired originally, not by the figure of the pope, the Schiller hero Fontana, or the satanic doctor, but by SS officer Kurt Gerstein, the spy for God about whom Hochhuth had intensively read and studied. In its mixture of fact and fiction as well as in its attitude towards history and politics, *The Deputy* does not adhere to the critical definition of documentary theater as offered by Weiss; rather, it incorporates into fictional situations direct quotations from documentary sources. These sources are expanded in the "historical sidelights" that are appended to the play but have a definite rhetorical relation to it. They illuminate some of the historical complexi-

ties that had to be omitted, and they convey three basic problems faced by
a playwright who makes history his subject matter: the admission that our
historical perception is always fragmentary; that our perception of history
is based on the selection of historical facts; and that there is far more
material than the playwright was able to include. Hochhuth decided to
focus on the indignant heart as the central motivating force of the play, a
heart that will not accept arguments based on *Realpolitik*. The characters
in the play are, therefore, judged according to the degree of their indignation against the Nazi outrage.[8] Hochhuth is indignant that Pius XII chose
neutrality over indignation. As a result, the play hovers between idealis-
tic gestures and ironic attitudes, "between historical drama and satirical
pamphlet as well as the combination of documentary drama and morality
play."[9]

Hochhuth does not naively assume that Pius XII could have averted the
fate of European Jews; his pessimistic view of history leaves no room for
the great man as savior. He realizes that we may have to choose between
nightmares. However, he prefers a myth that places responsibility on
individuals who act in spite of the absurd despite his awareness that
human beings frequently prefer to act as products of a mass society. The
moment, however, a person possesses an indignant heart, he steps out of
the mass, becomes individuated, and, very likely, tragically isolated if he
has no power. Furthermore, Hochhuth insists that each person experiences
his or her death in the isolation of being an individual, even when a person
is part of the mass led off to be murdered.[10] It is, therefore, essential for
drama to "insist that man is a responsible being."[11] Drama which
defines the individual as individual is engagé. Yet the epitome of evil in
which that individual may find himself cannot be represented on the
stage. Hochhuth admits that when we think of Auschwitz we can only
think of the train station, the "humane ante-chamber of hell." The
technical processing of people cannot be represented because it is no
longer human.[12] Since reality is absurd enough, Hochhuth also rejects
surrealistic devices to illustrate the extreme situation. Realism and absurdity should not be seen as opposites but should be presented in all their
photographic grotesqueness, including intellectual game-playing as well
as moments of unbelievably melodramatic action.[13] For Hochhuth the
stage is very much a moral institution in Schiller's sense, namely, that the
judicial right of the stage begins whenever the area of secular law
becomes impotent.

Aside from his secular, historical, and judgmental aims, Hochhuth
also intends the play to be a Christian's tragedy. As I pointed out, the

medieval mystery and morality plays could not be tragic because of their Christian message. A Christian's tragedy can only occur when the believer, in this case Father Riccardo, finds that the universe, instead of being filled with the creative and loving force of God, is only a vacuum, finds that the promise of eternal life is not fulfilled and that the tomb is simply empty without symbolizing the resurrection. The fifth act of *The Deputy* raises this question of the silence of God, just as the previous acts raised the question whether or not the pope would remain silent. Riccardo makes two crucial statements about the individual's need for an answer. When the pope has chosen to be in effect silent, Riccardo leaves him with the words "Gott soll die Kirche nicht verderben / nur weil ein Papst sich seinem Ruf entzieht" (God shall not destroy His Church / only because a pope shrinks from his summons).[14] The word *Ruf* means summons, call, vocation, and reputation, all applicable to the pope. The pronoun *seinem* is used ambiguously here, for it could be His summons (that is, God's call to man), or it could be the pope's refusal to live up to his calling and reputation. When Riccardo leaves the pope's throne room, he still believes in a heavenly father; but after having worked in the crematorium at Auschwitz, his dying words are *"in hora mortis meae voca me"* (in the hour of my death call me). There is no answer to this final, whispered, imperative call of man; the universe remains silent. The concept of the call informs the play from beginning to end; but if one follows the call, or if one remains silent, or if one provokes the silence by committing atrocities as the satanic doctor does, it makes no difference in Christian terms as long as one assumes that God is in the heavens. "Beware of the man whose God is in the sky" is the motto of the first act. Although Riccardo has his god in the sky, he also responds to the call of man and to the call of a Christian conscience when he suddenly encounters Gerstein in the papal legation in Berlin. As he follows Gerstein's call, he will slowly be stripped of all his illusions, foremost among them his belief that the pope will interfere with the arrest of the Jews of Rome. The structure and characterizations of the play are shaped by this notion of accepting or refusing the call or one's calling.

A. The Structure and Cosmos of *The Deputy*

By following the call, a person finds that he has to follow it in historical time and within forces more powerful than he is. The play's metaphors of evil define three centers of power: Berlin, where decisions are made that will lead to Auschwitz; Rome, where decisions made in Berlin are being carried out, but where counterdecisions are expected; Auschwitz, the industrial city shrunk to an infernal village where human beings succumb to decisions made in Berlin and not made in Rome. Each of these centers is also an analogical displacement of a mythical dimension. Berlin is the historical world, but we never see its center of power, the Reichskanzlei where Hitler works; he, too, is an absent god. Rome is for Riccardo the eternal city, with its center at the Vatican; but he discovers that this center is really part of a thoroughly human and fallen world and that its ruler is no more than a man, if not less. Auschwitz is the inferno where questions regarding the existence of God become most urgent, but where the ultimate pit, the crematorium, remains as unseen as Hitler in his office. In these broad and epic proportions, the play very much follows the pattern that Auerbach outlined in his definition of Christian drama. That drama, however, was comic in the sense of integration and final harmony, but the man who wishes to imitate Christ in the confines of the ironic mode must do so without hope. History does not end in a final judgment; rather, a traumatic era will simply run its course and finally exhaust itself like the plague.

Act I (Berlin), "Der Auftrag." The title, which applies to the three scenes of the act, can be translated as the mission, the message, or the order. The first scene takes place at the papal legation in the Rauch-strasse, an ironic name since *Rauch* (smoke) hangs perpetually over Auschwitz. The Nuncio is, as his name indicates, a messenger and, as such, a mediating neutral. SS officer Gerstein arrives with a "message for the Vatican" about the gassing of the Jews. Since the Nuncio fails as a messenger, Riccardo already implies that he will seek out Gerstein and become his messenger. Scene two reveals the *Jägerkeller* (hunter's cellar) where the persecutors are shown at their leisure. Air raids have forced them to go underground. Nevertheless, the shelter is exemplary in its bourgeois atmosphere of *Gemütlichkeit,* at least on the surface, for the conversation soon reveals the macabre preoccupations of the persecutors. Gerstein suddenly appears and reports about the effectiveness of the gassing, now in the tone of the medical engineer who has followed his orders. An air attack concludes the scene, electric lights fail, and dark-ness falls over this first underground and infernal scene of the play. The three personae of Gerstein are shown in scene three where we see him in his apartment in relation to the victim Jakobson to whom he has given refuge, in relation to the Doctor of Auschwitz who pays him a teasingly sinister visit, and in relation to the neutral Riccardo who is initiated here as a messenger to the Vatican. To test his sincerity, Gerstein asks him to exchange clothing with Jakobson. Riccardo agrees reluctantly and pins the Star of David, "stigma of the outlaw," on his chest, a gesture that is as yet mainly symbolic. Gerstein has called Riccardo to his quest and will eventually make a futile attempt to save him from his death at Auschwitz.

Act II (Rome), "The Bells of St. Peter." The act consists of a single scene, Riccardo's homecoming to the neutral ground of his father's house. The bells of St. Peter proclaim a message to the world: the dogma of the ascension of the Virgin Mary, to whose immaculate heart the pope dedicated the world that morning. "They ring and ring as though the world were paradise," says Riccardo, annoyed as he tries to inform his father of the true state of the world. Allusions to Rome as the heavenly city continue, as when Fontana the elder warns, "You are ambitious. Lucifer the favorite of his Lord also fell from ambition." Fontana and the visiting cardinal, after Riccardo's passionate persuasiveness, seem potential allies in his quest to persuade the pope; but the pope's preoccupation with the dogma of the Virgin at this moment in history makes it doubtful that he will come to terms with the polluted earth.

Act III (Rome), "Die Heimsuchung." The ironic use of visit and visitation underlies each of the scenes in this act. The first shows the Luccanis in their apartment in the Via di Porta Angelica preparing for their flight to a monastery; they are arrested. Scene two shows a monastery where several victims have found shelter. Here, Riccardo and Gerstein are able to persuade the cardinal that the pope should issue an official statement against the arrests. Riccardo, however, already intimates that the pope will refuse and that he, Riccardo, will accompany the victims to Auschwitz. When he hints to the abbot about the possibility of murdering the pope, his tragic isolation begins as the abbot rejects him as an outlaw. Scene three emphasizes the urgency of the situation and the necessity for the pope to speak out. Victims arrive and disappear into the Gestapo cellar as everybody waits for a message from the pope, a message that is sure to come, as Gerstein assures an SS officer.

Act IV (Rome), "Il Gran Rifiuto." The great refusal takes place during Riccardo's visitation of the pope where he discovers that a political being rather than the deputy of Christ lives in the sanctity of the Vatican. From Riccardo's point of view, this act is the turning point, but it resolves nothing; it merely isolates the protagonist from the community. Riccardo responds to the pope's empty symbolic gesture by fastening, now with provocative earnestness, the Star of David to himself. Rome proved to be the eternal city only in the symbolic sense in which it combined heaven (the Vatican), ordinary life (Luccani's apartment), and hell (Gestapo cellar). Since the fourth act immediately precedes the final act, a causal connection between the refusal and Auschwitz is unavoidable. The red throne room, symbolic of martyred blood, anticipates the smoky red of Auschwitz. One of the deepest ironies between the two acts is that the fourth act is largely dominated by discussions of money, while the question of God's existence plays an important role in the last act. Furthermore, the pope, stage manager of the grand refusal, is replaced by the Doctor as stage manager of Auschwitz.

Act V, "Auschwitz or the Question 'Where Are You God?'" again has three scenes. The first contains three monologues, spoken or thought on the transport train. These monologues are central to the theological problem of the act, for they are a thematic displacement of the trinity into the fallen world. Scene two shows the threshold of Auschwitz, the guardroom which the victims must pass. Here, Riccardo meets the Doctor and, while his fellow Italians go to their death, debates the existence of God with him. Such a conversation can occur only here, for, in the final scene, Riccardo, having worked several weeks in the crematorium, cannot defend his god with the same conviction. In Auschwitz, Rome seems indeed like paradise, and Riccardo is twice given a glimmer of hope to return to the eternal city, first by the Doctor, who, knowing how the war will end, plans to escape with Riccardo. The final illusion of reprieve comes with Gerstein, who, driven by his conscience, tries to free Riccardo. The rescue is complicated when Jakobson appears; he has been able to survive by claiming that he is a priest. Thus, the three figures at the beginning of the quest meet again, but the Doctor, who was then only a threat, is now in full power. Riccardo tries to shoot the Doctor but is gunned down and mortally wounded. His sacrifice and death have proven pointless, for he had no power. Only if there was a transcendent reality would his actions be meaningful, as he desperately hopes in the imperative of his dying words. Coincidence and melodrama dominate the last scene and make the perceiver forget the suffering of humanity at Auschwitz. Nevertheless, while this scene borders esthetically on a kind of grotesque *Kitsch*, the historical reality of Auschwitz, where children played ball before they were gassed and where little dwarfs were painted on the wall of a nursery school, makes the whole scene not an improbability. Although the symbolic use of the cloud of smoke and the cement mixer, as well as intellectual debate, may direct attention to theological questions at the expense of the victims, the play concerns a man-made world where the powerful act like gods behind the scenes to perpetrate crimes. The greater the power of an individual, be that power symbolic or real, the greater his moral responsibility.

B. Hochhuth's Categories of Individuals in *The Deputy*

In his study of Hochhuth's works, Siegfried Melchinger points out that the characters in *The Deputy* are carefully balanced in their appearances between neutrals, persecutors, and victims.[15] However, according to their propensities, characters overlap: Pius XII with Baron von Rutta, Eichmann with the Jewish manufacturer in the Gestapo prison in Rome. Besides the women in the play, only three characters stand by themselves: Gerstein, Riccardo, and the Doctor. For better or worse, each of them is a strong individual, while the overlapping of characters indicates a hierarchy of guilt accrued primarily through opportunism. As in Dante, the opportunists only follow their own advantage even though they might know the good. They usually have a displaced remnant of human decency that may be no more evident than in Eichmann's shock over the Doctor's pornographic and blasphemous song. The clergy are the group of opportunists who have the greatest potential for good. The cardinal, Fontana the elder, and the abbot are basically decent people who are fully informed about the persecution of the Jews and who are yet unable to protest successfully because, in the final analysis, they remain obedient to their superior, the pope who refuses to make a commitment. The sins of the neutrals are then the sins of omission, of a sloth that knows the good but does not want to pursue it.

The little men in politics and economics are by definition opportunists. For this reason, Eichmann and the Italian manufacturer are grouped together. The latter is an assimilated Jew who, in spite of the fact that he even agrees with Hitler's genocidal policies, is pushed into the Gestapo cellar. After he has been cut off from all hope, he will no longer be the opportunist but will accept his Jewishness fully and move with Riccardo into the camp of the victims. It is almost as if the opportunist must be robbed of all opportunities before he can become human. Eichmann and his cohorts have made crime an opportunity. In the *Jägerkeller* scene, Eichmann projects himself as the production manager of the final solution who tries to discover more and more efficient means for death. Jews are valuable to him because they can speak German and because they are more knowledgeable industrial workers. Baron von Rutta, socially superior to Eichmann, profits from the struggle between persecutors and victims. His surface, upper class refinement and his aristocratic Catholicism, which make him barely tolerate the petit bourgeois jollities in the *Jägerkeller,* give him an icy indifference which aligns him with the pope. Money is his prime motive, and Christianity is reduced by him to the appreciation of esthetic rituals.

The actor who plays Baron von Rutta should also play Pius XII, who heads Hochhuth's list of characters. Opportunism and lack of commitment find in Pius XII their horrible culmination because, of all the neutrals, he is the one who is most informed of the atrocities and the one who should know how to do good actively. But the good is no longer an ethical concept to him; it is a hollow esthetic gesture. Hochhuth does not personalize Pius XII but presents him as the highest representative of an institution whose ethos is being undermined. Pius had also been silent when Hitler invaded Poland, a silence that Hochhuth indicates when he has the character Pius XII speak the words that the historical pope uttered on that occasion. Rhetorically, this leads to an a fortiori argument: if the pope was silent about the fate of Catholic Poles, he will be even more silent about the persecution of people who are not even Christian:

> We are—God knows it—blameless of the blood
> now being spilled. As the flowers
> *(He raises his voice, declaims.)*
> in the countryside wait beneath winter's mantle of snow
> for the warm breezes of spring,
> so the Jews must wait, praying and trusting
> that the hour of heavenly comfort will come. [pp. 177, 220–21]

They will be liberated by the Red Army, the force that the pope fears most. The emptiness of the poetic cliché is obvious; but why have so many been outraged over Hochhuth's satiric portrait of Pius XII? After all, Dante did not hesitate to put most of his popes into grotesque, infernal postures. Carl Amery answers this question by arguing that "only in a world increasingly indifferent and blind to the real questions of Christianity, increasingly indifferent even of its vocabulary, could there arise the disagreeable possibility of building up the popes not as office holders, but as celebrities. Slowly the pope was associated with tremendous moral credit."[16] He has become a wish projection in a secular world, and Hochhuth has fallen for this mystique, as his deep chagrin over Pius's all too human failing makes evident.

Pius's opening lines align him with the world of Baron von Rutta, the guilty world of money, as he expresses his "burning concern" *(brennende Sorge)* for Italian factories by unwittingly using the words of his predecessor's encyclical. At the end, after he has dictated his shallow protest over the general conditions of war-torn Europe, he immediately turns his attention to the safety of the Church's Hungarian railway investments. The reader is, of course, aware that these very same rails will carry cattle wagons with victims to Auschwitz in the spring and summer of 1944. Money, the god of this world, has always been defined in opposition to the law of the New Testament "Love one another." Pius himself is aware of the ambiguity of his situation when he decides to dictate a protest so that "no one shall say we sacrificed the law of Christian love to political calculations" (pp. 170, 212). He wants to maintain his reputation of obeying that law, but it is not an inner human and spiritual need for him; instead he prefers to withdraw into that icy abstractness which gives the impression of "unearthly spiritualization," but which really is empty and cold rigidity. Although Hochhuth puts him ostensibly into the antechamber of hell, he is, as the representative of the creator of the universe, associated with ice which for Dante was the antithesis of life, a metaphor of evil.

On the one hand, Pius is very conscious of the gestures, symbols, and words he uses; on the other hand, he has lost touch with the meaning these should possess. It is in this that the satiric attack on Pius becomes most obvious, for his words and posturings will not become flesh, will not become deed. Beginning with his opening statement about his "burning concern," the emptiness of his language becomes more and more apparent. Anything that would violate neutrality is rejected, and he is visibly shaken when Riccardo fastens the Star of David to his chest: "In the name of the victims . . . this . . . this / arrogance as well! And this impertinence—/ the Star of David on the habit of Christ's servants!" His objection falls into two parts. In the first half, Pius is evidently thinking that Riccardo has arrogant, esthetic motivations which would be an insult to the victims; he cannot imagine that anyone could have other intentions. Riccardo himself is deeply sincere as well as rebellious, yet he has not really experienced what the star means. The last half of the pope's objection shows his true feelings about the Star of David; "he quivers with rage." This is the only time that Hochhuth attributes anti-Semitic motives to the pope, who is also outraged over the young Jesuit's Protestant opposition to established authority.

After Riccardo departs, Hochhuth completes his satiric portrait by having Pius wash his hands in an unconscious but, for the reader, almost too obvious imitation of Pontius Pilate. He draws the circle of his advisors around himself again, including Riccardo's reluctant father, whom he consoles with "who should know it better than We, to be a father is to wear a crown of thorns," a metaphor of suffering that loses its meaning because Pius seems to have forgotten that it is the son who wears the crown of thorns. Hochhuth obviously alludes to the Doctor when he

defines the pope as "once more completely stage manager of the situation" as he opens his arms to embrace the world in an empty benediction,
a world that hovers in suspension to hear a meaningful word from him.
Unwilling to stain himself through involvement in historical time, the
character of Pius XII remains a hollow form.

The antithesis to Pius XII is Kurt Gerstein, the Christian as SS officer.
If the pope retains the outer trappings, Gerstein claims an inner core of
Christian meaning. In spite of his many roles, he is not an opportunist; he
is victim as well as persecutor. In his case the ethical and psychological
problem arises of how long one can commit crimes through the persona of
the uniform before the uniform and the crimes touch one's real self.
Totally isolated, Gerstein concentrates on being a witness for God and
takes no comfort in human needs and love. Hochhuth calls him a marked
man who can perhaps be understood through the philosophy of Kierkegaard (pp. 16, 15), who defined the role of the sinner as spy for God: "I
am, as it were, a spy in the service of the highest. The police also use
spies."[17] Gerstein was instrumental in supplying the gas and observed
his first gassing in Belsen reported by the character Gerstein at the papal
legation in Berlin.[18]

In the play, Gerstein defines himself in Kierkegaardian terms: "I will
not survive the work that I must do. A Christian in these days *cannot*
survive if he is truly a Christian. I don't mean Sunday Christians—
beware the steady churchgoers—I am thinking of the Christians Kierkegaard had in mind: the spies of God. I am a spy in the SS. And spies are
executed—I am aware of that" (pp. 65–66, 79). His Christianity is
defined, not by an institution, but by an absolute and personal faith in an
incomprehensible god for whose sake he debases himself in sin and
betrayal, always remaining fully conscious that he does so and why he
does so. Without his faith he would merely be a criminal; as he is, he
retains the knowledge of what sin is in a time when crime is merely habit.
Pius XII refuses to become conscious in spite of his knowledge; Riccardo
wants to become conscious and to act with conscience, but he does not
realize to what sights and insights his consciousness will lead him.
Gerstein is fully aware of the historical situation and his many roles in it,
but his consciousness would destroy him were it not for that immutable
and absurd center of faith within him.

Gerstein seems to burst into the consciousness of those he wishes to
reach, but at the same time he appears to them as one who is hunted. For
Riccardo he is the sudden intrusion of reality into a comfortable and
neutral life. Yet Gerstein is able to win merely the powerless Riccardo

to his cause. Riccardo cannot fulfill Gerstein's hopes for a statement from the pope; he can only follow his own imitation of Christ without, however, committing the sins that Gerstein commits. No one, certainly no human being, wants Gerstein's uncomfortable consciousness. When Jakobson accuses him in Auschwitz that his resistance has failed to blow up even one railroad track to the camp, his involvement in history seems as futile and absurd as Riccardo's sacrifice, for which he feels responsible.

Riccardo Fontana, S.J., becomes involved with Gerstein and history from the moment he pledges, "Your name is Gerstein—I will find you" (pp. 26, 27). When he meets Gerstein again in Auschwitz, their roles are reversed as he greets him with "Gerstein! You should not have tried to find me" (pp. 215, 269). By this time he is in the know about human suffering as much as he will ever be, and he, too, clings, in spite of tremors, to his faith. One cannot, however, help but wonder if his faith is not an expression of sheer stubbornness, for it is the Doctor's aim to make him lose his faith. Riccardo is clearly aware of himself as a representative and symbol of Christianity, and he flaunts this attitude, not only in the Vatican, but also upon his arrival at Auschwitz. His Christianity is a provocation, while Gerstein's is a deep secret. In the course of the play, Riccardo has to learn that it is easy to define oneself as a symbol and very hard to find oneself a solitary man as the result of one's symbolic definition. Because of his heart's indignation, he becomes a pilgrim through time. During his pilgrimage he is stripped of all his illusions, even the illusion that he could be a martyr, for as the transport nears Auschwitz he attempts to tear off the yellow star. After he has regained courage, the audience sees him arriving with a child in his arms. He has become a physically involved father. But at Auschwitz he meets his new teacher, the Doctor, who replaces Gerstein and who tells him, "As long as you can believe, my dear priest, dying is just a joke" (pp. 194, 243).

Riccardo is at first unconvinced by the Doctor's argument that Auschwitz refutes creator, creation, and creature (pp. 198, 248). Since theological debates do not persuade him, he is sent to burn corpses in the crematoria, and, as he does so, he burns each day a fraction of his faith. At the end, he admits to Gerstein, "And with every human body that I burn a portion of my faith burns also. God burns. Corpses—a conveyor belt of corpses. History is a highway paved with carrion . . . If I knew that He looks on—I would have to hate—Him" (pp. 215, 270). Since Riccardo argued earlier that God is suffering with His creature in history, he is reaching the conclusion that God will die in history; but this seems better than that He look on and remain silent. As far as Riccardo is concerned, the question of the existence of God is left open, for he prefers death to the inexorable corrosion of his faith. His God was a highly personified father image of which the pope was the embodiment on earth; and, as he rejected Pius for his silence, he would reject God for his knowledge and silence. Riccardo's God, like that of Elie Wiesel in *Night,* is in the heavens, and this destroys faith; for Riccardo cannot internalize God as Gerstein does or as Father Kolbe must have done when he died the martyr's death in Auschwitz by sacrificing himself for another person. Riccardo shares with the historical Father Kolbe the Auschwitz number 16670.

Riccardo's quest and death are a Christian tragedy, as Hochhuth subtitles the play in the German edition, because they concern the inevitable failure of a Christian in historical time. As Walter Kaufmann writes in his discussion of *The Deputy,* ''The play ends tragically, and the hero is not merely a nominal Christian or a man who happens to be a Jesuit, but one who tries more desperately to become a Christian in the most demanding sense of the word. I doubt that a tragedy more Christian than that is possible.''[19] As the Christian's tragedy, however, it leaves the protagonist the choice of death or loss of faith, for certainly the rhetoric of the play moves towards the conclusion that ''He does not exist''—the Doctor leaves the stage like a successful lecturer; the announcement regarding the eventual liberation of Auschwitz by the Red Army is made by a technological and nontranscendent voice. God is either nonexistent or is silent in the sky. In a sense, therefore, Riccardo's tragic end is kind, for it leaves him apparently suspended in the illusion and hope for God's existence. He seems to have gained what he wanted upon his arrival in Auschwitz: a very easy death. I say *seem* because the Doctor's last statement about him destroys this illusion. When Gerstein shouts, ''He's still alive,'' the Doctor replies, ''The fire is a good physician. It will burn out the Jew *and* the Christian in him.'' Riccardo is to be thrown into the fires of Auschwitz alive; thus, his ultimate physical and spiritual destiny will end beyond the guardhouse.

In his analysis of evil, Volkmar Sander mentions in passing the dandy-like qualities of the Doctor in *The Deputy.*[20] Based on the infamous and historical Dr. Mengele, Hochhuth introduces through his Doctor the Antichrist of the mystery and morality plays, a figure whose tradition does not seems to fit the notion of the banality of evil. The Doctor is anything but banal and may at first appear as too blatant an anachronism. Yet he is not the devil incarnate, but, as his many references to the human need for escape indicate, he is a human being posing as the devil. Demonic powers are diminished and displaced as the satanic displays itself in the ironic mode, a process of secularization that Camus defines through the figure of the dandy. Camus sees the dandy as a metaphysical rebel whose highly developed self-consciousness lacks all ethical dimensions of conscience:

> The dandy creates his own unity by aesthetic means. But it is an aesthetic of singularity and negation. "To live and die before a mirror": that, according to Baudelaire, was the dandy's slogan. It is indeed a coherent slogan. The dandy is by occupation always in opposition. He can exist only by defiance . . . . Profligate, like all people without a rule of life, he is coherent as an actor. But an actor implies a public . . . . He can only be sure of his own existence by finding it in the expression of other's faces. Other people are his mirror . . . . The dandy, therefore, is always compelled to astonish. Singularity is his vocation, excess his way to perfection. Perpetually incomplete, always on the fringe of things, he compels others to create him, while denying their values. He plays at life because he is unable to live it.[21]

Although far more intelligent than the Eichmänner on whom he depends, the Doctor as dandy is another manifestation of demonic emptiness. Every time he is on stage, he uses others as reflectors, and he can be whatever others wish to see in him: the profligate, the intellectual, the theologian, the kind uncle, the reliable and reassuring camp official, the long lost lover. But all who trust him will die.

For different reasons, the Doctor is a provocateur like Riccardo. If Riccardo had unwarranted expectations from a self superior to his own ego, the Doctor secretly desires to be punished for his ever increasing self-inflation. Nasty and provoking like a spoiled child, he posits a cosmic though indifferent parent who refuses to be his nemesis and hence does not exist: "Since July of '42, for fifteen months, weekdays and Sabbath, I've been sending people to God. Do you think He's made the slightest acknowledgement? He has not even directed a bolt of lightning against me . . . . I took a vow to challenge the old Gent, to provoke him so limitlessly that he would have to give an answer. Even if only a negative answer which can be His sole excuse, as Stendhal put it: that He doesn't exist" (pp. 246, 247). It is part of his provocation, a perversion of prayer, that he mimics the role of final judge as he separates people to the left or to the right with his baton. The need to provoke springs from the inner

emptiness of a self without identity. "Boredom always plagues me," he
tells Riccardo (pp. 200, 250), and in his wrath against the emptiness of
boredom he creates a catastrophic world. Separation from a commitment
to genuine life leads to emptiness, the yawn of chaos that needs to be
filled, if need be, with negation, with corpses. No one in the play has as
much knowledge as he. He has the pope's bureaucratic knowledge, but,
since he looks at the individual child and sends her to her death, he also
has the physical knowledge of crime as he breathes the stench of Auschwitz. It is, however, a knowledge without empathy, hence without conscience and guilt. He can separate himself from other Nazis by means of
his perceptive irony; he shares their emptiness, a vacuity that is more
demonic in his case because he always knows what he does. He gives
lessons in death on the stage of history, and his vision of the world is a
symptom, a consequence of the refusal to do good.

If there is a healing vision in *The Deputy,* it remains implicit in the
emotions and actions of the indignant, loving heart and its sense of
responsibility. But such a heart remains powerless in this ironic version
of the mystery and morality plays, for here the divine comedy is changed
into the Christian's tragedy. At the opening of the last scene in the
Auschwitz act, Rutta asks Helga, "And now you are in Auschwitz. Do
you enjoy your new job?" Helga answers evasively, "A job's a job,"
and admits that her fiancé is here also. To this the SS man responds,
"Aha, so it was love that lured you here." No one is conscious of the
grotesqueness of these clichés in the present context. Such thoughtless
use of words reveals once more in encapsulated form a world where love
is betrayed, where all sex is pornographic, where eros and agape are
denied, where fathers are abstract and silent, and where mothers are
either dead (Riccardo's mother) or about to be murdered. It is a world
made by men who have a passion for death or, what is worse, are
indifferent to death. At the end, each of the major figures is isolated and
possesses at best an abstract and absurd love for God. Auschwitz has its
moment of liberation, but the liberators are human armies. Although they
open the tomb, they continue a nightmare of history in which the cosmos
is silent because of human silence.

III.
Peter Weiss's *The Investigation:* **Report about a Locale Called Auschwitz**

Peter Weiss witnessed many of the sessions of the Frankfurt Auschwitz
trials in 1964–65, but the drama he wrote about them has none of the

flamboyance of Hochhuth's *The Deputy*. *The Investigation* is detached
and cool. Its tone and purpose are summarized towards the end by witness
3: "I speak free of hate/I do not nurture the desire for revenge against
anybody/I stand indifferently before the individual accused/and only
wish to bring to mind/that they could not have carried out their trade/
without the support of a million others."[22] Weiss created an objectified
ritual in which horror is expressed through language. Stage directions are
also kept to a minimum. As a result, readers and viewers have to
interpret, have to investigate *The Investigation*. Yet, like all of Weiss's
work, this documentary drama springs from deeply personal sources
which are transposed to a political and therefore more objective level. As
Erika Salloch comments in her study of the play, "The play is neither
Auschwitz on the stage nor the Frankfurt trial, it is a concentration of
these events in the consciousness of Peter Weiss."[23] Weiss himself
admitted autobiographical motivations: "We have to confront these
details . . . we have to face these images in order to comprehend them
. . . . I wrote the drama also for myself, in order to clarify for myself
what happened there."[24]

The autobiographical aspects of Weiss's work have been considered
by several commentators, foremost among them being Otto Best. Best
shows that Weiss always struggles against an oppressive past, that is, his
familial past which he describes in two autobiographies, *Abschied
von den Eltern (Farewell to My Parents)* and *Fluchtpunkt (Vanishing
Point)*.[25] Crucial for his development were his middle class background
and his discovery that his father was Jewish. He belonged by definition to
the victims but did not want to belong. Hence, identification with and
repulsion of victims is an essential tension in Weiss's work, especially in
his prose. His dramas project this tension into the oppressor and oppressed dialectic of his political faith. This faith is to him a healing force
which is nevertheless continually cast into doubt by political reality; the
desire for a withdrawal from history becomes a temptation, as shown in
Hölderlin where the revolutionary poet escapes into a madness for which
only the young Karl Marx seems to have sympathy. As Reinhard Baumgart argues, "An author, who wanted to further the revolution through
his writings, invented in the end only radical individuals and through
them a moral, a justification, almost a sanctification."[26] Ironically, what
we remember from *The Investigation* is the emergence of individuals
from the anonymous mass of victims and persecutors. Also, Weiss has
the openness of an ironist who is acutely aware of the uncertainties of
present time and who interprets these uncertainties positively by means of

a dialectical dynamic. The fluctuations and possibilities of the present, however, receive their impetus from the repressive and projective psychological forces of the individual and the collective. Weiss's collective healing vision of the future is achieved at the expense of the memory of a catastrophic past which would in the future be split off as an antiworld. Thus, *The Investigation* raises an unusual question, namely, "How can one write about Auschwitz without referring specifically to the murder of three million Jews?" One does so in order to avoid the pathological concentration on personal pain and scruples for the sake of a collective state of well being. Weiss always hesitates to name specifically that which is most painful or most desirable to him.[34]

Since Weiss's father belonged to the middle class, defined as the oppressor by Marxism, and yet was victimized as a Jew, the problem of rebellion, guilt, and repression becomes all the more acute. Weiss can never escape either background, both of which hinder him from fully joining a new order. As a socialist, he will always be a convert and not a member of the true proletariat. As a young man, he was attracted to the frenzy provoked by Hitler's speeches until his stepbrother informed him that he could not join because his father was a Jew:

> The sudden change happened after one of the speeches which at that time burst through the loudspeakers and of whose incomprehensible power one was unaware, and when one became aware they turned into a confused shriek from hell. Next to me sat Gottfried, my stepbrother, and we listened to the hoarse screams, were overpowered by the screams, but only overpowered, for we did not grasp the content—there was no content but an unheard extension of emptiness, emptiness filled with screams. The emptiness was so overpowering that we lost ourselves therein; it was as if we heard God speak in oracles. And when silence finally returned, and when the storm of joyful shouts about death and self-sacrifice, which then appeared to us as a golden future, had passed, Gottfried said, too bad that you can't take part in it. I felt at these words neither surprise nor fear. And when Gottfried explained that my father was a Jew, it was for me a confirmation of something I had intimated for a long time. Repressed experiences rose up within me, I began to understand my past . . . .[28]

In *Fluchtpunkt (Vanishing Point)* he describes how a newsreel showed him in 1945 the fate that he had escaped through his wandering exile: "Everything turned to dust, and it would be impossible to search for new comparisons, touchstones before such ultimate images. This was no

kingdom of the dead. These were human beings whose hearts were still
beating. This was a world in which mankind lived.''[29]

Twenty years later, in 1964, Weiss visited Auschwitz, "the town for
which I was destined, but which I escaped.''[30] In his essay "Meine
Ortschaft" (My Locale) he describes the empty camp and his feelings
about it. He visits the *Stammlager*, the base camp which is projected on
the stage in many productions of *The Investigation;* what strikes him is
that "everything is so very small.'' As he walks through the political
division, through the gas chambers, past the gallows, his imagination of
Auschwitz is slowly replaced by the banal and bleak reality about him: ''I
knew once these roll calls, about those hours of standing in rain and
snow. Now I only know about this empty muddy square in the middle of
which are three posts rammed into the earth and bridged by an iron rail.''
The never experienced memory is magically evoked by defining sights
and relating them to the past. The similarity between Weiss's evocation
and Borowski's ''A Visit'' is striking:

> Here they walked, a slow procession, coming from all parts of Europe,
> this is the horizon they still saw, these are the watch-towers with the
> sun's reflection in the windows, this is the door through which they
> walked, the rooms flooded with bright lights, without showers, but
> only with these square columns of tin; these are the foundations
> between which they ended in sudden darkness, in gas that streamed
> from the holes. And these words, these realizations say nothing,
> explain nothing. Only heaps of stone overgrown with grass. Ashes
> remain in the earth of these who died for nothing, torn from their
> homes, their countries, their workshops, away from their children,
> their wives, husbands, lovers, away from everyday and thrown into the
> incomprehensible. Nothing remained except the total meaninglessness
> of their deaths.

Towards the end he walks into the barracks where the bunks filled with
straw intimate a human presence to the intruder, "but after awhile,
silence and paralysis take over.'' The living man cannot really comprehend and is excluded: "He only stands in an extinct world. He can do
nothing here. For awhile utter silence reigns. Then he knows it is not yet
over.''

Weiss's walk through Auschwitz, related in the first person and through
the immediacy of the present tense, is comparable to a Christian's
pilgrimage along the Via Dolorosa. It is a walk through the silence
of a past whose fragments have become museum pieces visited by

thoughtless school children, but reverberating for the responsive perceiver with imagined memories. Detachment and identification provide
tension throughout the account as the narrator, whose name was on the
list of the victims, creates cumulative sentences that describe the ultimate
fate of the Jewish people who came here from all over Europe. He names
the all too familiar ritual of this locale, but he cannot name the victims
whose steps he retraces. Instead, he turns in the end to his knowledge of
other prisons where "it is not yet over," thus refusing to differentiate
Auschwitz from analogous recurrences in other parts of the world. By
doing so, he has the chance to fight against an existing Auschwitz and
thus atone for his locale.

The Investigation, then, transcends the personal through the ritual
politics of past, present, and future. Erika Salloch views the play as an
antithesis to a metaphysical world view, an antithesis already evident in
the subtitle An Oratorium in Eleven Cantos which removes the ritual of
the Frankfurt trials by undercutting their immediacy through traditional
form.[31] I would suggest, however, that The Investigation is less an
antithesis than a parody of a sacred world view, for that implies regret
over the loss of such a view as well as a yearning for it. Weiss's
preoccupations with Dante certainly indicate such mixed feelings. In
form the play is both an oratorium and a series of cantos in Dante's sense.
This form, once filled with sacred content, now mocks the little men who
committed great crimes, and by doing so it becomes a parody. Grove's
Dictionary of Music defines oratorio as "a dramatic poem, usually of
sacred but not liturgical character, sung throughout by solo voices and
chorus to the accompaniment of a full orchestra, but—at least in modern
times—without assistance of scenery, dresses, or action." Its origin is to
be sought in the Christian mystery plays, especially the Passion.

The solo voices of The Investigation, especially the voices of the
witnesses, are primarily vessels, "speaking tubes" as Weiss calls them,
through which the matter of the oratorium is transmitted. While the
witnesses are most anonymous in that they are only numbered and a
compound of various personae, they are also individualized through the
precision of their memories. The accused, who are identified by name,
are on the other hand very predictable in their tendency to deny or justify
their crimes in the same refrain. Their language is the most cliché-ridden
in the play. The attorneys—the prosecutor representing an East German
point of view, the defense attorney representing West German attitudes—
are predictable in the questions and responses, while the judge, who
functions primarily as a questioner, often couches his inquiries in such

precise terms that he becomes a namer and definer. In spite of the question and answer ritual, the familiar story is told by solo voices who do not really communicate with each other.

The influence of Dante is evident both in the form and content of *The Investigation*. Best argues that on the most obvious rational level the purpose of this ritual may be to demonstrate to us that the capitalist inferno is a condition preceding the socialist paradiso.[32] Such a belief would, of course, assume that mankind learns from history the way Dante learned in his pilgrimage through hell. In the artifact of his *Commedia,* Dante transposed the personal, historical, and eschatological levels of perception into a timeless realm, a work of art, an inner vision, a religious projection. Weiss, however, maintains that inferno and paradiso tend to fuse in *The Investigation,*[33] and they must fuse because historical time is not transcended in the play. Weiss insists that he knows "only the Inferno section in the way a contemporary reader can know it . . . . I lack the theological and philosophical bases to understand the Paradiso . . . . I can understand the last section in which Dante repeatedly states that his voice failed, that he lacks words to describe a condition."[34] Dante projected hell as a model of divine justice. The Nazis established the hell of Auschwitz under similar assumptions, but we cannot accept that man-made hell where the sinners are sinless and where they do not desire their damnation as they do in Dante. Furthermore, the damned and the persecutors meet gradually at a dim line of cooperation. In the courtroom the persecutors become the sinners who have repressed their crimes to such an extent that they can lead comfortable lives as nurses, teachers, and beauticians. In their eyes the accusations of the witnesses are damnable lies. Yet, like Dante's sinners, the accused are paralyzed in their status quo because they refuse to become conscious. There is, then, consciousness on the part of the witnesses (except for the first two) and lack of consciousness on the part of the accused. To achieve paradise on earth would entail the mutual consciousness and conscience of oppressor and oppressed and the will to overcome that dialectic. As long as this does not happen, history will be the paradise of the oppressors, their comedy in the sense of a happy end. For this reason Weiss ends the oratorium not with a judgment, but with the approbation extended to the chauvinist outburst of Accused 1. The vision of a healed world is not maintained in *The Investigation;* if there are glimpses of it, they are undercut by the world as it was and is.

In his verse essay "Preliminary Exercise to the Three Part Drama divina commedia," Weiss admits that Dante provided him with "mere forms . . . perhaps not even forms, only suggestions, constructed patterns into which content had to be newly poured.''[35] New content and matter were discovered by Weiss during the Frankfurt trials where he watched witnesses and accused, wondering if the former belonged to the choir of angels and the latter to ''Lucifer, the three-headed one, the cannibal.'' He concludes, ''They belonged only to us, they belong / to no hell, to no paradise, they grew up with us / and what they did, what happened to them / belonged to us.'' Dante's three realms are now secular history, and today Dante would have to revise his vision:

> The Alighieri of today must give up the play of illusions, he cannot wake the dead, he has nothing but the reality of words which can still be uttered, and it is his task to find these words and allow them to live in an absolute void . . . .
>   . . . Spoken perhaps
> by witnesses, as I saw them, before the court, stepping forward, searching individual memory . . . .

Perceived with these lines in mind, Weiss's Auschwitz oratorium transcends the simplistic charge of communist propaganda. The dream of justice, of the dissolution of the dialectic between oppressor and oppressed, is not even intimated. Dream and nightmare occur in the same world. Awareness merely leads to the painful recognition of an incomprehensible emptiness which the poet tries to fill with words. These words shape, in spite of all reliance on documents, Weiss's vision of Auschwitz, his comprehensible explanation. However, since the dialectic of the play is part of historical time, it is subject to changes and ironies that the playwright cannot predict. In a utopia of reason and consciousness, Weiss's play, if not banned, would be considered prophetic, but at the expense of those for whom the extermination camps were primarily established—the Jews. If we imagine a future in which Weiss's oratorium is the only document of the holocaust to survive, we become immediately aware of the limitations of documentary theater as a conveyor of facts. By emphasizing the sufferings of the political prisoners, Weiss shows the individual dignity of the believer's agony. His death, torturous as it may have been, was more likely to be remembered than the death of an unnumbered Jew. When Weiss does describe the latter death in several cantos, he does so without writing the word *Jew,* for that word remains a problem for him.

Structurally, *The Investigation* is akin to the *Inferno* in its division of thirty-three cantos subdivided by eleven subjects. The thirty-fourth canto of the *Inferno* is not needed, aside from the numerical balance, because the previous life of the inmates is not of interest. Any wrong they may have committed is irrelevant to their imprisonment. A further parallel with the *Inferno* is the movement of the oratorium from the periphery of the ramp to the center of destruction, the fiery ovens where the person was totally obliterated. In the icy circles of Caina, the damned were forever frozen in their individuality, but in Auschwitz those designated as damned simply vanished. The base camp of Auschwitz could be overviewed from almost any position with the result that everyone was in the know (pp. 62, 83). The perceiver is made aware of the center of extinction beginning with the first canto when the wagons marked with the number of victims arrive and when the smoke and fire of the crematoria are visible in the night. There is no descent to the pit; the topography of damnation is horizontal.

The "speaking tubes" of *The Investigation,* the voices who report or deny what they have seen, hover between individuality and anonymity. Anonymity is established by numbering both witnesses and accused; but the accused have names, while the witnesses project anonymous personae. Anonymity is, of course, found in the very mass of human beings going to their death, a mass that impresses itself on the memory of the individual witness recalling specific moments of agony and brutality. Even saints' legends are possible in the memory of Auschwitz. Political identity, as I pointed out, preserves some semblance of personal identity and makes death seem less meaningless, especially since Weiss emphasizes that political prisoners still languish and die in prisons. Historically, Weiss is justified in emphasizing the politicals of Auschwitz for whom the camp was originally established. After 1942, Auschwitz increasingly became a camp for the extermination of the Jews. Even then, political prisoners had the chance to postpone their death; but as they did so, they cooperated with the oppressors and thus entered the hierarchy of guilt. As Witness 3 points out, "Those prisoners who / by their privileged position in the camp / managed to postpone their own death / made one step towards / the rules of the camp / in order to maintain / the possibility of survival / they were forced / to give the appearance of cooperation" (pp. 77, 106). Because they were too much in the know, they would eventually be destroyed as bearers of secrets *(Geheimnisträger).* The witnesses in the play, then, may be politicals or Jews, or both, but only their political identity is mentioned.

Anonymity in *The Investigation* is more obvious to the reader of the oratorium than to the member of the theater audience; since the latter associates the words with the actor as speaker, they become embodied. For the reader, on the other hand, the report about Auschwitz flows from the accused to the witness without pause, emphasizing thereby the speaking-tube quality of the numbered witnesses and accused. The questions, comments, and objections interjected by the judge, the East German prosecuting attorney, and the West German defense attorney could well be interjected by the reader. The mechanics of the court are in and of themselves peripheral in comparison to the revelation of factual material. A defense of Auschwitz is by definition impossible, and any attempt at it immediately destroys the ethos of the defender. The ritual of the court can neither justify nor judge the deeds of the accused. *The Investigation* remains without action; it is a world of words created through memory and denial of memory as well as through the rhythms of inquiry, statement, and analysis. Although the play ends with the triumphant voices of the accused, who appear to be winners, the great number of lines given to the witnesses reveals that it is their day in court. Named and pointed out at least once, all the accused deny individual responsibility by insisting on their administrative functions and their political conditioning. They want to be "mere numbers" and are anonymous in their predictable responses, while the witnesses become individuals through their utterances.

The numbering of the accused and the witnesses emphasizes their anonymity; but since numbers have symbolic values, the reader, not the member of the audience, attaches meaning to them, especially with regard to the hierarchy of guilt. Mulka, after whom the trial was named, is Accused 1 and has the last word in the end. He is followed by Boger, head of the political division and the sadistic inventor of the notorious "swing." Next comes the doctor group (3, 4, 5, 6) arranged according to degrees of guilt; all are, however, implicated because they violated at the very least the ethics of their profession. Of less authority, but not of less brutality, are SS officers Kaduk 7 and Hoffman 8. Hoffman passively admits, "I only did my duty / Whatever I am assigned to do / I do my duty" (pp. 17, 16). He had personally nothing against the persecuted: "After all they are human too" (pp. 17, 16). Here, as well as in an account of a brutal act commited by Kaduk, Weiss omits the word *Jew*. During the actual trial a witness reported about Kaduk: "He told the second one, the Jew, to lie on his back. Kaduk placed the blood-soiled iron across the neck and stood at one end. A prisoner had to stand at the other. Thus the man was strangled."[36] Weiss omits the reference to the other prisoner and thereby also omits the guilty relationship between oppressor and oppressed. He cools the language by avoiding images such as "blood-soiled iron": Once Kaduk hit one of the prisoners / in our work detail / knocked him down / then laid his walking stick / down across his throat / put one foot on each end of the stick / and rocked from side to side / until the man choked to death" (pp. 43, 53). Accused 9, 10, and 11 are implicated in the mass murder of people by means of phenol injections. Accused 12, SS Corporal Stark, stands by himself and is followed by a group of SS officers of greater and lesser criminality. The 18th accused is again isolated. He is Emil Bednarek, the only inmate standing trial. In terms of the hierarchy of guilt, he is thus technically in the position of being a witness.

The witnesses are outnumbered by the accused two to one, which puts them symbolically, in spite of their many personae, into a more power-less position. The first two witnesses are the most guilty, projecting not inmates but outsiders who cooperated to varying degrees with the Nazi regime and who were promoted to important positions in the social and economic structure of West Germany after the war. As so-called decent men, they remained at the threshold of the horror and avoided uncomfort-able knowledge as much as possible, thus aiding the smooth functioning of the machinery of destruction. Witness 1 projects in the first canto the persona of a stationmaster who regulated the punctual arrival and depar-ture of the trains at Auschwitz but denied that he had anything to do with their content: "I was not initiated into the matter." As the oratorium funnels to its historical and symbolic center, the fiery ovens, the first two witnesses become more involved in "the matter," driving the trucks to the gas chambers, observing how the gas was poured in, and noticing that "when the lids were taken off / I heard a humming sound / as if a lot of people were underground" (pp. 168, 249). The subterranean sound is the truth of a reality that the witness attempts to deny through *as if* phrasing. The most positive projection of the first two witnesses is Witness 1's account of how he was sent to Auschwitz as an investigating albeit impotent judge.

The various personae of Witness 3 penetrate every level of the camp from the ramp to the crematoria. His testimony is absent only in the cantos about the swing, those about Lili Töfler's saint's legend, and those about Corporal Stark; for these cantos focus primarily on individuals, their crimes, their attempts at survival, and their martyrdom. Witness 3, however, brings the specific experiences of Auschwitz onto a general political and economic denominator. His many selves each time project a well-informed, objective, and rational individual who is very conscious of the role he played in the camp, conscious that he and every survivor

took at least one step towards the persecutors and thus implicated themselves in the hierarchy of guilt.

Witnesses 4 and 5 are women, their personae clearly differentiated
from each other. The voices of Witness 4 are more passive, the examples
of horror concentrating on the individual human experience. Her last
report concerns the medical experiments inflicted upon her, leaving her
unable to bear children. Witness 5 refuses to bear children after she had
seen the murder of children in the camp where she worked under Boger in
the political division. Her personae are precise in their observations and
in their memory of what attitudes and actions aided survival. In her
consciousness and insights she is very much like Witness 3, except that
she does not draw political and economic conclusions from her experiences. Instead, she is merely aware that survival could only be furthered
by always insisting on one's advantage. In her last line she reports the
sardonic sentence of Lili Töfler: "I am always fine."

None of the remaining witnesses interpret Auschwitz; they report
instead with great precision what they have seen. As these facts accumulate, they take on a power against which the rational explanations of
Witness 3 seem pale and impotent. The socialist message of the drama is
thus definitely undercut. Witness 8 has the most lines of all and reports in
one of his voices his personal experience and survival of Boger's torturous swing. Although he offers no explanations concerning the why and
wherefore of the camp, his descriptions overwhelm the audience in their
keenness and precision. Neither he nor the other witnesses suffer consciously from survivor guilt. Their suffering precludes and expiates all
guilt accrued in the struggle for survival.

The structure of *The Investigation* funnels memory into an open
present, comparable to the point of constriction in Celan's "Engführung." The internal pattern follows the ritual of arrival, initial traumatization, adjustment, ways of survival, and manner of death, liberation
being omitted. Weiss's suggestion that an intermission could follow the
cantos about Stark hints at a clear divison of the oratorium. The first half
concerns itself primarily with the arrival and survival attempts of the
witnesses, with the brutalities of the political division, and with the
portraits of saint and criminal. Individuality is much more important in
the first half, while the second recounts increasingly efficient means of
mass murder. Yet the perceiver must always keep in mind that arrival and
annihilation are simultaneous; everybody is always aware of the chimneys and the smell. Periphery and center, the fiery ovens, are one, as is
made clear in the opening cantos.

Here the witnesses report about the beginning of their physical and psychological stripping shortly after the brief illusion of reprieve at the sight of the Red Cross trucks. Female Witness 5 immediately realized that here one's own advantage counted the most, as the abnormal became the normal. In a relentless inversion of the Sermon on the Mount, she defines those who failed in the concentrationary universe:

> Only the cunning survived
> only those who every day
> with relentless alertness
> took and held their bit of ground
> The unfit
> the retarded
> the slow
> the gentle
> the bewildered and impractical
> the ones who mourned and the ones
> who pitied themselves were crushed [pp. 34, 40]

She is also aware that every individual, oppressor and oppressed, at least had a choice of attitude. For the prisoner this may have meant the choice to struggle for survival at all cost; for the persecutor it meant that "everyone . . . had the choice to resist conditions and to change them" (pp. 47, 57–58). Witness 7 reports that this choice of attitude was realized even in a nine-year-old boy who was completely in the know when loaded along with ninety other children onto a truck to be driven to the gas chambers. He calmed the children, but, as they all were driven off, he shouted to the guard, "You won't be forgiven anything" (pp. 36, 43), an absurd faith and a final assertion of human dignity and individuality.

The nature of the political department under the leadership of SS Oberscharführer Boger is revealed in the three cantos about the swing, a torture instrument to which the victims were tied and then beaten while being swung back and forth. Each of the eleven sections of the oratorium starts either harmlessly or with a simple factual inquiry or statement. Thus, the first canto about the swing opens with a report by Witness 5 about her working conditions and responsibilities in the political depart-ment; judicial inquiries lead her to a description of the swing, followed by descriptions of Boger's murder of a child by smashing it against a wall, his eating of the child's apple, and his ordering Witness 5 to wipe off the wall. Since then she has never wanted a child. Later testimony will reveal how Boger shot a little girl at the Black Wall. Weiss is deeply conscious of this slaughter of the innocents as he reports their fate in a language that cools down the language of the actual testimony. Yet the image of the child with the apple, the image of the little girl in the red dress, and the image of the children playing ball before their death impress themselves in the perceiver's consciousness with stark simplicity. Those same images moved Judge Hofmeyer to conclude the trials in Frankfurt with the following words: "There will be many among us who will not be able to look into the glad and trusting eyes of a child without having in mind a vision of the anxious eyes of those children who went their last walk in Auschwitz."[37]

The next two cantos about the swing give examples of one who died because of the torture and of one who survived it. These reports lead into three cantos describing the possibility of survival as determined by three factors: failure of the technical apparatus of destruction, the prisoner's cooperation with the system, and the evacuation of the camp. Witness 3 experienced the first two possibilities; Witness 4 survived medical experiments only because the camp was evacuated. These cantos also deal with the interrelations between the prisoners and the guards. Using the metaphor of the theater, Witness 3 says, "Many of those who were destined / to play the part of prisoners / had grown up with the same ideas / the same way of looking at things / as those / who found themselves as guards . . . / they could equally well have been guards" (pp. 78, 107–8). While the guard had total power and the prisoner none at all, the first could use his power to preserve life, and the second did not need to give in completely by succumbing to death. Witness 3 considers the camp the ultimate exploitation, a political and economic system using even the bones of the exploited (pp. 79, 108). Because the same exploitative system still functions, the witness concludes "that millions could again stand waiting to be destroyed." It is this canto which gives the oratorium its apparently Marxist line, and it is significant that a tentative hint at an alternative for survival appears in the central canto. Whether one agrees with this line or not is not as important as agreement with the argument that the fundamental interactions between peoples and nations must change in order to prevent a recurrence of Auschwitz.

The physical details of the camp, its causes and effects, are reported when the investigation turns to focus on the individuals Lili Töfler and SS Corporal Stark. Both are projected as young people; both illustrate the possibility of choice for the powerless and the powerful. Töfler uses her radically limited power of choice to a far greater extent than Stark, who almost claims to have been a robot because of his Nazi indoctrination.

Stark, a member of the political division, is projected in three roles: as former student in a humanistic gymnasium, as SS officer, and as teacher in an agricultural school after the war. His case is especially shocking because it makes clear that neither youth nor a humanistic education are a guarantee against dehumanization and the committing of atrocities. His language especially reveals his insensitivity. Mixing colloquialisms and officialese, he shrugs off his work and his education as something that had to be *erledigt* (gotten rid of). Involved in shootings as well as gassings—he objected to the latter because they appeared to him unmanly—he is asked by the judge if he ever had doubts about his activities. To this question he responds with a lengthy analysis of his situation, for his humanistic education had given him the ability to use words with some skill when necessary. His sophistic defense comes to the conclusion that "we weren't supposed to think / others did that for us" (pp. 110, 158), to which the other accused assent with laughter. Through Stark, Weiss projects the portrait of a youthful and relatively educated criminal who abrogates all personal responsibility for his crimes by rationalizing that he lost his individuality to the Nazi conditioning. Because he once possessed the potential for a different kind of life, he, even more than the other voices of the accused, presents a truly hopeless case.

The second part of *The Investigation* begins with the three cantos about the Black Wall and moves from there to increasingly efficient mass murder. About 20,000 people were shot before the wall, which was four meters broad and three meters high and covered with a black, tarred cloth to catch the bullets. The evidence of the ritual of judgment reveals here that the murderer was still directly involved with the victim, who was shot in the back of the neck as he faced the wall. An officer could not hand over the execution to an inmate functionary because no prisoner was allowed to carry a weapon. The abrogation of responsibility by the officials is evident in the three cantos concerning the phenol injections which killed 30,000 inmates. Inmates attempted to deceive the victims by claiming that the procedure was medical. Officers and inmates were in the know and cooperated, but victim and executioner still faced each other since each victim was murdered individually. The three cantos about the bunker block show how the victim was separated from his persecutors by being buried alive. Only one functionary, the Bunker Jacob, was now needed, and he remained unmoved by the killings. It was in the bunker block that the first experimental gassings were used to kill Russian prisoners. When they were successful, the commandant concluded, "Now I'm relieved / Now that we have this gas / we'll be spared all those bloodbaths / The victims too / will be spared / until the last moment'' (pp. 155, 228). Technological killing had begun.

The three cantos about Cyklon B are strictly a report about the nature of the gas and its cost—200 people killed at the expense of forty marks. Once more the familiar road of the victims is traced as they conveniently disappear from sight. The judge asks the first witness, "Where did the people go?'' He answers evasively, "Into a house / I didn't see anything else after that''; but when pressed he admits, "They were burned up / right then and there'' (pp. 166, 244–45). In the final three cantos about the fiery ovens, *The Investigation* returns to the ramp, the beginning of the victims' experience which was repeated so many times in the history of the camps. Now, however, the perceiver learns, not about the arrival of those who became survivors, but about the arrival of those who were selected for immediate gassing. The first of the three cantos leads up to the moment when the gas was thrown in. Judge and Witness 7 calmly exchange questions and answers about this event, and yet there exists between them a subtle understanding: each repeatedly uses the word *Menschen* (human beings) as if only that accumulated reiteration could convey the message of one who actually being killed in the gas chamber. When the judge asks if the victims knew what was about to happen to them, the witness answers, "No one returned / to report about it.'' In the next canto, the doors are opened and the dead are revealed in the words of Gerstein's famous report. Before cremation, the final plundering of the dead takes place as their dental gold is extracted. After cremation the ashes are taken to the nearby river. Witness 1 concludes his report by describing his visit to the crematoria during the time when he was sent to investigate fraud at Auschwitz. He found nothing in the center of hell except female prisoners feeding potato pancakes to drunken functionaries. There was not "even a speck of dust'' of the dead, the modern inferno displaying itself harmlessly as a bourgeois kitchen. The witness seems to lament his inability to bring action against the killings. He could not have indicted the government, and if he had simply told outsiders, no one would have believed him. He would very likely have been executed.

The final canto of *The Investigation* once more indicts the accused, who respond with rationalizations. Witness 3 reiterates the number of all of those who knew about and cooperated with the institution of the camps, and he evokes once more the mystic number of the victims. Fixed in mathematical metaphysics, the dead lose all meaning to the living, who are busy repressing their memories and constructing a new life. Mulka, the main accused, ends the oratorium with the following peroration:

> Today
> when our nation
> has worked its way up
> after a devastating war
> to a leading position in the world
> we ought to concern ourselves
> with other things
> than blame and reproaches
> that should be thought of
> as long since atoned for
>   [Loud approbation from the Accused]

The ritual of judgment ends as a comedy for the accused, whose last words reject the rationale of the trial itself. In *The Investigation,* the delinquent confirms his good conscience, for the presumptuous and rationalizing attitude of the delinquent is not contrary to that of the polis; it is the attitude of the polis where the judge becomes impotent. If the ritual of judgment in *The Investigation* concluded with the passing of sentences, the audience would view the criminals as *erledigt;* they would exorcise the criminals from their collective consciousness. As it is, Weiss's conclusion is as open-ended as Hochhuth's, for historical time continues with all its corruptions. The Frankfurt trial also left no sense of liberation after the sentences were passed; rather, as Langbein points out, "The trial was ended when the last witness had given his testimony, when the last protocol had been read. What followed then was a judicial epilogue that had to be insufficient because Auschwitz cannot be put into a paragraph."[38]

In the documentary drama of the 1960s, the chaos created by the myths which make history becomes a metaphor of evil within the confines of the stage. The setting of a room, a guardhouse, a courtroom reveals through language the horrendous deeds of humankind. This is not the language of confession leading to exculpation, for in this ritual the victimized, the survivors, tend to feel guilt rather than the accused, whose guilt, if it exists at all, remains subconscious. The witness reports events that no man or woman should have witnessed, for such events should never have occurred. From the point of view of the accused, what the witness has seen is a taboo that should never be expressed in language but should be repressed until it disappears from memory. In the final analysis, the ritual of judgment, acted out in the courtroom or on the stage, is in its attitudes, words, and gestures a show without ethical force.

People come to see this show; they see how the myths that shaped religion and politics have become shattered by the actuality of historical events. The theater still provides that moment of communal experience during which people can see a displaced reality enacted by living persons. Hochhuth and Weiss remind us of our collective guilt and try to make us conscious of it during the theater experience. Hochhuth not only indicts the organization man but also indicts Christians who are not Christians if they are silent about their knowledge of evil. The viewer is shocked and chagrined over the failure of the pope to fulfill that role. Thus, the pope receives the medicinal and mythical aura of a scapegoat; for no matter how much Hochhuth refers to shared guilt, the image of one pope remains in our minds and permits us to project communal guilt onto one figure. In this way we achieve an illusory catharsis of our own vaguely realized scruples. Although Weiss provides no scapegoat, although he, too, emphasizes individualism through moral choice, defiant gesture, or even biological reflex, his report about the locale called Auschwitz exonerates those involved through emphasis on the collective experience of oppressor and oppressed, which was analyzed collectively at the Frankfurt trials. Neither play is a mimesis of an actual trial, not even Weiss's which, while it has its own austere order, begins and ends *in medias res* as far as the historical trial is concerned. Outrages continue on narrow ground and in global expansion.

Stimulation of guilt, confession, insight, and eventual integration were the didactic aims of the Christian morality plays. In documentary drama, however, while guilt may be stimulated and insight may sometimes be gained, confession and integration are impossible for the audience witnessing the enactment of these rituals of judgment, rituals which cannot dispense a justice that would satisfy the victims and the members of the polis. Through change of dress, the accused as everyman denies or is indifferent to what he has been as he verbally rationalizes a new self for himself. We may be shattered or outraged over the destruction of our myths, we may fabricate new myths, or we may sit through a performance indulging in communal castigation, experiencing momentary embarrassment or melancholy and thus expiating guilt through fleeting discomfort. Yet the better world remains a utopia as we, like medieval everymen, go on sinning and corrupting even the hope for a secular paradise. Like peripatetics, we circle with our teachers, the documentary playwrights, without achieving a genuine peripeteia.

7

Towards the Point of Constriction: Nelly Sachs's "Landschaft aus Schreien" and Paul Celan's "Engführung"

Of all literary forms it is the lyric which has been most severely challenged as being appropriate for the images of the holocaust. Yet it is the defined and confined space of the lyric, its few words, which has given many a human being a momentary sense of order in the chaos and rigidity of the holocaust, of war and defeat.[1] Northrop Frye has argued that the lyric can "be on any subject and of any shape." It reveals its content through the recurrent dynamic rhythms of images rather than narrative pattern; it assumes a turning away from the audience and insists on an element of privacy even when communally sung as a hymn rising from the heart of each singer in a ritualistic participation mystique.[2]

Such a participation mystique is found in Nelly Sachs's "Landschaft aus Schreien" (Landscape of Screams) and Paul Celan's "Engführung" (Point of Constriction). The two poems also reveal mythic and oracular images and rhythms uttered, not by a priestly representative, but by the prophetic spirit of an imagination threatened by and defending itself against disintegration. Such lyrics reveal the urgency as well as the precariousness of defense through verbal structure even more than an autobiography. For the lyric's confined space crowds the rhythms and associations of images to such a degree that their inherent energies are driven to a pitch and maintained at a point of balance whence they might break forth creatively or destructively; or they might congeal into a rigidity that may be nothing but dead letters on a page or a form demanding animation. Sachs's "Landschaft aus Schreien" and Celan's "Engführung" are hermetic poems forged by the imagination of two survivors who internalized the chaos of history and struggled with it until their deaths in 1970.

The encapsulated and seemingly hermetically sealed word images of these poems nevertheless project with utmost precision the ambiguous and intricate relationships between victims, persecutors, and bystanders. Words are the elements in the retort of these poems, while Sachs and Celan are the alchemists of words who seek to distill their matter in such a way that it will point towards, if not reveal, "the something quite other." They will fail, for only the corrupt ground of history and their personal reaction to it through the insufficiency of words provide the sole certainty for both poets. Yet, as Octavio Paz points out, "the hermetic poem proclaims the greatness of poetry and the wretchednes of history." It is distinguished from the poem of facile communication by its precision of language, which becomes so much more than "a mere medium of exchange."[3] The hermetic poet aims to make the word timeless, aims to rescue the word from a diachronic line into synchronic roundness by imploding into it all the abusive, banal, and glorious meanings it accrued through its evolution in historical time. Two traditions inform the use of the word by Sachs and Celan: the word in Jewish and Christian mysticism and in the secular mysticism of *symbolisme*. Both traditions seek to liberate the word from its guilty historical and social contexts. But Sachs and Celan, as they reach for such timelessness, cannot escape into it; their consciousness of historical time and its ethical implications permits no transcendence of the creative imagination. Alienated in its consciousness of historical evil and urged by guilt and the ethical necessity to bear witness for the landscape of the dead, the lyric self has only the impotent power of the word with which to address, aggressively challenge, and provoke "the quite other." This quite other—God or the larger self—is a projection of the ego, separated from it so that the ego can maintain itself in opposition or in expectancy of it. But the ego never relinquishes its rigid self-definition and hence cannot achieve a mystic union. The projection of the other and the memory of the landscape of the dead remain unreal and silent and cast the ego back into alienation, no matter how much the ego sought contact through the word.

The poems of Sachs and Celan are frequently riddles that demand to be solved. As André Jolles has argued in his study of simple forms, "To be unable to solve a given riddle means annihilation, to ask a riddle that no one can answer means life . . . . At its deepest meaning, the riddle is a matter of life and death."[4] Such a riddle is at the core of the poetry of Sachs and Celan, a riddle directed to the silent cosmos. The riddle is a matter of life and death for the poet and the poet's god. If the god does not answer, he is nonexistent and annihilated, but the poet, too, is robbed of all meaning for existence. On the other side of this paradoxical coin is the riddle that no one can answer: life. Both poet and god offer such a riddle—the world and the poem—and thus retain the possibility for existence and the hope for life.

The topography of "Landscape of Screams" and "Point of Constriction" projects a hermetic vision, an enclosed world that suggests both the ironic and mythical mode. In approaching these poems, the reader is at first barred from perception by the seemingly absolute literalness of the words as abstract signs on the page. Yet an empathetic circuit between perceiver and poem will release energies in both and surround the words with auras of meanings until human existence in all its ambiguities is realized. The fiction of a dialogue between witness and god about the landscape of the dead remains an ambitious fiction. The lyric self would be doomed to wholly converse with itself were it not for the human reader who takes the time to meditate over and thereby reanimate, albeit imperfectly, the black symbols on the white page. What the reader discovers is not so extraordinary: it is the longing for empathy and love and the difficulty of having that longing fulfilled.

Because "Landscape of Screams" and "Point of Constriction" are so intricately related in content and form to the use of the hieroglyphic word in mysticism and *symbolisme,* I will briefly review the influences of both on Sachs and Celan and show how both are related to the hermetic poet's bondage in history and use of metaphors of evil.

I.
The Power of the Word in Mystic and Modern Poetry and Its Displacement into History and Guilt

As the most primal and sophisticated of literary expressions, the poem and its maker parallel the first myth of evil in which the creative god struggles with chaos and achieves salvation through the act of creation.[5] The human poet, however, lives after Babel where the struggle with unorganized reality is never concluded. In the mythical world of Genesis, word and act are one as the spirit of God moves across the waters and calls light and form out of the formless deep. Adam, in a sense the perfect and original poet, can find names for the animals and is able to retain a dialogical relationship with God even after the fall when the divine voice becomes accusatory. An angry or compassionate but always concerned dialogue between God and man pervades the Old Testament. In the Gospels the word becomes flesh and enters the ambiguities of historical

time through the person of Christ. Christ's verbal powers are at times
strictly those of a god, as when he calls forth Lazarus, but his powers fail
him at the nadir of his bondage when the cry "God, my God, why hast
Thou forsaken me?" remains unanswered.

By projecting the image of a deity who can make word and deed
coincide, humankind overcomes the deficiency of its own use of language magic. The conventional image of an external and divine being is
comforting even when it threatens, for the ego can turn to it as *the other*.
Ideally, however, the ego establishes with it that dialogical contact which
Jung called the ego-self axis. The mystic, in contrast, experiences the
divine in a moment of external-internal envelopment wherein egocentricity is dissolved as the god-man or man-god is realized. The possibility of
the annihilation of God is inherent in the conventional and mystic experience of the divine. In the first, God withdraws from the dialogue; He
neither listens nor responds but becomes as egocentric as the world He
has created. When the individual perceives the divine in this fashion, he
or she becomes all the more conscious of the alienated loneliness of the
ego; and the ego inflates itself, becomes central in order to survive, as we
saw in young Eliezer's rebellion against the silent god. In the Judaic-
Christian mystic tradition, the possibility for annihilation exists both
for the god and the human being. God is perceived as the no-thing that is
simultaneously the everything from which creation emerges like consciousness from unconsciousness, like ego from self. In the mystic
experience, the ego (man) is not connected with the self (god) through an
axis but merges with it and must emerge again in order to resume normal
human life. The no-thing can be negatively experienced as sheer nothingness, as empty chaos. It is likely to be viewed as such when the world
appears empty and rigid to the ego, a world of marionettes or a landscape
of the dead, of rigid corpses or of bodies evaporated in smoke. As the ego
gravitates towards and identifies with that void, there comes the annihila-
ting realization that it, too, is nothing, that it has no subconscious or self,
no well of creativity. At this point of constriction, madness and suicidal
impulses become a possible escape from painful awareness. The poetry
of Sachs and Celan expresses the ambiguities both of the ego's sense of
identity and alienation as well as of mystic longing. For the anxious lyric
self yearns towards and demands attention from a silent cosmos, yearns
towards the landscape of the dead by means of the word whose silent
constellations of letters preserve its efficacy and impotence.

The primary influences of Judaic and Christian mysticism on Sachs
and Celan come from the theosophic doctrine of the Zohar as translated

and discussed by Gershom Scholem, from Hasidism and Martin Buber's interpretations of it, and from Christian mysticism, specifically that of Jakob Boehme, who has himself a deep affinity with Kabbalism. Such cross-fertilizations of mystic trends are not surprising since, in spite of variables in image patterns, the mystic experience is basically the same psychological experience, namely, the *personal* working out of the myth of individuation in terms of the ego's relation to cosmic metaphors of the self. It is the psychological validity of mystic images which makes them relevant to the poetry of Sachs and Celan, who would have arrived at similar image clusters even if they had not been familiar with the mystic tradition. They ask questions that mystics have always asked, and they experience the frustration of mystics when they attempt to express the inexpressible. Sachs and Celan do not intimate in their poetry the memory of a positive mystic experience; at best, they only can realize a state of suspended yearning. Yet their poetry is informed by three intricately related problems that concerned traditional mystics: the probability of the existence of a deity and the nature of its manifestation, the power of the word in cosmic and poetic creation, and the origin and nature of evil.

In his discussion of the Zohar, Scholem points out that the process of cosmic individuation requires the separation of a previously undifferentiated totality into ten emanations, the Sefiroth. The goal of the process is the return to a harmonious integration, better now because of the experience of separation, inflation, and alienation. The fact that the emanations can be named and discussed separately implies division. The problem of separation has been especially pronounced for two of the divine emanations: *Din,* the power of God as chiefly manifested in stern judgment and punishment, and the *Malkuth* or *Shekhinah,* the kingdom of God, His immanence in the world, and the archetype of the community of Israel after the diaspora (cf. p. 213).

Viewed positively, the Shekhinah is "the presence and immanence of God in the whole creation. It is the point where man, in attaining the deepest understanding of his own self, becomes aware of the presence of God" (p. 216). When the separateness of the Shekhinah is emphasized, it becomes anthropomorphized as the female half of God, comparable to the Great Mother and to Sophia, the divine wisdom of the Gnostics. As such she is the divine fallen, spellbound and exiled in the world of matter where her captured energy is also the source of creative and generative forces. In the Shekhinah, the State of Israel, Rachel the mother wanders as exile through the world, seeking redemption from matter and reintegration with the larger selfhood. Whenever a human being recognizes this divine spark in matter and, in empathy with the divine, speaks the right word, the process of redemption is futhered. The problem of evil is, therefore, inextricably tied to the process of individuation, of consciousness which necessitates inflation and alienation before integration; the latter, however, remains an ever unrealized goal.

Just as the Zohar does not say why God wanted to become manifested, neither does it give an unequivocal answer to the problem of evil which is part of the theosophic process as well as part of the moral nature of man (pp. 238–39). Separation, disunity, and false unity—namely, the rigid and confining enclosure of the divine in matter, in the bark of the tree or in the shell of the nut—generate the various metaphors of evil in Judaic and Christian mysticism. We again see here the radicals of the archetypal energies of evil: chaos and rigidity.

The Zoharic interpretation of Genesis showed how a dark flame grew out of the mystery of the innermost recess of the Infinite, which only later produced radiant colors and light. Consciousness begins with an eruption of energy from out of a condensed point. Negatively, this power is, according to Scholem, aligned with the wrath of God, a fire that always burns within Him and must be tempered by His mercy. "When it ceases to be tempered, when in its measureless hypertrophical outbreak it tears itself loose from the quality of mercy, then it breaks away from God altogether and is transformed into the radically evil, into Gehenna and the dark world of Satan" (p. 237). In Christianity the same wrath is isolated from mercy in Dante's *Inferno,* the creation of the justice of the Father and the evil other placed coeternally with God. Jakob Boehme also perceived the wrath of God in terms of the constricted energy of *Grimm* and *Zorn.* It is the first principle of God's unfolding, "an *Angst* fire which can readily be compared to a hypothetical pure energy whose eruptive primal forces press towards the outside, towards materialization."[7] In Boehme's mysticism, God's son is the metamorphosis of wrath into love. These metaphysical projections of the cosmic process of individuation parallel the encapsulated "dark nucleus" of the human sense of deprivation, a no-thingness experienced first in childhood or later through a traumatization that threatens the individuating ego; aggression is often the only means by which the ego can maintain itself. Sachs and Celan are well aware of this but fear the inflationary result of a "hypertrophical outbreak." Both temper the encroachment of aggressive emotion through images and attitudes of humility, helpless rebellion, patience, and endurance.

Incapable of provoking the unknowable and silent aspect of God, the lyric selves of Sachs and Celan empathetically turn just as often to the Shekhinah, the alienated and exiled emanation of the divine who, like the gnostic Sophia, has fallen into the rigidity of matter from whence she seeks liberation and unification with the divine. Time and again the lyric selves reenact the myth of individuation, fluctuating between inflation and alienation, and capturing the yearning for being in the momentary illusion offered by the constellation of words, the poem.

Nelly Sachs identifies herself many times with the Shekhinah but also sees herself as an archetypal image of the exile whose memory of primal unity has left her with the wound of consciousness:

> Beyond the rims of the world
> the exiled soul of Genevieve always waits
> with the child rich in pain
> in the radiance of longing.
>
> You can also call her Shekhinah,
> crowned with dust,
> sobbing through Israel.
>
> And the sacred animal woman
> with seeing wounds in her head,
> that do not heal
> in memory of God . . . .[8]

The Shekhinah pervades Celan's poetry through manifestations of the anima archetype. She is the lost and longed-for mother, the sister, the erotically loved woman, or even mown grass bending towards God, i.e., human beings falling into silence. Sexual union becomes in Celan's poetry on the anagogic level the imitation of the *hieros gamos* and is as such a challenge to the absent god who, because divided, does not house:

> Dioecious, Eternal, you are un-
> inhabitable. Therefore
> we build and build. Therefore
> this wretched bedstead
> stands,—in the rain,
> there it stands . . . .[9]

The bedstead of human love is wretched and miserable, *erbärmlich*, but it cannot provoke the absent god to be *barmherzig* (compassionate).

Nevertheless, the act of love between human beings remains meaningful for Celan, while an act of love by the deity belongs to the realm of once upon a time (A 103).

Martin Buber points out that the Israelites conceived of prayer as a process of address and answer: "God in all concreteness as speaker, creation as speech . . . the life of every being as dialogue, the world as word,—that message was Israel's. It taught, it showed: the real God can be addressed because he is the addressing God." God is housed amidst those who address Him. But when the god seeker negates the immanence of God in creation and searches only for His absoluteness, then "God disappears with the world and only it, the soul is there; what it calls God is only an image within it; what it considers a dialogue, is only a monologue with distributed roles because the real partner of the relationship is no longer there."[10] Caught in the theological metaphors, the lyric self of Sachs and Celan finds itself in a comparable situation. A living god cannot be immanent in a dead world, an intolerable world from which the ego seeks escape and absorption in some kind of all-embracing absolute. As sole perceiver of the landscape of the dead, the lyric self in contemporary hermetic poetry remains caught in its individualized consciousness, experiencing inflation as it challenges the cosmos and deflation as it is thrown back again into its loneliness. At best, it imitates the Shekhinah by collecting the multifaceted shards of a shattered world, but it is unable to find the longed-for integration. A dead time and world, not a living mystical experience, overwhelm and envelop it. While Celan's lyric self occasionally establishes a I-Thou relationship with a friend, a lover, or even with the memory of the dead mother, the lyric self of Sachs knows no such respite. It speaks to a silent, absent Thou about those who live in silence and those who are dead.

Unable to achieve a dialogical relationship with a cosmic Thou, the poet still has the word, impotent as it may be. Sachs's poem "In meiner Kammer" (In My Chamber) is the lyric poet's attempt to imitate the god's struggle against chaos, accompanied by the realization that the poet is bound to fail because she is overpowered by the memory of how the earth really is:

> In my chamber
> where my bed stands
> a table a chair
> the kitchen stove
> the universe kneels as everywhere

to be redeemed
from invisibility—
I draw a line
write down the alphabet
paint on the wall the suicidal words
that make the newborn burgeon at once
I have just fastened the planets to truth
when the earth begins to hammer
night works loose
drops out
dead tooth from the gum—[11]

The dash after "invisibility" is literally the line the speaker draws, an open-ended line that needs to be inscribed, as the King inscribed the divine aura to make it visible. But the human being is confined in a chamber; therefore, the creative wrath becomes a suicidal slogan, aggression flowing back to its origin. Yet the slogans generate connotations that lead to a moment when the lyric self is almost able to grasp the constellations of truth. The reversal is not achieved, for at the point of epiphany the brutal rhythm of the earth makes itself felt. Night cannot be transformed into "the wound called day," but repressively contracts into the hollow rigidity of a dead tooth, the impotent word. Celan, too, knew that he had to "chew this bread [reality] with the teeth of writing" (Sch. 32). When the word is potent with spiritual powers, however, it becomes food that human teeth have to chew (Revelations 10:9–10). Thus, words and their grammatical constellations contain the potential for good or evil depending on whether they are mere words, husks, or can lead to epiphanies. The hermetic poet always risks that the reader will only perceive the husk, the rigidity of the word and not the meaning, for she or he experiences the mystic's urge to communicate an overwhelming experience that cannot be communicated.

In this case, words are dead teeth, containers or boxes of the spirit, as Boehme puts it. For Boehme, good and evil are divided by a fine line, the hyphen or *Bindestrich* (connecting line) that Nelly Sachs and Paul Celan use so frequently. Boehme argues that the hyphen can determine whether an individual lives in *All-Einheit* (all-oneness) or in *Allein-heit* (aloneness). If the choice falls on the second, then separation, egocentricity, and all of its negative consequences occur.[12] Sachs and Celan fluctuate between the yearning for All-Einheit and the pain of Allein-heit. Sachs is especially interesting in her frequent attitude of loving and passive expectancy, which should be interpreted as an attempt to avoid the inflationary tendencies of wrath. She is always mindful that the hunted can become the hunter, and yet what gives her poetry its energy is that smoldering aggression so evident in "Landschaft aus Schreien." The lyric self of Celan, however, can be openly aggressive towards the silent cosmos and accuse the god, defined as loveless, of tolerating, if not creating a loveless world. God can become the evil other and as such denies the lyric self what it most desires, as Celan's poem "Tenebrae" (Sp. 23) illustrates:

> We are near, Lord,
> near and at hand.
>
> Handled already, Lord,
> clawed and clawing as though
> the body of each of us were
> your body, Lord.
>
> Pray, Lord,
> pray to us,
> we are near.
>
> Wind-awry we went there,
> went there to bend
> over hollow and ditch.
>
> To be watered we went there, Lord.
>
> It was blood, it was
> what you shed, Lord.
>
> It gleamed.
>
> It cast your image into our eyes, Lord.
> Our eyes and our mouths are open and empty, Lord.
> We have drunk, Lord.
> The blood and the image that was in the blood, Lord.
>
> Pray, Lord.
> We are near.   [trans. Michael Hamburger]

The lyric self, one with and speaking for those who no longer exist, must, in order to speak at all, project its inner sense of void as a cosmic otherness against which it can assume a rebellious attitude.

Language is a temporary shelter for the exiled poet, but it always retains the potential and the openness for the unexpected reversal—the Lord may start praying and answer the imperative challenge. As the words of the Torah pulsate in the perception of the mystic (Scholem, p. 14), so the words of contemporary hermetic poets become texts that intimate polysemous meanings. These meanings are not merely private; they are archetypal in their expression of the poet's response to his or her desire to escape from the historical-ethical level of experience to an anagogical realm beyond good and evil. The universality of such hermetic poetry unfolds when the reader allows the words to reverberate until a sudden salience connects the reader's consciousness with the words of the poet, at least establishing on a human level the longed-for dialogical relationship.

In modern poetry, the mysticism of the literal level of the word receives a great density as the poet attempts to make the word a universal in miniature, an absolute and self-contained metaphor.[13] Since language is a medium of exchange, however, the poem can never be quite free of a social context; it inevitably has a connection with external reality. Sachs and Celan are poets in the tradition of *symbolisme* but go beyond that tradition in their insistence on a historical-ethical consciousness. Celan differentiated his work consciously and intellectually from *symbolisme,* while Sachs became acquainted with it through her work as a translator. What is more interesting, she chose the self-contained hieroglyphics of hermetic poetry through an inner need as appropriate for what she wanted to express. If Mallarmé wanted to free the word from its guilty social context so as to reveal the beauty of its universal essence, Sachs and Celan relate the absolute metaphor to the problem of negation; as such, it becomes a fitting expression for the vertical ascendence into a silent cosmos and for the horizontal, empty rigidity of the landscape of the dead.

Historical trauma and the poet's reaction to it prompted Celan to make the following statement in 1958: ''The German lyric goes, I believe, into a different direction than the French. There are dark things in its memory, there are highly questionable things about it; therefore, in spite of all awareness of the tradition with which it is associated, it can no longer speak the language which many an inclined ear still seems to expect from it. Its language has become more factual, it mistrusts the 'beautiful,' it tries to be genuine. It is therefore . . . a greyer language which, among other things, also wants to settle its musicality at a different locale where it would no longer have anything in common with the 'mellifluousness' which unconcernedly sounded during and next to the most horrible events. This [new] language aims at precision in spite of its insistent polysemousness. It does not transfigure, does not 'poeticize,' it names and defines, it tries to measure the realm of what is given and what is possible. To be sure, in this, language is never in and of itself at work, there is only and always an I speaking from the special inclination of its existence, concerned about contour and orientation. There is no reality, reality wants to be sought out and won."[14]

The historical experiences of Sachs and Celan generate the symbols of transcendence in their poems, whose authenticity as verbal universes can alone contain the vicissitudes of time. Sachs and Celan were Jews, both lost a beloved person in the holocaust, both experienced the terror of the Nazi era, and both survived and attempted the possibility to write poetry about such a time and with a language whose surface meanings have been corrupted. Their work evolves towards increasingly hieroglyphic and enigmatic constellations of words, but even in such poems the memory of the dead refuses to be repressed and erupts frequently in powerful and singular images. Critical studies about Sachs and Celan, however, usual-ly deemphasize the historical level and concern themselves more with the theological and linguistic aspects of their work. While certain images are explained as allusions to historical events, commentators frequently warn against seeing historical reality as a major influence in the work of both poets.[15] Among the few studies that emphasize the impact of history on the work of Sachs and Celan are Marie Syrkin's article "Nelly Sachs: Poet of the Holocaust," Jerry Glenn's book *Paul Celan,* Lawrence L. Langer's discussion of Celan's "Todesfuge," and several poems by Sachs in *The Holocaust and the Literary Imagination*.[16] Historical expe-rience and its ethical implications are indispensable to an understanding of the poetry of Sachs and Celan, for here the dead are the force of gravity in those three ecstatic moments of human experience when we can lose consciousness of our ego confinement: the act of love, the act of artistic creation, and the act of integration with the larger selfhood of the divine.

Because the dead did not die a natural death and because the poets survived by taking flight from the destiny that awaited them, their memory is heavy with the ethical urgency of guilt. In reading Sachs's comments about her mystery play *Nachtwache* (Nightwatch), the reader can infer the nature of her guilt feelings. Sachs points out that all human beings become guilty but that the degree, share, and consciousness of guilt are different; for the more sensitive an individual is, the more lacerating are the feelings of guilt. The criminal who awakens the beast in

man, the puppeteer who pulls the strings, is the most evil but feels the
least guilt. Next come those who murder under orders and protect
themselves with the cowardly thought that they will remain unpunished.
Those who watch murder and do not interfere are also actively evil; but if
they all of a sudden recognize in one of the hunters a person whom they
once loved, they feel guilt because of that love. Betrayal is also an evil,
especially the betrayal of love, but it can lead to a very conscious guilt
which can be expiated. The sensitive person who feels love, looks on
evil, and takes flight is torn apart by guilt. Many of Sachs's and Celan's
poems are rituals of expiation enacted again and again. The network of
words does not allow them to elude the guilt of their memories of the dead
and of the flight both poets took from death. Death and its object lessons
become their teacher. The hieroglyphic images in their poems are,
therefore, condensed points of memory whose density implies the rigidity of repression as well as the yearning for liberation when "the stone
deigns to bloom" (Celan).

The lyric self of both poets often uses the collective *we* as it provides a
voice for the silent ones in the landscape of the dead. The landscape and
its inhabitants communicate: this is not good. If world history is an esthetic experience, then this is negative esthetics. It is a world that human desire rejects; but just as the beautiful and the ugly are physical expressions
of good and bad, so history, no matter how amorally presented, will be
evaluated ethically. The perceiver of such a world must define himself or
herself in terms of the negative world. Thus, a healing self-love is
impossible, for it would again become immoral over and against such a
world. In the case of Sachs and Celan, therefore, the empathetic consciousness and conscience are a displacement of the guilty conscience
that screens itself through expressions of love for those who are the
burden and inspiration of the lyric self. Yet there is a further dilemma: it is
artistic energy and invention that permits a conscious conscience to
empathize with and speak for the dead, who remain as void and silent as
the universe to whom the lyric self addresses itself.

Both poets, then, share not only the same religious and literary tradition, but also similar historical experiences and ethical responses to them.
It is, therefore, not surprising that similar images are found in their
poems. Celan's poetry is much more hieroglyphic than Sachs's, however,
and hence seems more inaccessible, cooler, and self-contained in silence. The poet's companionship in exile and their mutual concerns have
been movingly expressed in Celan's "Zürich: Zum Storchen" (N 12).
Here, while stopping at the transient resting place of an inn on Ascension

Day, both poets find a dialogical moment. Celan's lyric self admits with melancholy rebellion that it can only have "the heart that I had/hope for His highest, rasping, His wrangling Word," the "Why has Thou forsaken me?" The dialogical thou of Sachs looks at the wrangler and speaks to his eye and ear: "We don't know, you know, we don't know what counts."

II.
"Landscape of Screams": The Shackled Leaps of Nelly Sachs[17]

"How did a literary phenomenon like Nelly Sachs become possible?" asks Bengt Holmquist in his introduction to *Das Buch der Nelly Sachs,* a collection of her poems and plays as well as critical essays about her work.[18] In the discussions and laudations written during her lifetime, Sachs emerges as a legendary figure. Only a few facts and hardly any personal revelations are known about her life since she did not feel the need to aid future biographers in their work (p. 24). Herein she shares a desire for anonymity characteristic of Jewish mystics, but as a result her persona is also mythified with a numinosity enhanced by words such as *Sehnsucht* (longing), exile, and epiphany. Her frequent and justified use of mythical projections such as the Shekhinah are transferred from the images in her work to the poet herself so that she becomes a gatherer of shards, "the single witness of Jewish Fate under National Socialist rule."[19] Paul Kersten, who wants to view her poetry as poetry, finds that this strange combination of critical analysis and sanctification has been partially furthered by the poet's own admission that the word, the main concern of her poetry, was her means for survival and shaped her primal theme: a mystic experience of death that nourishes a longing after a dematerialized transformation of this reality into a world beyond where birth and death are unified in an invisible universe.[20]

The radical difference between the image of the poet and Auschwitz, between saintliness and criminality, has led to the tendency to see her as an anima figure in a soulless time. As a Jew she was a pariah in 1940; as a Jew she became a sacred taboo in the late 1950s and throughout the 1960s because the Germans were afraid of accepting anything Jewish as their own. But her Scandinavian biographer, Lagercrantz, admonishes the reader that "it is easy, too easy, to define her as a great Jewish poet. It seems to be much harder to understand and realize that Nelly Sachs is a contemporary poet of the German people."[21] If her letters and medical records should ever become available, we may know more about the person than the persona of Sachs. Her struggle with madness, which persisted to the end of her long life (1891–1970) and to which she often tried to give shape in her work, will then reveal her less as a saint, but rather as a complex human being painfully touched in her isolation by the events of the twentieth century.

Her isolation was there from the beginning. As the only child of assimilated, cultured, upper middle class parents, she felt a difference early between herself and others, "turned inward and was very shy and sensitive about meeting strangers"; while her relationship with her parents was, as she put it, "almost wordless" (Holmquist, p. 26). She fell in love at the age of seventeen with a man who is said to have been murdered years later in a concentration camp. It is this man who becomes the mythified bridegroom in the work of the exiled poet. Whereas the image of woman in Celan's poetry is grounded in the experience of woman as mother or beloved, the nameless man in Sachs's poetry is an absence that she longs to fill and does so through the animus projection of logos, the word which proves yet insufficient to provoke the cosmic animus projection, a failure she shares with Celan.

Isolated and unacquainted with the historical, intellectual, and artistic currents of her time, Sachs was eventually forced to become conscious of history. After the death of her father and until her flight to Sweden by airplane on 16 May 1940, she experienced in Berlin the collective isolation inflicted on Jews during the Hitler regime. With the order to report for a work camp already in her pocket, being a Jew did not mean to her obedience to "Mosaic law, but to endure suffering and fear *[Angst]*. All human beings who suffered became Jews: to be a Jew meant to be a genuine human being." Her physical constriction brought about by fear was so intense that she suffered for several days from a paralysis of the larynx after having been questioned by the Gestapo.[22] Many years later, after literary recognition had come to her, she still remembers, "When the great terror came / I became mute— / Fish, the death side / turned upward / air bubbles paid each struggling breath . . . ."[23] She arrived in Sweden with her mother, a few hand-carried items, and her beloved German language. Although worldly honors reached her, including the Nobel Prize in 1966, she remained an exile in Stockholm. As Lagercrantz reports in his tribute on the occasion of her death, she lived her last years in a single room where she displayed a collection of fossils,[24] the imprint of the spark of life caught in stone as her poems caught her memory of those who once lived.

Sachs attempted even less than Celan to define her poetics intellectually; as a result it has to be culled from the context of the poems themselves.
A statement to Gisela Dischner is among the few direct comments she has
left: "The terrible experiences which brought me to the edge of death and
darkness were my teachers. If I had not been able to write, I could not
have survived. Death was my teacher. How could I have occupied myself
with anything else, my metaphors are my wounds. Only through this can
my work be understood."[25] Her metaphors are wounds that enable the
poet to repress and release pains and desires that cannot be communicated
directly. A wound is a memory of pain; in the state of inflammation it is
closest to the moment of infliction. But a wound can also be bandaged,
can become encrusted, can turn into a scar, or can heal. The last does not
happen in the work of Nelly Sachs, for in that case her creative activity
would cease. No matter how much she desires a healing transcendence,
the memory of the dead remains her teacher. Dischner points out that
memory functions in her poems as a warning; the basis of the terror must
be exposed, and that basis is the forgetting of what is human. Exact
memory saves the individual from succumbing to the pathology of what
has happened, while the mechanisms of repression, which retreat from
the realizations of pain, lead to an escape into madness.[26] Both exact
memory and repression shape her work. Hieroglyphs encapsule memory
and repress it until it breaks with violence or yearning. They are confined
in the poem as the human being is confined in a room; within the human
being is the heart as fugitive, whose shackled leaps towards liberation
from pain make it a wound. In Sachs's poetry the wound is a cosmic and
divinely inflamed pattern; it is the eye of the blind seer, the mouth that
issues the silent scream, and the mute letter slashed across the whiteness
of the page.

"Landschaft aus Schreien" was published in 1957 in the collection
Und niemand weiss weiter–And Nobody Knows How to Go on. It is a
forceful and aggressive poem that projects its hieroglyphic track by
means of grotesque and sublime images into the landscape of the dead.
On one level the poem is a horizontal journey through a landscape of
pain that extends in time from Genesis to the New Testament, from Hiroshima to Maidanek. From this silent world of pain, silent screams move
vertically upward into infinity in search of an ear. The poem begins and
ends with an expectant state of crisis:

Drawing: Jehuda Bacon

Landscape of Screams

In the night where dying begins to sever all seams
the landscape of screams
tears the black bandage open,

Above Moria, the cliff's downward plunge to God,
hovers the flag of the sacrificial knife   5
Abraham's Heart-Son-Scream
saved at the great ear of the Bible.

O the hieroglyphics of screams
carved into the entrance gate of death.

Wound-corals of broken throat flutes.   10

O, o hands with dread-plant-fingers
buried into wildly rearing manes of sacrificial blood—

Screams, locked in the tattered mandibles of fish,
Woe tendrils of the smallest children
and the gulping train of breath of the old,   15

Slashed into singed azure with burning tails.
Cells of prisoners, of saints,
tapestried with the nightmare pattern of throats,
feverish hell in the doghouse of madness,
of shackled leaps—   20

This is the landscape of screams!
Ascension of screams towards the sky
from the bony grate of the body,

Arrows of screams
freed from bloody quivers.   25

Job's Four-Wind-Scream
and the scream concealed in Mount Olive
like a powerless insect caught in crystal.

O knife of sunset red tossed into throats,
where the trees of sleep surge blood-licking from the ground, 30
where the time falls off
the skeletons in Maidanek and Hiroshima.

Ashen scream from the seer's eye tortured blind—

O you bleeding eye
in the tattered eclipse of the sun
suspended for God-drying   35
in the cosmos—

The fundamental irony in the poem is that no image projects anyone
screaming directly in agony and liberation. The scream is either caught in
constricted space or lost in infinite space. Like Celan's "Engführung,"
Sachs's poem is a verbal landscape whose track of images leads into a
revelation of suffering in the horizontal nightmare of each victim and
demands, albeit passively, that the cosmos respond to the vertically
ascending scream.

In the first three lines, images of violence establish an inextricable
relationship between creation and destruction on a cosmic scale. In the
secrecy of night, the process of dying begins to sever what has been
created or made. Implied is a metaphor of death as a scissor or knife
slowly beginning the process of separation. In contrast, the landscape of
screams tears the black bandage of secrecy open and makes the wound
conscious. Screams and the severing force of death also suggest the
comet, that bent line of violence and suffering which will be made more
explicit later in the poem (l. 16). The element of wrath in the opening
lines echoes the Zoharic concept of creation and the nature of evil, the
process of becoming individuated, conscious, but also separated. Divine-
tempering mercy is absent in the poem and is replaced by the human
creative act, the poem in whose enclosure the scream is harbored and
preserved. The poem must, however, reconcile the need for protective
enclosure with the need for liberation and openness, for otherwise the
poem itself would become an expression of wrathful rigidity. The word
open (auf) which concludes the first stanza foreshadows, with its
meanings of upward and open, the reconciliation of the paradox.

As we have seen, hermetic poetry tends to implode images of infinite
immensity to intimate immensity. The first part of "Landschaft aus
Schreien" funnels from cosmic expansion into the constricted space of
the doghouse of madness, from which the enclosed and shackled spirit
seeks to leap. Before reaching this demonic epiphany, the poem's second
stanza individualizes the scream through Abraham, the first suffering
Israelite, who is caught here in the moment of suspension between
deepest agony and relief. The pattern of the first stanza is repeated as the
sacrificial knife hovers like the flag of a comet over Mount Moria while
the scream rises upward from the landscape. Mount Moria does not

ascend to God, but is a "Klippenabsturz zu Gott" (a plunging downward of cliffs towards God). Etymologically, *Sturz* and *stürzen* not only mean fall and falling, but also starting or rearing up suddenly, with the connotations of panic and rigidity. Another meaning of *stürzen* is to stand something on its head. The *Klippenabsturz* is an image of an impatient downward transcendence, an urge towards a negative union with God; on the anagogical level, however, God's height and depth are measureless. The *Klippenabsturz* directs the eye downward, whereas it glances upward when the angel of God calls to Abraham from the heavens that no human sacrifice is demanded. In the poem, the god does not send his messenger; there is no communication other than the moment of extreme tension when the potential murderer Abraham recognizes in the victim his beloved son and when Isaac realizes that his father will be his killer. At this moment the communal scream of pain and love is wrenched— "Abrahams Herz-Sohn-Schrei"—but does not ascend in an infinite line; instead it is preserved and proven true *(bewahrt)* at the great ear of the Bible that stores like a vessel the verbal record of suffering.

The next two lines, "O the hieroglyphics of screams, / carved into the entrance gate of death," define the structure of the second half of the first part of the poem: a series of hieroglyphic images of screams. As hieroglyphs the screams are not only images like Egyptian pictographs but are also sacred and enigmatic writing cut and engraved above the incomprehensible gate to extinction. Caught in stone, they become a silent memorial to those who have disappeared from the memory of humankind, but they also demand to be deciphered.

The first hieroglyphic image is "Wundkorallen aus zerbrochenen Kehlenflöten" (wound corals of broken throat flutes). Among wind instruments, the flute, originally made from bones, hollowed twigs or reeds, is one of the oldest instruments; and next to the rhythmic drum beat of the heart it is perhaps the most organic musical extension of man. It is closely aligned here with the image complex of breath and the choking of breath. When properly functioning, the human throat emits a harmonious sound, but the broken throat flute is the broken scream of Gehenna. The throat flute also communicates the pathos of all broken instruments, as they suggest a harmony forever gone. When the throat flute has been broken and its sound stifled, there remain only fragmented images suggesting sound. Here the broken throat flutes become wound corals, connoting, among other things, the folk motif of the bleeding tree within which a human spirit awaits liberation. Red coral is, of course, a tree-like structure composed of marine animals; its branches are used for jewelry.

Coral and necklace are symbols for words and poem: "This chain of enigmas / laid around the neck of night / King's word written far away / illegible / perhaps in comet journeys / when the open and torn wound of the sky / hurts . . . ."[27] With its meanings of chain and ornament, *Kette*, as metaphor for poetry, communicates the bondage of suffering and the transformation or, rather, enclosure of suffering in the work of art.

Wounded corals and broken throat flutes are examples of Sachs's use of the metaphysical grotesque. As images of Gehenna they are violently fragmented and fused only in imitation of organic wholeness. They are metaphysical in that they point to something quite other than their own thingness. The broken throat flute is empty but not vacuous; it suggests a sacred emptiness. "Landschaft aus Schreien" reveals a chain of fragmented images, each a reinforcing variable of the same idea, just as documentary photographs of mountains of glasses, shoes, or hair say finally the same thing and point to something beyond their thingness. The next hieroglyph is also composed of fragments: "O, o hands with dread-plant-fingers / buried into wildly rearing manes of sacrificial blood." Implied is a metaphor of a rider subduing and yet fearful of the horse that carries him through a nightmare. Here the intimate relationship between hunter and hunted comes to the fore as the killers are terrified by their victims—the projected parts of themselves which in the nightmare are no longer the weak outcasts but, rather, the upsurging subconscious powers, evanescent like the hair of the mane, the fleeting tail of the comet (cf. *cometa*, hair). From the point of view of the victims, the dreading fingers planting death echo also the sacrificial knife and scream (ll. 4–7).

The scream of relief is not granted to the victims fossilized in isolated images, and it is also stifled in the two final sections of the first part of "Landscape." Next we see three concrete examples of silent suffering beginning with "screams, locked in the tattered mandibles of fish." Lagercrantz points out "that the fish with its long silent agony is a foremost symbol of martyrdom for Nelly Sachs."[28] The mute creation suffers, but the old and young also cannot express the fear about the horror that awaits them. The smallest children can only raise "woe tendrils," tiny parallels of protest to the wildly rearing manes of sacrificial blood, while the old swallow and drag their breath like a chain. Although the stanza begins with the word *scream*, no screams come from fish, child, or old people; instead, the screams, as bent and crooked lines of suffering, are "slashed into singed azure with burning tails." The screams repeat the action of the landscape which tore open the black bandage of night in the first stanza. But now there is a change for the worse. The azure sky of day has been artificially darkened through the unnatural death by fire. Screams tear into this sky with burning tails, but they do not expose anything; they are simply an addition to it. The cloud over Auschwitz or Hiroshima, the cloud that turns day into night, is the historical reality behind the cosmic image.

At this point the poem reaches a frantic pace by means of a series of violent images that end in frustration. The hieroglyphics which stood earlier above the entrance gate of death are now within the claustrophobic cells of prisoners and saints. The walls of the cells are tapestried with the nightmare pattern of throats, an image which, because of its syntactical position, can also refer to the "feverish hell in the doghouse of madness." The external nightmare closes in on, penetrates, and destroys the human mind. The universality of Sachs's image nevertheless leaves the possibility of specific historical memory open, the experience, for instance, of being confined in the "bunker" of Auschwitz. In the struggle with evil, the human being grows mad yet has the blind desire to escape, tugging with shackled leaps at the chain like a mad dog. Characteristically, "with shackled leaps," the line that concludes the first part of the poem, ends with the open dash. The images of that last stanza also define the dilemma of the lyric self: she wants to express the inexpressible but nears insanity in her attempt as the perception of evil contracts in her mind. The battle with madness must be controlled by the artifact of the poem even if it can be no more than an expression of shackled leaps. Having funneled to this point of constriction, the poet can either conclude with such desperate intensity or introduce a shift in attitude.

Nelly Sachs does the latter with the declarative and cool line that opens the second part of the poem: "Dies ist die Landschaft aus Schreien" (This is the landscape of screams). The topography of the landscape again consists of words expressive of silent screams. Three sections shape the second part: the release and frustration of screams, the sunset of Maidanek and Hiroshima, the function of the poet-visionary and her relation to God.

The first set of images shows the release of screams from "the body's grate of bones" and from "bloody quivers," while the screams of Job and Christ are either lost or hidden. Only the dying are granted the "Himmelfahrt aus Schreien" (ascension of screams towards the sky), an ironic parallel to the transfigured ascension of Christ to which the word *Himmelfahrt* specifically refers. The body's grate of bones suggests the image of a ladder as well as a lyre upon which ascending screams create a cacophonous tonal ladder. There is, however, no last rung in the ladder as there was in the ladder of Jacob's dream, where the Lord stood at the top and promised, "I am with thee, and will keep thee in all places whither thou goest" (Genesis 28:15). The screams rise *empor,* a word that connotes the urgency of their escape and the excited if not rebellious nature of their ascendence. The word *Gitter* (grate or grille), here a metaphor for the rib cage, also has a prominent place in the imagery of Celan. The open spaces between the grille are important to both poets, for through their emptiness one can reach out of one's confinement towards something else.

"Arrows of screams / freed from bloody quivers" is again an ironic contrast to the arrow symbolism in the Christian-Judaic tradition. Job laments, "The arrows of the Almighty are within me" (6:4). "His archers compass me round about" (16:13). Although he expresses through this image the suffering of one severely tested, the arrows come from God. They are also an expression of God's concerned and loving word, while the person engaged in prayer sends God's word-arrow back to His heart. In Sachs's use of the symbol the arrows come from within the bloody quiver of the human body, a flayed body. They are screams that are *erlöst,* freed and expressive of suffering, but not necessarily saved in the sense of redeemed. They shoot upward without the intermediary of archer or bow; therefore, they can neither know nor find their aim.

The lost and stifled scream is projected through Job and Christ, the archetypal sufferers of the Old and New Testaments. Job's scream is scattered to the wind—"for the speeches of one that is desperate are as the wind" (6:26)—and loses in this diffusion the aggressive concentration of the scream as arrow or comet. Yet by naming Job, the poet as recorder fulfills the sufferer's wish: "O that my words were now written! O, that they were recorded in a book." Christ, always the sufferer in her poems, is directly named only twice in her poems written during and after the Hitler regime. Since names held a magical quality for her, she could no longer use the name of Christ because it had been abused and corrupted by the persecutors. "The Jews were marked as God's murderers, which meant that they bore the guilt of the crucifixion of Christ. In her youth she had published a collection of legends in which Christ is present everywhere . . . . Now Christ is prohibited to her, but he returns in mysterious ways."[29] The expansion of Job's scattered scream and the concentrated stifled scream in the Garden of Olives are as powerless as an insect caught in crystal, but they are no more powerless than the screams that trace the line of suffering through cosmic infinity. The insect caught in crystal, like the breath-crystal of Celan, is another metaphor for the artifact of the poem which includes the life of the lyric self within the rigidity of the printed word. The lyric self makes no reference to the eventual harmonious reintegration of Job and Christ; the cosmos of the poem truncates such a possibility even though it is constantly desired through the metaphor of the ascending scream. The question of an afterlife was not important for Nelly Sachs, but she needed the faith in a transcendent being who would empathetically bend towards suffering humanity.

As the poet-seer turns to twentieth-century suffering, the topography of Maidanek and Hiroshima is expressed through images of violent insanity expanding the doghouse of madness to global proportions: "O knife of sunset red tossed into throats / where the trees of sleep surge blood-licking from the ground, / where time falls off/ the skeletons of Maidanek and Hiroshima." Rapidity of movement characterizes the stanza, which employs once again the motion from above, the response from below, and the *Klippenabsturz* motif of the first part, now shrunk to human skeletons that have dropped out of time. Only the use of personification reminds the reader that all this violence is perpetrated by human beings; to the speaker of the poem it seems so great that it could only be a cosmic event. The knife of Abraham was comprehensible in that Abraham obeyed a test imposed upon him by his eventually benign god. Now the cosmos cuts throats even before the scream, the message, can escape. Death occurs on a large and mechanical scale. Stimulated and realized by the blood, the hieroglyphic trees of sleep surge from the ground, suggesting again an overwhelming and destructive manifestation of the subconscious. These are not slow-growing, natural trees but are a demonic vision of the tree of life. Their aim is death and agreement to death, and in their presence they suggest the sudden terror of the unfolding atomic blast, resembling a tree as well as the human neck and skull from which it ultimately originates. As time drops off the skeletons of Maidanek and Hiroshima, it is not gathered in the eternal memory of God but simply falls into an oblivious timelessness, leaving the skeletons as ossified hieroglyphics. They demand an interpreter who cannot do what only a god can do: to give meaning to suffering that is inexpressible. For this reason, the poem concludes with a description of the failure and desire of the poet-visionary.

Her dilemma is imagined by means of another hieroglyph: "Ashen scream from the seer's eye tortured blind." The lucid ball of the eye has become a dark socket, an open mouth issuing an ashen, silent scream. The seer's eye has been tortured blind by the reality of the atrocities of history; it internalized that reality and was destroyed by it, destroyed by its empathy with suffering. The center, the core in the seer is gone, for it could not contain suffering as the ear of the Bible or the crystal could. The tortured, blind eye now projects its own state of being onto the cosmos by means of the ashen scream that contains the memory of the dead. A line is established between the scene of suffering, the scream of the eye, and the infinite; but the infinite is like the eye of the seer.

The last stanza begins with an apostrophe to the bleeding eye hung "in der zerfetzten Sonnenfinsternis" (in the tattered eclipse of the sun). With this image of suspension, implying a cloth as well as a crucified body, the poem reaches its point of demonic epiphany: in the darkness of the universal eye, the poet's eye-scream-poem is hung "zum Gott-Trocknen," meaning that either a god will dry its wound or that it will dry the suffering god and receive his imprint, as Veronica received the true icon on her cloth. If that should happen, the true dialogical relationship would be established, but it is far more likely that the imprint of meaning will not happen. The cloth metaphor of bandage and flag, introduced in the first and second stanzas, is now projected as a cloth of nothingness. If one true icon is possible for the contemporary poet, then it is the poem which can fuse, while still being meaningful, the shredded mandibles of fish, Job's scattered scream, Christ's stifled scream, the bleeding eye of the seer, and the dark center.

The poem remains open-ended as the lyric self stands expectant for the I-Thou relationship with the tattered eclipse of the sun, whose corona suggests a crown of thorns as well as hidden glory. In discussing modern man's relation to God, Martin Buber points out that "an eclipse of the sun is something that occurs between the sun and our eyes, not in the sun itself."[30] While intimating such hope, Nelly Sachs's poem does not follow the easy optimism of the eclipse analogy. Her lyric self, isolated by the I-It relationships that make human history, awaits suspended in a transcendent I-Thou contact, wanting to comfort and desiring comfort. It is ready, but at the same time the very passivity of its loving expectancy inadvertently creates an expression of outrage at the silence of the cosmos, which seems to persist in a state of eclipse. This state of tension in "Landscape of Screams" communicates what remains perhaps the only believable attitude possible for the religious human being who writes lyric poetry about and after Auschwitz.

III.
Through the Point of Constriction: Celan's "Engführung"

Celan's language is a defensive system that pulsates between shimmering points of contraction and networks of wandering, detouring words that, in spite of all openness, seek to return home, if it must be, through a point of constriction. The trope of personification allies Celan the wanderer with the word as wanderer, wandering being a disguised search for a point in a landscape as well as the avoidance of a point. With characteristic circumlocutions, Celan evokes in 1958 his hometown of Czernowitz, a war-tossed town that finally passed from Rumania to the Soviet Union in 1944: "The landscape from which I come—through what detours! but is there such a thing: detours?—, the landscape from which I come to you is probably unknown to most of you."[31] Celan does not name the town, for the single word may provoke memory to a point of pain. In the same speech, he also does not name the language that was his from the beginning, German (pp. 17–18 above), and that accompanied him through his losses and exile: "In this language I have tried to write poetry in those years and in the years afterwards: in order to speak, to orient myself, to discover where I was and how things would go with me, in order to design reality for myself." For Celan, poems are messages in a bottle: "They direct themselves towards something. Towards what? Towards something open, something that can be seized, perhaps an addressable Thou, an addressable reality." This is the topography where poet, language, and poem are on their quest through time and in search of a point of rest. Language is the companion in exile of the lyric self; the lyric self is "tentless" and uncannily free, as both it and language are "wounded by reality and seeking reality."

Celan's language went through "the thousand darknesses of death-bringing speech" during the German occupation of Czernowitz. In 1942 his parents were sent to the extermination camp Am Bug. On the day of their arrest, Celan found refuge in the house of a girl friend. He escaped not only the fate of his parents but was also able to escape from a Rumanian forced labor camp where he received the news of his parents' death.[32] After his escape, he joined the Soviet troops as a medic. In 1944, he returned to Czernowitz, tried to study Romanic languages, helped edit a communist newspaper, but left Czernowitz in 1947 to go to Vienna. In 1948 he went to Paris, the main locale for the rest of his life. Here he studied German literature and philology, married the graphic artist Gisèle de Lestrange, had a son, and taught German language and literature at the

Ecole Normale Supérieure. Literary honors and prizes began to reach him from Germany after the publication of *Mohn und Gedächtnis* (1952) and *Von Schwelle zu Schwelle* (1955).

His mother's death deeply affected him and is often directly alluded to in his earlier poems. His father's death is never mentioned; it is an absence and a silence comparable to the absence and silence, the unknowable no-thingness of God which the lyric self so often wants to provoke. In contrast, the image of the dead mother becomes the Shekhinah, the traveling companion through exile who leaves him the word as ward: "This word is your mother's ward / Your mother's ward shares your camp stone for stone. / Your mother's ward bends towards the crumb of light" (M.u.G. 64). Like the poet, the word wants to bend and concentrate on the crumb of light, the scattered part of something greater. As *Muttersprache* (mother tongue) language receives much of its power, but here the word is merely her ward, whose origin is somewhere else. Mother and word are dead and impotent, as the lyric self realizes that no magic word or rite can accomplish that "which never has been / A human being arose from the grave" (M.u.G. 31–2). Nevertheless, the lyric self rigorously pledges itself to the "word—you know: a corpse" (S.z.S. 49).

In spite of his awareness of himself as a Jew caught in the nightmare of twentieth-century history, Celan, according to his friend Hans Mayer, did not consider himself a Jewish poet: "The Jewish themes belonged to the substance of his life and, therefore, emerge again and again. They must not be misunderstood as a religious faith."[34] He uses Jewish tradition in such a way that it elucidates our twentieth-century condition but hides that tradition often behind Christian motifs or his own neologisms. His word *Atemwende* (breath reversal) is a case in point: it is a displacement of the Kabbalistic concepts of *Tsimtsum,* the myth of creation projected by the exile Isaac Luria. Summarizing this Kabbalah, Scholem states that God, in preparation for creation, concentrated or contracted into himself, thus clearing a primal space which was not God. The concentration resulted in the rigidifying of God's *Din* or wrath. Creation, then, is a release for God as he sends out the letter *yod,* the first of His powerful name. It breaks the vessels that ought to contain it: creation and catastrophe become a simultaneous event. The next stage is an attempt at restitution accomplished by the human being who discovers the divine sparks and raises them home to God in meditation. Scholem concludes, "Just as the human organism exists through the double process of inhaling and exhaling, and the one cannot be conceived without the other, so also the whole of creation constitutes a gigantic process of divine inhalation and exhalation. In the final resort, therefore, the root of evil is latent in the act of Tsimtsum'' (p. 63). The experience of deprivation leads to crystallization of the energy of wrath, which then flares out often in substitutions masked by the word *creativity.*

Through its metaphors of evil, Celan's work intimates the fear that the clearing and the contracted point may simply be nothingness, that there is no well of energy either without or within the human being. Shortly before his death, Celan attended a conference in Stuttgart concerning Hölderlin, a poet who meant much to him. He was deeply moved by Martin Walser's analysis of Hölderlin's perception of selfhood: "He could not accept the idea that he could create from within a self, deep and firm as a cistern. He did not have a self. Yet, he had one, but only to the extent that he was assured of it from the outside."[34] Celan, like Hölderlin, does turn to others. In the end, however, the lyric self identifies most closely with the words it utters, for that which obsesses it, namely, absences, can only be expressed in words. As Horst Peter Neumann writes about Celan's kinship with Hölderlin, "His self, too, stood and fell with his calling as a poet. As Hölderlin before him, he had bound the lyric self of his poems so irrevocably to the poem that an equation of both persisted even in negation as a unit of 'Nichts' and 'Genicht' [inhalation, poem-noem]." This equation turned his poems into oracles about his very own constriction *(Enge),* oracles whose dark meanings he understood as "mantic," not, as Neumann points out, in the sense of prophetic seeing, but rather as a mad, silent, devouring yet praying mantis: "You prayer-, you blasphemous-, you / prayer-sharp knives of my / silence . . . ." (N. 35)[35]

A poem is a two-fold defense system for the lyric self which, as Celan admits, always seeks to return to its point of origin.[36] At one time, the locale of the beginning was free and rich with many attributes, but it became constricted and rigidified with the sense of pain and loss. As a displacement of and defensive screen against the experience of deprivation, the poem can be mere techne or can promise an *Atemwende.* As techne the poem is a rigid and seemingly empty pattern of syntactical structures and words. It is, as Celan allegorizes in his meridian speech, a Medusa or an automaton and appears "dark" to the reader (p. 141) who will be alienated from the poem. The poet as maker, having gone into his own constriction and deprivation, sends forth the poem as an, if not catastrophic, then incomplete and crippled creation, locked into itself in an aggressive withdrawal that nevertheless can be an aggressive challenge to the reader. An *Atemwende* is possible for poet, poem, and reader: "Poetry *[Dichtung]:* that can mean a breath reversal. Who knows, perhaps poetry goes the way—also the way of art—for the sake of such a breath reversal? Perhaps it succeeds because the alien, the abyss *and* the head of Medusa, the abyss *and* the automatons seem to lie in one direction,—perhaps it succeeds to differentiate between strangeness *[Fremd]* and strangeness *[Fremd]*, perhaps the head of the Medusa shrinks here, perhaps here the automatons fail—fail for this singular short moment? Here perhaps, with the self—with the alienated self set here and *in that* manner free—something else is set free" (pp. 141–42). The two kinds of strangeness are the sense of alienation from ordinary reality and the truly strange, namely, a metaphysical other.[37]

Celan admits that the poem shows a strong tendency towards silence, that it maintains itself at its own periphery (p. 143), and that "nobody can say how long it will hold its breath." "But the poem speaks! It is mindful of historical time, but it speaks. To be sure, always in its very own language only" (p. 142). The perceiver is blind to the poem because of its "darkness" just as he would be blind to the light of God that breaks the vessels. The reader must be willing to go into his own point of constriction with the poem and liberate himself and the poem there (p. 146). Because a Celan poem is in the ironic mode, this shamanistic ritual does not lead to any transcendent awareness, but at best to an empathetic contact with the poet-poem's sense of deprivation. Thus, the third stage of the cosmic myth of Tsimtsum is imitated as the reader meditates and liberates, albeit imperfectly, the sparks of pain and hope from the rigidity of words. The poem may be alien and new, but it promises the rediscovery of something that was always sought.

In search for the home, the place of beginning and pain, reader and poet need a guide for utopia, the place that does not exist. Celan finds the meridian, "something—like language—immaterial yet earthly, terrestrial, circular, something that returns unto itself across the two poles and thereby—happily—even crosses the tropics" (p. 148), *Tropen* meaning both tropics and tropes. Celan's association of the meridian with language is crucial, for the meridian functions in topography, as do the topoi, the places and lines of argument, in rhetoric and poetics. Both create slots of meaning and combine the image of line and focal point. The meridian and Celan's linguistic topography are thus part of the associative cluster around the metaphor of the *Sprachgitter,* the speech grille or grate that confines and yet permits communication. In stasis the meridians enclose the earth like a system of imaginary bars; but as they

turn with the sun from time zone to time zone, the abstract line wanders
and aligns itself with light, thereby being metamorphosed into a *Faden-
sonne* (sun-thread). Light is a possibility, a promise revealed and fulfilled
in the breath reversal that shapes the poem "Es ist alles anders"
(Everything is Different) (N. 82–84). Here, at the end of a dark night of
the soul, the "Tekiah" is sounded, the call from the ram's horn that gets
man in touch with God. God and humankind are at peace, and love
returns to the beds:

> . . . the hair
> of women grows again,
> the retracted
> bud of their breast
> emerges again, life-,
> heart-line directed it wakes
> in your hand that climbed up the thighpath . . . .

Subtly, the image alludes to Dante's breath reversal, his climb down the
thigh of Satan, through the center of gravity, and upward and out. Only in
the topography of language can memory and repression blend into each
other in this way.

    Sprachgitter (1959), which concludes with the nine cyclical poems of
"Engführung," has been acclaimed as an expression of Celan's maturity
as a poet. Much attention has been given to the poem "Sprachgitter," but
for the purpose of understanding "Engführung" only a brief explanation
of the term is needed. All speech grilles are screens that hinder and further
communication. As Alfred Kelletat points out in his investigation of the
term, the word refers most specifically to the *fenestra locutaria* through
which hermetic nuns talked with the outside world. By extension, the
eye, an important symbol in Celan's poetry, "is in all its parts a complicated protective apparatus, a many-levelled graduated grille before the
enigmatic event which happens inside the pupil, in the retina, when
physical phenomena are translated into intellectual and spiritual ones . . .
and an equally enigmatic transfer occurs in language between sound and
meaning, between the sensuous and the semantic quality of a word."[38]
With its microcosmic mimicry of radiance, the eye is a natural mandala, a
symbol of the self, whose dark and seemingly vacant center is controlled
by the iris's reaction to light. Here experience in time and space can be
contracted to a shimmering point.

    The dark point and the shimmering point remain in perpetual tension in
Celan's poetry, a poetry whose verbal structure contains and projects the

word on the literal level as a sign and motif in a language that seems both familiar and alien. His poetry expresses the private and physical experience of love and death and includes a public historical dimension in which the lyric self is a confederate and prisoner of the beloved dead. On the metaphysical level this poetry expands and implodes being and nothingness into points of light and darkness; but on all these levels the creative word is also the anagogic container, potent in its ability to emanate memory and desire and impotent to actively affect memory and desire through the ritual of its sympathetic magic.

"Engführung" has been analyzed primarily in linguistic terms in Dietlind Meinecke's and Klaus Weissenberger's studies about Celan's poetry.[39] Most influential in my reading of the poem have been Peter Szondi's posthumously published essay-notes "Durch die Enge geführt: Versuch über die Verständlichkeit des modernen Gedichts" (Through the Point of Constriction: An Attempt about the Comprehensibility of the Modern Poem). Szondi, who insists strongly on the historical dimensions of the poem, argues that all meanings connoted by Celan's ciphers coalesce into points: "Plurality of meanings has become the means of understanding and makes the unity of that visible which only seemed separate. It serves precision."[40] "Engführung" carries the process of contraction so far that certain images combine persecutors, victims, and witnesses into conceits that a German poet who is not Jewish would not dare to forge.

The title "Engführung" must be taken in the literal sense as leading to a point of constriction which is less a dead end than a funnel from which the constriction flows out. The German word is also a technical term in music, namely, the *stretto*. This latter meaning connects "Engführung" with Celan's earlier and most famous poem "Todesfuge" (Fugue of Death), where victims and persecutors directly confront each other. Here the fugue element is brought out through the alternate voices of the dead, who "schaufeln ein Grab in den Lüften da liegt man nicht eng" (shovel a grave in the air where one does not lie tight). In keeping with the Latin derivation *fuga* (flight), the "Todesfuge" is a musical-poetic statement of *Todesflucht* (flight from death) brought about by the dissolution of the human body into air (cf. Sachs's "O the Chimneys"). The German cluster of meanings associated with *fügen, Fug,* and *Fügung* gives the "Todesfuge" such meanings as connection, point of transference, artifact, destiny, and acquiescence. "Todesfuge" is thus a point of destiny through the dissolution of form in air, and it expresses both death and flight from death through the artistic analogy with the fugue.

At the end of the fugue comes the Engführung, the stretto. According to *Grove's Dictionary of Music*, the stretti of a fugue can combine to a point of excitement at the climax; the more intense, contracted, and tighter the stretti are, the greater is the excitement as the subject of the fugue is driven home. In Celan's "Engführung," levels of meaning form into stretti as they fuse or, rather, bundle together. The guidance into constriction, actually into rigidity, is accompanied by excitement and trepidation caused by the fear and rebellion against constriction *(Enge)*. It is the wrathful *Angst* experienced by the contracted god and by the victim through *angina,* the spasmodic strangulation of the throat, or *angina pectoris,* strangulation due to anemia of the heart muscle. The failure of breath and the failure of heart (love) lead the lyric self to its own point of constriction and attempt to free the lyric self there through a breath reversal:

Towards the Point of Constriction

*

Passed into
the land
with the indubitable track:

Grass, written apart. The stones, white,
with the shadows of haulms: 5
Read no more—see!
See no more—go!

Go, your hour
has no sisters, you are—
are at home. A wheel, slowly,   10
rolls out of its own volition, the spokes
climb,
climb upon a blackish field, the night
needs no stars, nowhere
does anyone ask after you.   15

*

                              Nowhere
                                        does anyone ask after you—
The place where they lay has
a name—it has
none. They did not lie there. Something   20

lay between them. They
did not see through.

Did not see, no,
spoke about
words. None awoke,   25
sleep
came over them.

*

                            Came, came. Nowhere
                                          anyone asks—
It is I, I   30
I lay between you, I was
open, was
audible, I ticked towards you, your breath
listened, I
am still there, you   35
still sleep.

*

                         Am still there—
Years,
years, years, a finger
gropes down and up, gropes   40
about:
seams to be felt, here
it gapes wide apart, here
it grew together again—who
covered it?   45

*

                     Covered it—
                        who?
Came, came.
Came a word, came,
came through the night,   50
wanted to shine, wanted to shine.

Ashes.
Ashes, ashes.
Night.
Night-and-night. —Go   55

*

Go
to the eye,
the moist one—
Hurricanes.
Hurricanes, as always,   60
particle blizzards, the other,
you
know, we
read in a book, was
opinion.   65

Was, was
opinion. How
did we clasp each
other—with
these hands?   70

It was also written that.
Where? We
placed a silence over it,
stilled with poison, large,
a green silence, a sepal, the   75
notion of vegetation attached itself—
green, yes,
attached, yes,
beneath a malicious
sky.   80

Yes, of
vegetation.
Yes.
Hurricanes, par-
ticle blizzards, there remained   85
time, there remained
the trying out of the stone—it [he]
was hospitable, it
did not interrupt the word. How
well off we were: 90

Granular,
granular and fibrous. Stalk-like,

dense;
grape-like and radiating; nodular,
flat and   95
lumpy; loose, inter-
twined—; he, it
did not interrupt the word, it
spoke,
spoke gladly to dry eyes, then closed them.   100

Spoke, spoke.
Was, was.

We
held fast, stood
amidst, a   105
porous structure, and
it came.
Came towards us, came
through, patched
invisibly, patched up   110
the last membrane,
and
the world, a milli-crystal
shot up, shot up.

*

                Shot up, shot up.   115
                     Then—
Nights, unmixed. Circles
green or blue, red
quadrangles: the
world pledges its innermost   120
in the game with the new
hours.—Circles,
red or black, bright
quadrangles, no
flight shadow, no   125
table of offerings, no
soul of smoke ascends and joins the game.

*

                Ascends and
                    joins the game—

In owl flight time, at   130
the petrified exposure,
with our separated, fled hands, during
the latest diaspora,
above the bullet-catch at
the shattered wall: 135
visible a-
new: the grooves, the

choirs, at that time, the
psalms. Ho, ho-
sanna.   140

Thus
there are temples still. A
star may well have yet light.
Nothing,
nothing is lost.   145

Ho-
sanna

In owl flight time, here,
the discourses, day-grey,
of ground water traces.   150
     *

                              (—day-grey,
                                        of
                                  ground water traces—

Passed
into the land   155
with
the indubitable track

Grass.
Grass,
written apart.)   160

The meridian that will guide me through the verbal constellations of "Engführung" is the definition of the poem as an elegiac quest of the lyric self through an intimately immense landscape of the dead, those who are dead literally, hence absent, and those who live with a "little life in dried tubers" (T.S. Eliot). Persecutors, victims, the lyric self, and the reader share this existence, an existence of delusion and repression flaring up occasionally into murderous madness, ambiguous epiphanies, and questionable hopes.

The nine sections of the poem fall into five parts. Introduction (ll. 1–5) and conclusion (ll. 151–60) repeat the same words, parenthetically rearranged, however, in the conclusion where the word *grass* appears twice. The important words in the poem are repeated three times, usually consecutively, but *grass* is a wandering word. After its first appearance, it hides behind the pattern of the speech grille only to emerge with double strength at the end, laden with connotations. This insistence on the number 3 indicates that the poem emphasizes a process, a dialectic that does not reach completion in a fourth state unless the poem itself is to be such a completion. The three central parts of the poem follow the process of tsimtsum, albeit in a very ironic sense. Each part opens with a state of almost fluid disorganization wherein all attributes are dispersed. Then, an organism separates itself and contracts into a repressively rigid structure. The immensity of space and the intimacy of the contracted organism are then challenged by a force that could prove to be a breath reversal. The force is somehow frustrated, however, so that the process leads, not to creation or insight, but to a new turn in the quest. All three quest rituals prove to be diversionary tactics, defense systems that leave the lyric self on the horizontal plane of a day-grey existence where only traces of ground water tell of depths that cannot be explored. Only the indubitable track of grass remains, written apart and provoking further repetition of the ritual of questing.

The introduction opens with deceptive absoluteness: "Passed into / the land / with the indubitable track: / Grass, written apart." An event has happened and left its mark. On the literal level, the poem has passed into the open page; its track displaces the reader—the German *verbracht* also connotes something brought about wrongly—into the scene of the text. The reader can recapitulate the quest of the lyric self, which begins, easily enough, with a track agglutinated with associations of script, meridian, train track, plough, or scythe. But the track, like the topoi or lines of argument in language, is too well traveled and circuitous and will lead the quester sooner or later to a dead end. The end of the line, lost in the countryside, was a well-known point of constriction for the victims of Nazism.

Grass, however, is not an image for real grass but for grass no longer existent; it is "a word, you know, a corpse." The stones are white with the shadow of haulms, suggesting a photographic negative, white shadows over dark stones, the reversal of black print on the page, and the merging of white shadows with white stones. Grass and stone are, of course, traditional metaphors for humanity, the former communicating the coming and going of generations, the latter, the hardness and endurance of humankind. The stone, always an important *chiffre* in Celan's work, suggests in "Engführung" a repressive though protective shutupness; rarely do we find the stone from which the divine spark is released. The track and stones in the expanse of a landscape where grass is the shadow of a memory define the locale in which an imperative voice now gives a directive to the reader and the lyric self: "Read no more— see! / See no more—go!" Read, see, go—each intensifies participation as the poem becomes the anagogic container whose intimate and inclusive reality the questing self recognizes, submits to, and explores. This may sound very shamanistic, but in order to achieve empathy with such a poem, the reader must be willing to return to the nominal realism with which the child perceives the word's relation to reality. Peter Weiss describes a similar quest less enigmatically, hence less defensively, in his Auschwitz essay "Meine Ortschaft."

The first of the three quest rituals (ll. 8–56) is an attempt by the ego consciousness of the lyric self to make contact with the invisible absent ones in a great realm of night. Alienation, the dark night of the ego, is inevitable as the ego naively accepts the directive which seems to be given by a larger aspect of its being, the self which promises a homecoming: "Go, your hour / has no sisters, you are— / are at home." Ego consciousness is urged and tricked into a timeless realm where night is unbroken by and does not need stars. Only a wheel rolls slowly of its own volition, a mechanical and windowless mandala, a perversion of wholeness signaling the blindness of the ego. The lyric self realizes that in this ironic homecoming "nowhere does anyone ask after you," a realization that implies questions such as "Where are they?" and "Why is no one concerned about me?"

As yet the ego consciousness separates itself from the absent ones, the *they.* This separation leads to an accusatory attitude and a defensive explanation of the cause of their absence, defensive because the lyric self does not yet implicate itself. It recalls that "the place where they lay has /

a name—it has none'' (ll. 18–20). Since naming the place would immediately evoke complex historical and ethical associations, it is avoided. Yet it is also true that naming the place would necessarily be a falsification. The German *der Ort* (the place) still means today, in the specialized language of miners, ''the end of the line.'' The place where they lay was a dead end, a point of constriction called Auschwitz or Dachau. But those names no longer signify a reality; those who lay there are gone, while the place itself has changed into a tourist attraction. Even when the past was present, the name of the place, if known, had no reality that could be imagined by those who would lie there. They spoke about words *(von Worten)* focusing on the black letters, the bars of the speech grille, and not the open spaces through which the aura of words passed. Thus, ''they did not see through.'' The verbal universes of victims and persecutors obscured reality until ''sleep overcame them.'' It is the sleep of escape, the sleep of not wanting to be conscious that makes betrayal, murder, and the sleep of death possible. The reader or listener of ''Engführung'' will also be lulled into that sleep if he or she does not penetrate beyond the incantatory quality of the poem, which then becomes a spellbinding speech grille.

Enveloped in the landscape of a timeless night, the ego attempts to make contact (ll. 28-36). Six times the word *I (ich)* asserts itself only to fall back into the alienating realization that ''you still sleep.'' Here the I can be seen not only as ego consciousness, but also as a negative and alienated expression of God and the Word, to whose potential the sleepers were oblivious because they talked about words. As the ego remains egocentric without contact, so the Word remains locked in its wordness unless love would release its divine spark. Likewise, God (self) must have contact with the creature (ego) in order to be realized. The I is larger than the ego; it is self, word, God. It is always present: ''I was open, was audible, I ticked towards you.'' We have here an ironic reversal of Michelangelo's God ticking (in the sense of tapping and touching) with his finger towards Adam, the sleeper who awakes as the pulse of the larger Other passes into him. Mutual nonrecognition might lead to destruction, as Celan hinted when he pointed out that there was a ''time bomb'' in the poem.[41] Only an involuntary breathing pattern responds to the I; a breath reversal does not occur. With a fading ''—am still there,'' the I disappears from the poem, and ego consciousness turns from the external night and explores a dark, inner landscape.

It is really a timescape into which the pain of memory has been contracted through ''years, years, years'' (ll. 37–45). Ego consciousness is metamorphosed into a finger, a part of the whole, that touches the mendings, scars, and wounds of its own self; but because that self is objectified into an organism, the exploring consciousness does not recognize its kinship with it. The blind finger reads the braille of pain, of wound and defense against wound, and asks, "Who covered it?" Who designed the bandage that represses so well? It is an empathetic question, but the blind searching consciousness will not tear the "black bandage" open to reveal the landscape of screams; instead the answer will come circuitously, will be acted out, and reveal: we did it and we want it that way even though we long for liberation.

Night, ego consciousness, and contracted organism are unable to break into light without a true breath reversal. Such a reversal wants to occur through the Word that "came, came, came" through the night and wanted to shine (ll. 48–51). It came with an urgency comparable to the first letter that the King sent out to pour light into the vessels even if it meant breaking them. But here the word fails; it does not even flash brilliantly for a moment as in Gottfried Benn's poem "Ein Wort." Celan's word cannot realize itself at all; it remains as frustrated will and desire, overwhelmed by the words "Ashes. / Ashes, ashes. / Night. / Night-and-night" which counteract the five-times-repeated, pressing use of the word *came (kam)*. Ashes and night, annihilation and absence are so abysmal that they cannot be penetrated by the creative urge. The breath reversal does not occur. Instead, a new directive indicates another variant of the quest ritual, a new direction: "Go to the eye, the moist one" (l. 56). It remains to be seen if a more human topography can be found.

The second quest ritual is the sixth and longest section of the poem (ll. 59–114) and begins with a reiteration of the directive to go to the moist eye. The ego consciousness of the first ritual now loses itself in the comfort of a collective we, a false community held tenuously together by shared anxiety, guilt, and defense systems. These defense systems express themselves in metaphors of increasing rigidity moving from a vegetating to a crystalline state of being, the contracted "millifold crystal" that provokes a catastrophic change.

A state of primal disorganization, where possibilities and attributes are fluid, opens the second ritual and reveals, not the chaos of night, but a powerful wind that creates a particle blizzard (l. 61). It is a state of terrible freedom, feared and desired by the lyric self in another poem: "A ROAR: / truth itself / has appeared / among men / amidst the / blizzard of metaphors" (A 85). Quoting Democritus, Celan wrote into Hans Mayer's copy of *Sprachgitter,* "There is nothing but atoms and empty space;

everything else is opinion.''[42] Looked at positively, the great wind is reminiscent of the Lord's presence in the whirlwind or of the pentecostal storm of the Holy Ghost, moments in which the human being was touched by a cosmic breath reversal.

But the first stanza undercuts the sense of direction that always accompanies the breath reversal. The particle blizzard *(Gestöber)* is governed by chance direction; and besides, it is *von je,* the usual particle blizzard as found in even the most sublime verbal constellations. In a positive sense, atoms and particles are constants, for they are formally finished like the crystal snowflake and remain so no matter how much they are buffeted about. In grammar, the particles are the short and unchanging parts of speech that signal the position of words in a sentence but carry little meaning in and of themselves. Rather, they define the slots through which words project their infinite variety of meanings. Thus, they can capture ''the other'' in a book (l. 61) which then becomes mere opinion and not a cosmic force. It is clear in the first directive that opinion is to be overcome: ''read no more see, see no more go.'' Celan's lyric self had a precursor who both saw and went, namely, Dante. The first stanza of the new turn in the quest alludes to Dante's circle of the carnal sinners where Francesca tells the moist-eyed traveler Dante how she and Paolo looked up from a book about love, saw each other's eyes, and read no further. Yet the experience of love led to crime and guilt so that they, too, could ask, ''How did we clasp each other with these hands?'' (ll. 67-70 As Dante saw at the beginning of his quest, the sinners ''swept together so lightly on the wind'' *(Inferno, V),* so the beginning of this new course of the quest projects a turmoil from which no genuine creation can emerge; the wind will eventually congeal into rigidity.

The first state of repression, the vegetative state, implies an answer to the earlier question ''Who covered it?'' Something that has been written is vaguely remembered (l. 71), but ''we placed a silence over it, / stilled with poison, large / a green silence, a sepal.'' A sepal, of course, encloses something that could unfold. Hence, the vegetable state is not an ideal defense system, for something can emerge from within even if the sepal is *giftgestillt* (nursed or quieted with poison). Furthermore, the contracted, vegetating existence of the collective we is exposed to the open space of a ''malicious sky.'' It, too, is quiet and has contracted its knowledge. The cosmos reflects the condition of humankind as God has withdrawn into his own malicious space. A false peace has been created into which the memory of hurricanes and particle storms nevertheless intrudes (ll. 84–85).

To avoid that memory, the collective we recalls the search for a deeper repression, the past tense implying that the repression did not work: "There remained time, there remained the trying out of the stone—it [he] was hospitable, it did not interrupt the word. How well off we were." The world of the poem has now shrunk from the vegetative state beneath the malicious sky to the repressive-protective density of the stone which does not threaten to release the bloom and which provides a partition between human existence and sky. Celan, aware that human beings need defense systems in order to exist, wrote in another poem, "Whatever stone you lift— / you expose those who need the shelter of the stone; / whatever word you speak, / you owe to disaster" (S.z.S. 53). Creation is an act of aggression against another's defense system, but the created in turn becomes the defense of the creator. The defense of a stony environment is such that finally petrifies the heart, a repetition of the dialetic of outer night leading to inner darkness in the first ritual. The heart, a vulnerable organism, is discernible in the word-accumulation *(Wortaufschüttung)* following the colon that punctuates the nostalgic "how well off we were" (ll. 91–97). "Granular, fibrous, stalk-like, dense; grape-like and radiating; nodular, flat and lumpy: loose, intertwined" suggest the heart as a biological organism separated, like the finger earlier, from organic wholeness and therefore impotent to conduct the pulse of life. In German, *er, es* (he, it) refer to stone and heart respectively. Both were hospitable because they did not interrupt the word, which in turn also became hard as it "spoke gladly to dry eyes, then closed them" (l. 100). The quest has not led to the empathetic, moist eye but, rather, to eyes that are either closed to human suffering or can no longer cry before they are closed in death.

Before the final constriction is recalled (ll. 103–14), two words, uttered twice, intrude upon the collective consciousness: "Sprach, sprach. War, war" (Spoke, spoke. Was, was). Since the German *war* suggests a pun on *wahr* (true), something that no longer exists spoke truthfully, namely, the heart and the word *(es)* that brought death (l. 100). The collective we, avoiding this truth, remembers the process towards so dense a point of constriction that the only catharsis possible had to be an aggressive explosion into the chaos from which it had separated itself. It could well be that this state of being expresses the psychology of hunter and hunted, but the images of the poem have reached such a point of defensive density that the act of reading becomes an act of aggression against that density, resulting very likely in a misreading.

The collective we remembers, "Wir liessen nicht locker" (We held fast) (l. 104). The German *locker* (loose) is related to *Loch* (hole); therefore, the we denied its "porous structure" (l. 106), its vulnerable biological organism. The porous structure belongs to the associative cluster of images around the concept speech grille, for it too is a pattern that can be penetrated and is penetrated in spite of the fact that the collective we tried to hold fast. Something invisible penetrated and patched up even the last membrane, the most delicate tissue (ll. 106–11). This is the aura words receive in "the thousand darknesses of death-bringing speech." It is the uncreating word that does not shape but patches up, providing the cover, which the finger of ego consciousness pondered over earlier. The membranes, skin and parchment, have lost their open spaces and no longer permit penetration and interpretation. The world has become fixed in a neologism, the *Tausendkristall* (the millicrystal). Of all forms in nature, the crystal appears most victorious over chaos as it repeats its structure according to a definite mathematical law. For Celan, it is analogous to the poem, but only as *Atemkristall,* as the breath crystal with a porous structure. The *Tausendkristall,* however, retains breath rigidly in its projection of a new age of man, as the word *Welt* (world) implies. No longer storm tossed, the energies within the structure are released with aggressive direction. They shoot forth for worse or better, for *Schoss* suggests shoot as well as lap, the origin of life. At best this is again a catastrophic creation that initiates the third quest ritual.

The world of the millicrystal pledges its innermost in the game with the new hours where the nights become "unmixed" (ll. 117–22). Rigid ego defensiveness is abandoned for total ego loss, again a defense mechanism. The colorful circles and squares, generated by the "innermost," recall patterns projected by the nervous system at the moment of death or in the ecstatic moment of erotic, creative, or mystic experience; the poem leaves it open as to which is meant. Time has begun again with the game of the new hours, and the poem moves toward an awareness of present time into which specific points of memory intrude. Three "mixed" words refuse to participate in the intense yet playful dance of the new hours; the words are three compound nouns with sacred, worldly-aggressive, and literary connotations. Corrupted with the meanings of historical time, they cannot be part of the archetypal shapes within a creative chaos; but they do exist and hence challenge the possibility of truly new hours. The first, *Flugschatten* (flying or flight shadow), suggests a threatening intermediary between earth and sky—a transcendent being, a plane or bird of prey in "owl flight time"—as well as the shadows of letters on the printed page. The *Messtisch* (l. 126) could be an altar from which prayers rise, a table at an officer's mess, or even a display at a book fair *(Buchmesse)*. Both words also hint at the dead, who receive their own word in *Rauchseele* (the soul of smoke), signifying those whose home and grave became air. With the naming of the soul of smoke, the poem must approximate that which its diversionary tactics have covered so well: it must confront the word's relation to historical experience.

The image of *Eulenflucht,* owl flight time before night falls or day breaks, conveys the historical experience of time, the day-grey realm of our world where the depths emerge only in "ground water traces." The deceptive certainty of historical time and fact is made ironic by the nonexistence of the past and by the fear and desire of individual perception, an irony that the poem brings about through syntactical structure (ll. 129–39), the time element of sentences. The repetition of "ascends and joins the game" can mean that the soul of smoke, which does not participate in the game of the new hours, participates in owl flight time at the "petrified exposure." The poem now drives home to that point of narrowness which constricted the breath of the victims during the "latest diaspora" at "the bullet catch before the shattered wall," where hands were separated and the *we* was annihilated. *Kugelfang* and wall strongly evoke the wall at Auschwitz covered with a tarred cloth to keep the bullets which missed their victims from ricocheting. The body, too, was literally a *Kugelfang* as it caught the small, concentrated, and aggressively propelled piece of matter that shattered it. The poem, throughout its rituals, has been a *Kugelfang* as well; but as an artifice rather than an organism, it provided a defensive cover for the pain of memory which the lyric self sought to explore.

In historical time, the breath reversal at the point of constriction led to death. Unable to accept death's absurd absoluteness, the lyric self attempted to rescue it into a meaningful transcendence. Grammatically, the opening of the eighth section of the poem reads, "In owl flight time . . . visible anew: the grooves, the choirs . . . ." The hope for a life-giving breath reversal reduces the words *exposure, fled hands, diaspora, bullet catch,* and *shattered wall* to dependent clauses. But historical reality intrudes relentlessly into the yearning for epiphany. The word *Rillen* means grooves, grooves that separate the two sides of a coin or grooves on a record, and rivulets, the ground water traces that remain on the poem's surface. Thus, as the coin turns, as the sound of salvation is heard, the rivulets of memory and forgetfulness do their work. The hosanna itself is undercut; for, as Walter Killy points out, its chopped syllables echo not only the singing of those about to die but also the rhythm which terrified Celan, the staccato of the German military march: "Wir sind des Hitlers braunes Heer, heia, hoho."[43] Yet with a tone of triumphant protest the lyric self insists, "Thus / there still are temples. A / star may well have yet light. / Nothing, / nothing is lost." The light of the star is, however, only a hopeful assumption comparable to the word that sought to penetrate the night. Moreover, the assertion that nothing is lost can mean that all the shards have been gathered, but it can also mean that the transcendent no-thing is nonexistent. The final hosanna may, therefore, be a triumph or a faint exhalation, a breath reversal towards owl flight time, horizontal time and place, where ground water traces discourse, talk and negotiate with and about words. In passing through the point of constriction, the poem and the lyric self have not transcended anything; rather, both remain with the reader on the surface space of an intermediary time where traces from a hidden source relay a message about the indubitable track. The quest for transcendence led the poet as God seeker back to the poet of human reality.

In the ninth and final section of the poem, the day-grey water traces are *verbracht,* passed into or displaced in the land with the track that continues to leave the grass written apart. The momentary hope for a breath reversal has become diffused almost as soon as it appeared. There are no new hours but only surfaces upon which the lyric self will compulsively engage in rituals of repetitions from poem to poem. The lyric self never reaches an end, never ceases to demand *kumi ori* (let there be light) or to find its meridian. The poem aids the lyric self and the reader in exploring the topography of nowhere where the indubitable track is lost in time and space at a point designated for death. Only at that point of constriction can the lyric self be set free by the last breath reversal that exhales all memory into silence.

In his use of metaphors of evil, Celan has universalized the holocaust and the shadow of Nazism to such an extent that, with the few exceptions of condensed and specific images, both seem to have disappeared and yet are universally present as they adhere to the connotative aura of the words in the poem. The defense against and the inescapability of the memory of human experience in historical time are thereby as truthfully revealed as in the specific notations and recollections of the diarist or autobiographer, the ambiguous ambience of the novelist's narrative, and the masks of the dramatis personae of the documentary playwright as pedagogue. If the reader has borne with me, he or she will have realized the rhetorical intent of my investigations of metaphors of evil, namely, that the history of the holocaust and Nazism must be studied in all its specificity and not merely shelved into that time and that place: it must be universalized and remain present in human consciousness so that we may prevent future chaos and rigidity.

Yet the word does not suffice as we hover between memory and forgetfulness. Ground water traces—words that course across the page— are finally only surface intimations of creative or catastrophic depths. As the living memory of the holocaust will pass, the surfaces of written records or photographic images and the site of a concentration camp itself will rigidify, will become historical scar tissue impervious to the memory of pain. This is no genuine healing but is an inevitability of human reality. The monstrosity that was once real is increasingly becoming a flattened shell that, like Gregor Samsa's deprived form, will eventually be viewed without horror.

Notes

CHAPTER ONE

1 Jean-Paul Sartre, *Antisemite and Jew,* trans. G. J. Becker (New York: Schocken, 1948), p. 88, and George Steiner, "K," in *Language and Silence* (New York: Atheneum, 1970), p. 121.

2 Ernst Cassirer, *An Essay on Man* (New Haven: Yale University Press, 1944/65), p. 9.

3 Lawrence Langer, *The Holocaust and the Literary Imagination* (New Haven: Yale University Press, 1975), p. xii; unfortunately, I was no longer able to consult the collection edited by Wagener, *Die Nachkriegsliteratur und das Dritte Reich* (Stuttgart: Reclam, 1977).

4 Georg Lukacs, *The Theory of the Novel,* trans. Anna Bostock (Cambridge: MIT Press, 1971), p. 90.

5 Paul Ricoeur, *The Symbolism of Evil,* trans. E. Buchanan (Boston: Beacon, 1969), p. 9.

6 Erich Neumann, *Art and the Creative Unconscious,* trans. Ralph Manheim (Princeton: Princeton University Press, 1969), p. 164.

7 As quoted by Aniela Jaffé, "Symbolism and the Visual Arts," in C. G. Jung, *Man and His Symbols* (New York: Dell, 1967), p. 310.

8 Henry V. Dicks, *Licensed Mass Murder* (New York: Basic Books, 1972), p. 238 and p. 246.

9 *Paradiso,* XXIX. All quotations from Dante's *Divine Comedy* are taken from John Ciardi's translation (New York: New American Library, 1957/61). References will henceforth be given in the text.

10 Theodor Adorno, "Erziehung nach Auschwitz" in *Stichworte: kritische Modelle II* (Frankfurt: Suhrkamp, 1970), p. 98.

11 Paul Celan, *Von Schwelle zu Schwelle* (Stuttgart: Deutsche Verlagsanstalt, 1955), p. 53.

12 Cassirer, p. 191.

13 Detlev Grieswelle, *Propaganda der Friedlosigkeit* (Stuttgart: Ferdinand Enke, 1972), pp. 64–70.

14 *Der Angriff,* 4 March 1933. See also Haig Bosmajian, "The Use of the Symbol 'Unknown' in Nazi Persuasion," *Folklore* (Summer 1966), 116–22.

15 Siegfried Bork, *Misbrauch der Sprache: Tendenzen Nationalsozialistischer Sprachregelung* (Munich: Francke Verlag, 1970), p. 83.

16 As quoted in Alan Bullock, *Hitler: A Study in Tyranny* (New York: Harper and Row, 1964), p. 672.

17 Viktor Klemperer, *Die unbewältigte Sprache,* 3d ed. (Darmstadt: Joseph Melzer, 1966), p. 26.

18 As quoted in Jost Nolte, *Grenzgänge* (Vienna: Europa Verlag, 1972), p. 237.

19 Nelly Sachs, *Das Leiden Israels* (Frankfurt: Suhrkamp, 1968), p. 77.

20 Adolf Hitler, *Mein Kampf,* trans. Ralph Manheim (Cambridge: Houghton Mifflin, 1962), p. 57.

21 Nolte, p. 236.

22 As quoted in Gerhard Schoenberner, *Der gelbe Stern* (Hamburg: Rütten and Loening, 1961/69), p. 103; trans. as *The Yellow Star* (New York: Bantam Books, 1973), p. 133.

23 Northrop Frye, *The Anatomy of Criticism* (Princeton: Princeton University Press, 1957). My discussion and application of the concept of irony in this and the following chapters is indebted to Frye's definition.

24 Martin Walser, "Unser Auschwitz," in *Heimatkunde* (Frankfurt: Suhrkamp, 1968), p. 11.

25 Hans Egon Holthusen, "Günter Grass als politischer Autor," in *Plädoyer für den Einzelnen* (Munich: R. Piper, 1967), pp. 42-43.

26 Hans Magnus Enzensberger, "Reflexionen vor einem Glaskasten," in *Politik und Verbrechen* (Frankfurt: Suhrkamp, 1964), p. 19.

27 Theodor Adorno, *Noten zur Literatur II* (Frankfurt: Suhrkamp, 1965), p. 127.

28 George Steiner, "Postscript," in *Language and Silence,* p. 163.

29 Peter Weiss, *Fluchtpunkt* (Frankfurt: Suhrkamp, 1962), p. 196.

30 Paul Celan, "Ansprache anlässlich der Entgegennahme des Literaturpreises der Freien Hansestadt Bremen," in *Ausgewählte Gedichte* (Frankfurt: Suhrkamp, 1970), p. 128.

31 Eugen Gürster-Steinhausen, "Rätsel Deutschland," *Die Neue Rundschau* (Summer 1947), 269.

32 Thomas Mann, "A Brother," in *Order of the Day,* trans. Loewe-Porter (New York: Knopf, 1942), p. 156.

33 Lukacs, p. 75.

CHAPTER TWO

1 David Rousset, *The Other Kingdom,* trans. Ramon Guthrie (New York: Reynal and Hitchcock, 1947), pp. 101–2.

2 Leon Poliakov and Joseph Wulf, *Das dritte Reich und die Juden* (Berlin: Arani Verlag, 1955), p. 215.

3 Erich Kahler, *The Tower and the Abyss* (New York: Viking Press, 1967), chapter 3.

4 Mircea Eliade, *The Sacred and the Profane,* trans. Willard R. Trask (New York: Harcourt Brace, 1957), p. 47.

5 Eugen Kogon, *Der SS-Staat* (Stockholm: Berman Fischer, 1947), p. 14.

6 Richard Rubinstein, *After Auschwitz* (New York: Bobbs-Merrill, 1966), pp. 34–36.

7 Eliade, p. 175.

8 William Grenzman, "Nietzsche and National Socialism," in *The Third Reich* (London: Weidenfeld and Nicolson, 1955), p. 238.

9 James Olney, *Metaphors of the Self* (Princeton: Princeton University Press, 1972), p. 307.

10 Olney, pp. 171–72.

11 Paul Ricoeur, *The Symbolism of Evil,* trans. E. Buchanan (Boston: Beacon, 1967), p. 7.

12 Northrop Frye, *The Anatomy of Criticism* (Princeton: Princeton University Press, 1957), p. 37.

13 Odd Nansen, *Day After Day,* trans. Kathrine John (London: Putnam, 1947/49), p. 800. Henceforth page references will be given in the text.

14 Chaim Kaplan, *The Warsaw Diary,* trans. and ed. Abraham I. Katsh (New York: Collier, 1965/73), p. 104. Henceforth page references will be given in the text.

15 All biographical data have been taken from Katsh's introduction to *The Warsaw Diary*. Katsh relates how the diary was smuggled out of the ghetto and passed on to a Pole who emigrated eventually with it to the United States.

16 Lawrence Langer, *The Holocaust and the Literary Imagination* (New Haven: Yale University Press, 1975), pp. 78–79.

17 Elie Wiesel, *Night,* trans. Stella Rodway (New York: Avon Books, 1971), p. 12. Henceforth page references will be given in the text.

18 Langer, pp. 75–87.

19 Harold Bloom, *Kabbalah and Criticism* (New York: Seabury, 1975), pp. 79–80.

20 Tadeusz Borowski, *This Way for the Gas, Ladies and Gentlemen,* trans. Barbara Vedder (New York: Penguin, 1976), p. 40 and p. 48. Henceforth page references will be given in the text.

CHAPTER THREE

1 Siegfried Lenz, "Ich zum Beispiel," in *Beziehungen* (Munich: Deutscher Taschenbuch Verlag, 1972), p. 12. Biographical references are taken from this and other essays in *Beziehungen.* Henceforth page references will be given in the text.

2 Lenz defines himself thus in his speech "Der Künstler als Mitwisser. Eine Rede in Bremen," in *Beziehungen,* pp. 201–6.

3 Dietrich Peinert, "Siegfried Lenz: 'Deutschstunde,' " *Deutschunterricht,* 23 (February 1971), 53.

4 I have used the following editions of the novel: *Deutschstunde* (Hamburg: Hoffmann und Campe, 1968), p. 163; *The German Lesson,* trans. Ernst Kaiser and Eithne Wilkins (New York: Hill and Wang, 1972), p. 134. For the convenience of the reader of either the German or English version page references will henceforth be given in the text. The first number refers to the German, the second to the English edition.

5 Albrecht Weber, *Siegfried Lenz: Deutschstunde,* with contributions by Birgit Alt and Hendrick Rickling (Munich: R. Oldenburg Verlag, 1971), p. 68.

6 Weber, pp. 30–31.

7 Weber, pp. 109–11, points to the similarities between *The German Lesson* and Grass's *Tin Drum* and argues that Lenz, by using the litote instead of the hyperbole, "maintains the child perspective on the level of probability." He does not see Siggi as a demonic child.

8 Soeren Kierkegaard, *The Concept of Dread,* trans. Walter Lowrie (Princeton: Princeton University Press, 1967/73), p. 119.

9 A serious mistake in translation occurs at this point. The German reads "als Altpapier verkaufen" (p. 559) which is translated as "sell them for publication" when it should read "to sell them for re-cycling like old papers" (p. 470).

10 Weber, p. 84; Peinert, p. 47.

11 Hannah Arendt, *Eichmann in Jerusalem* (New York: Viking, 1964), pp. 136–37.

12 Kierkegaard, pp. 118–19.

CHAPTER FOUR

1 Günter Grass, "Die Vogelscheuchen," in *Gesammelte Gedichte* (Berlin: Luchterhand, 1971), pp. 103–4. I am quoting and translating the last stanza.

2 Günter Grass, *Hundejahre* (Berlin: Luchterhand, 1963), p. 681; *Dog Years,* trans. Ralph Manheim (Greenwich, Conn.: Fawcett, 1965), p. 569. All quotations are from these two editions. Henceforth page references— German first, English second—will be given in the text.

3 Günter Grass, *Aus dem Tagebuch einer Schnecke* (Berlin: Luchterhand, 1972), p. 347; *From the Diary of a Snail,* trans. Ralph Manheim (New York: Harcourt Brace, 1973), p. 292. Henceforth page references to both editions will be given in the text.

4 Günter Grass and Pavel Kohout, *Briefe über die Grenze* (Hamburg: Christian Wegner Verlag, 1968), p. 44.

5 Heinz Ludwig Arnold, "Gespräch mit Günter Grass," *Text und Kritik,* 1 (October 1971), 21.

6 Manfred Durzak, *Der deutsche Roman der Gegenwart* (Stuttgart: W. Kohlhammer, 1971), p. 146. Durzak analyzes the novel as a political grotesque.

7 Christoph Eykman, *Geschichtspessimismus* (Munich: Francke Verlag, 1970), p. 122.

8 This problem has been philosophically treated in Theodor Lessing, *Geschichte als Sinngebung des Sinnlosen* (Munich: C. H. Beck, 1921), p. 28.

9 Quoted by Lothar Tank, "Deutsche Politik im literarischen Werk von Günter Grass," in Manfred Jürgensen, ed., *Grass: Kritik, Thesen, Analysen* (Munich: Francke Verlag, 1973), p. 174.

10 Arnold, "Gespräch . . . ," 7; see also Manfred Bouré, in Gert Loschütz, ed., *Von Buch zu Buch–Günter Grass in der Kritik* (Berlin: Luchterhand, 1968), p. 200.

11 Arnold, "Gespräch . . . ," 24.

12 "Rede von der Gewöhnung," in *Über das Selbstverständliche* (Berlin: Luchterhand, 1968), pp. 164–65.

13 "Was ist des Deutschen Vaterland?" in *Über das Selbstverständliche,* p. 41.

14 For background material on Danzig, see Herbert Levine, *Hitler's Free City: A History of the Nazi Party in Danzig, 1925–39* (Chicago: University of Chicago Press, 1973).

15 Albrecht Goetze, *Pression und Deformation: Zehn Thesen zum Roman Hundejahre* (Göppingen: Alfred Kümmerle, 1972), p. 68.

16 "Der Inhalt als Widerstand," *Akzente,* 4 (June 1957), 230.

17 Arnold, "Gespräch . . . ," 5.

18 Durzak, p. 141.

19 Norman O. Brown, *Life Against Death* (New York: Random House, 1959), pp. 301–2.

20 Norman O. Brown, *Hermes the Thief* (New York: Random House, 1947), chapter 5.

21 Brown, *Life Against Death,* p. 302.

22 C. G. Jung, *Psychology and Alchemy,* trans. R. F. C. Hull, *Collected Works* (London: Routledge and Kegan Paul, 1953), 12:461. I am indebted to this reference to Michael Hamburger's discussion of the phenotype in Gottfried Benn in *Contraries,* p. 338.

23 Otto Weininger, *Geschlecht und Charakter,* 15th ed. (Vienna: W. Braunmüller, 1916), p. 414.

24 Marcel Reich-Ranicki, "Günter Grass: Hundejahre (1963–67)," in Jürgensen, pp. 27–28.

25 "Die Ballerina," *Akzente,* 3 (December 1956), 534.

26 Alan Bullock, *Hitler: A Study in Tyranny* (New York: Harper and Row, 1964), p. 789.

27 Breon Mitchell, "The Demonic Comedy, Dante and Grass's *Hundejahre,*" *Papers on Language and Literature,* 9 (Winter 1973), 65–77. Mitchell draws convincing parallels between the *Divine Comedy* and *Dog Years.*

CHAPTER FIVE

1 Uwe Johnson, *Jahrestage: Aus dem Leben der Gesine Cresspahl* (Frankfurt: Suhrkamp, 1970), 1:386; volume 2 (1971), volume 3 (1973). Volume one and part of volume two have been translated as an authorized abridgement by Leila Vennewitz as *Anniversaries: From the Life of Gesine Cresspahl* (New York: Harcourt Brace Jovanovich, 1975). I base my entire discussion on the complete original German text. All quotations and references to that text are designated by month, day, and page number.

2 Wilhelm Johannes Schwarz, *Der Erzähler Uwe Johnson* (Munich, Francke Verlag, 1970), p. 88.

3 *Ibid.*, p. 90.

4 *Ibid.*, p. 7.

5 *Ibid.*, p. 90.

6 Mark Boulby, *Uwe Johnson* (New York: Fredrick Ungar, 1974), p. 4.

7 Schwarz, p. 94.

8 *Ibid.*

9 Reinhard Baumgart, ed., *Über Uwe Johnson* (Frankfurt: Suhrkamp, 1970), pp. 157–58.

10 *Mutmassungen über Jakob* (Frankfurt: Fischer Bücherei, 1962), p. 127.

11 Karl August Horst, "Im Bauch des Trojanischen Pferdes," in Baumgart, ed., p. 121.

12 Horst Bienek, *Werkstattgespräche mit Schriftstellern* (Munich: Hanser Verlag, 1962), p. 97.

13 Schwarz, p. 91. See also Ree Post Adams, "Antworten von Uwe Johnson," *German Quarterly,* 50 (May 1977), 241–47.

14 Paul Ricoeur, *The Symbolism of Evil,* trans. E. Buchanan (Boston: Beacon Press, 1967), p. 139.

15 Norman O. Brown, *Life Against Death* (New York: Random House, 1959), p. 240.

16 Sigmund Freud, *Beyond the Pleasure Principle,* trans. James Strachey (New York: Bantam, 1959), p. 70.

CHAPTER SIX

1 Yosal Rogat, *The Eichmann Trial and the Rule of Law* (Santa Barbara, Calif.: Center for the Study of Democratic Institutions, 1961), p. 4; see also Hannah Arendt, *Eichmann in Jerusalem* (New York: Viking Press, 1969), p. 229.

2 Erwin Piscator, *Das politische Theater,* foreword by Wolfgang Drews (Hamburg: Rowohlt, 1963), p. 7.

3 Piscator, pp. 74–75.

4 Peter Weiss, "Notizen zum dokumentarischen Theater," in *Dramen* (Frankfurt: Suhrkamp, 1968), 2:465.

5 Erich Auerbach, *Mimesis* (New York: Doubleday, 1957), pp. 137–38.

6 Erika Salloch, *Peter Weiss' Die Ermittlung: Zur Struktur des Dokumentarstheater* (Frankfurt: Athenäum, 1972), p. 37. In her detailed analysis of the play, Salloch convincingly compares certain passages from the *Divine Comedy* with lines from *The Investigation.*

7 Dolores Baracana Smith, "Rolf Hochhuth: The Man and his Work," in D. Baracana Smith and Earl Smith, *The Deputy Reader* (Chicago: Scott Foresman, 1965), p. 63.

8 Rolf Zimmermann, "Rolf Hochhuth der Stellvertreter," in Manfred Brauneck, ed., *Das deutsche Drama von Expressionismus bis zur Gegenwart: Interpretation* (Bamberg: Büchner, 1970), pp. 236–37.

9 Heinz Geiger, *Widerstand und Mitschuld: Zum deutschen Drama von Brecht bis Weiss* (Düsseldorf: Bertelsmann Universitätsverlag, 1973), p. 141.

10 Rolf Hochhuth, "Soll das Theater die heutige Welt darstellen?" in Wolfgang Kuttenkeuler, ed., *Poesie und Politik: Zur Situation der Literatur in Deutschland* (Stuttgart: W. Kohlhammer, 1973), p. 284.

11 Hochhuth, p. 286.

12 Hochhuth, p. 288.

13 Hochhuth, p. 292.

14 All references to *The Deputy* are taken from the following editions of the play: *Der Stellvertreter* (Hamburg: Rowohlt, 1967), and *The Deputy,* trans. Richard and Clara Winston (New York: Grove, 1964). I have occasionally made minor adjustments in the translation. Henceforth page references to the German and English edition will be given in the text.

15 Siegfried Melchinger, *Hochhuth* (Hannover: Friedrich Verlag, 1967), p. 60.

16 Carl Amery, "The Harrassed Pope," in Eric Bentley, ed., *The Storm over the Deputy* (New York: Grove, 1964), p. 152.

17 Soeren Kierkegaard, *Journals* quoted in Robert Bretall, ed., *A Kierkegaard Anthology* (Princeton: Princeton University Press, 1946), p. 172.

18 Gerstein's famous report is reprinted in Gerhard Schoenberner, *The Yellow Star,* trans. Susan Sweet (New York: Bantam, 1969), pp. 171–75. For a discussion of the man Gerstein see Pierre Joffroy, *A Spy for God: The Ordeal of Kurt Gerstein,* trans. Norma Denny (New York: Harcourt Brace, 1970).

19 Walter Kaufmann, *Tragedy and Philosophy* (New York: Doubleday, 1968), p. 387.

20 Volkmar Sander, *Die Faszination des Bösen* (Göttingen: Sachse and Pohl, 1968).

21 Albert Camus, *The Rebel,* trans. A. Brower (New York: Vintage Press, 1956), p. 51–52.

22 All quotations from *The Investigation* are from the following editions of the play: *Die Ermittlung: Oratorium in 11 Gesängen* (Hamburg: Rowohlt, 1971) and *The Investigation,* trans. Jan Swan and Ulu Grosbard (New York: Atheneum, 1967). I have occasionally made minor adjustments in the translation. Page references to both editions will henceforth be given in the text.

23 Salloch, p. 139.

24 *Der Spiegel,* 43 (20 October 1965), 164.

25 Otto Best, *Peter Weiss* (Munich: Francke Verlag, 1971), p. 191.

26 Reinhard Baumgart, "In die Moral entwischt? Der Weg des politischen Stückeschreibers Peter Weiss," *Text und Kritik,* no. 37 (January 1973), 8–18.

27 See Peter Weiss, "Zehn Arbeitspunkte eines Autors in der geteilten Welt," in Kuttenkeuler, pp. 297–98.

28 Peter Weiss, *Abschied von den Eltern* (Frankfurt: Suhrkamp, 1964), pp. 86–87.

29 Peter Weiss, *Fluchtpunkt* (Frankfurt: Suhrkamp, 1962), pp. 135–36.

30 Peter Weiss, "Meine Ortschaft," in *Rapporte* (Frankfurt: Suhrkamp, 1968), 1:114 ff.

31 Salloch, p. 48; see also pp. 42–46.

32 Best, p. 134.

33 Salloch, p. 53.

34 Peter Weiss, "Gespräch über Dante," in *Rapporte,* 1:142–43.

35 Peter Weiss, "Vorübung zum dreiteiligen Drama divina commedia" in *Rapporte,* 1:125–41.

36 Hermann Langbein, *Der Auschwitz Prozess, eine Dokumentation,* 2 vols. (Frankfurt: Europäische Verlagsanstalt, 1965), p. 253.

37 Langbein, p. 901.

38 Langbein, p. 906–7.

CHAPTER SEVEN

1 For a discussion of form as an ethical expression against chaos see Theodore Ziolkowski, "Form als Protest," in *Exil und innere Emigration,* ed. R. Grimm and J. Hermand (Frankfurt: Athenäum, 1972), pp. 153–72.

2 Northrop Frye, *Anatomy of Criticism* (Princeton: Princeton University Press, 1957), pp. 293–303.

3 Octavio Paz, *The Bow and the Lyre,* trans. Ruth Simms (Austin: University of Texas Press, 1973), pp. 33–36.

4 André Jolles, *Einfache Formen* (Tübingen: Max Niemeyer Verlag, 1968), p. 133.

5 Paul Ricoeur, *The Symbolism of Evil,* trans. E. Buchanan (Boston: Beacon, 1967), p. 172.

6 Gershom Scholem, *Major Trends in Jewish Mysticism* (New York: Schocken, 1973), p. 216. Henceforth page references will be given in the text.

7 Gerhard Wehr, *Jacob Böhme* (Hamburg: Rowohlt, 1971), p. 83.

8 Bengt Holmquist, ed., *Das Buch der Nelly Sachs* (Frankfurt: Suhrkamp, 1968), p. 184. Unless otherwise indicated, all my translations of Sachs's poems are based on this text. Henceforth page references will be given in the text.

9 Paul Celan, *Die Niemandsrose* (Frankfurt: S. Fischer Verlag, 1963), p. 45. All my translations and references to Celan's poems are taken from the following editions which will be noted in the text by a parenthesis including the first letters of the title and the page number. *Mohn und Gedächtnis* (Stuttgart: Deutsche Verlagsanstalt, 1952). *Von Schwelle zu Schwelle* (Stuttgart: Deutsche Verlagsanstalt, 1955). *Sprachgitter* (Frankfurt: S. Fischer Verlag, 1959). *Atemwende* (Frankfurt: Suhrkamp, 1967). *Fadensonnen* (Frankfurt: Suhrkamp, 1970). *Schneepart* (Frankfurt: Suhrkamp, 1970). The most extensive translation of Celan's poems has been made by Joachim Neugroschel, *Speech-Grille and other Poems* (New York: Dutton, 1971).

10 Martin Buber, *Die Chassidischen Bücher* (Berlin: Schocken Verlag, 1927), pp. xii–xv.

11 From *O The Chimneys* by Nelly Sachs, translated from the German by Michael Hamburger. Copyright © 1967 by Farrar, Straus and Giroux, Inc. Reprinted with permission of Farrar, Straus and Giroux, Inc.

12 As discussed in Hans Griensky, *Jacob Boehme* (Stuttgart: Frommanns-Verlag, 1956), p. 225.

13 Gerhard Neumann, "Die absolute Metapher: ein Abgrenzungsversuch am Beispiel Mallarmés und Paul Celans," *Poetica*, 3 (January-April 1970), 195.

14 Paul Celan, "Das grauere Wort" (1958), *Die Welt* (November 21, 1970). (First printed in the Almanac of the Librairie Flinker, Paris, 1958).

15 Such a deemphasis of history is evident in the studies by Dietlind Meinecke, *Wort und Name bei Paul Celan* (Bad Homburg: Verlag Gehlen, 1970), and Klaus Weissenberger, *Die Elegie bei Paul Celan* (Munich: Francke, 1969).

16 Marie Syrkin, "Nelly Sachs—Poet of the Holocaust," *Midstream*, 13 (March 1967), 22–23; Jerry Glen, *Paul Celan* (New York: Twayne Publishers, 1973); Lawrence Langer, *The Holocaust and the Literary Imagination* (New Haven: Yale University Press, 1975).

17 My discussion of Sachs's poem is an expanded version of my article " 'Landschaft aus Schreien': The Shackled Leaps of Nelly Sachs," *Bucknell Review*, 21 (Spring 1973), 43-62.

18 Holmquist, *Das Buch . . .* , p. 23.

19 Such mythologizing of Sachs is especially evident in the collection *Nelly Sachs zu Ehren, zum 75: Geburtstage, Gedichte, Beiträge, Bibliographie* (Frankfurt: Suhrkamp, 1966).

20 Paul Kersten, "Analyse und Heiligsprechung—Nelly Sachs und ihre Kritiker," *Text and Kritik* (July 1969), 44.

21 Olof Lagercrantz, *Versuch über die Lyrik der Nelly Sachs* (Frankfurt: Suhrkamp, 1967), pp. 48–49.

22 Lagercrantz, p. 17.

23 Sachs, *Suche nach Lebenden* (Frankfurt: Suhrkamp, 1971).

24 Olof Lagercrantz, "In den Wohnungen des Todes, zum Tode der deutsch-jüdischen Dichterin Nelly Sachs," *Die Zeit* (May 26, 1970), p. 13.

25 Gisela Dischner, "Zu den Gedichten von Nelly Sachs," in Holmquist, p. 311.

26 Gisela Bezzel-Dischner, *Poetik des modernen Gedichts: Zur Lyrik von Nelly Sachs* (Berlin: Verlag Gehlen, 1970), p. 9.

27 Nelly Sachs, *O The Chimneys* (New York: Farrar, Straus and Giroux, 1969), p. 238. My translation of the original in this bilingual edition of her poems.

28 Lagercrantz, p. 26.

29 Lagercrantz, p. 59.

30 Martin Buber, *The Eclipse of God* (New York: Harper and Row, 1952), p. 152 and p. 167.

31 Paul Celan, "Ansprache anlässlich der Entgegennahme des Literaturpreises der Freien Hansestadt Bremen," in *Ausgewählte Gedichte,* afterword by Beda Alleman (Frankfurt: Suhrkamp, 1970), p. 127.

32 Heinrich Stiehler, "Die Zeit der 'Todesfuge': Zu den Anfängen Paul Celans," *Akzente,* 19 (February 1972), 11–39.

33 Hans Mayer, "Erinnerung an Paul Celan," *Merkur,* 24 (December 1970), 1160.

34 Martin Walser, "Hölderlin zu entsprechen," *Die Zeit* (March 31, 1971), pp. 9–10; also quoted in Horst Peter Neumann, "Ich-Gestalt und Dichtungsbegriff bei Paul Celan," *Etudes Germaniques,* 25 (July-September 1970), 306.

35 H. P. Neumann, p. 308.

36 Celan, "Der Meridian" in *Ausgewählte Gedichte,* p. 148.

37 Klaus Voswinkel, *Paul Celan, verweigerte Poetisierung der Welt* (Heidelberg: Lothar Stiehn Verlag, 1974), p. 24.

38 Alfred Kelletat, "Accessus zu Celan's 'Sprachgitter,' " *Deutschunterricht,* 18 (December 1966), 97–98.

39 Cf. Dietlind Meinecke, *Wort und Name bei Paul Celan,* pp. 184–85, and Klaus Weissenberger, *Die Elegie bei Paul Celan,* pp. 47–54.

40 Peter Szondi, *Celan Studien* (Frankfurt: Suhrkamp, 1972), p. 11.

41 Meinecke, *Wort und Name* . . . , p. 179.

42 Mayer, p. 1159.

43 Walter Killy, *Elemente der Lyrik* (Munich: C. H. Beck, 1972), p. 61.

Index